German Yearbook on Business History 1981

German Yearbook on Business History 1981

Edited by
the German Society for
Business History, Cologne

in Cooperation with
the Institute for Banking History, Frankfurt/Main

Editors:
Wolfram Engels and Hans Pohl (Editor in charge)

Editorial Staff:
Manfred Pohl and Horst A. Wessel

Springer-Verlag
Berlin Heidelberg New York

ISBN 3-540-11230-8 Springer-Verlag Berlin Heidelberg New York
ISBN 0-387-11230-8 Springer-Verlag New York Heidelberg Berlin

Type-setting and bookbinding: G. Appl, Wemding
Printing: aprinta, Wemding
2142/3140-543210

Introductory Remarks

For at least one hundred years Germany besides England and France in Europe and besides the United States and Japan in the world has been that country with the most private and public enterprises. This is easily explained by the fact that our economy has been predominantly characterized by small and medium-sized enterprises. Yet, until the Gesellschaft für Unternehmensgeschichte e. V. (Business History Society) had been founded in 1976, there was no institution in the universities and outside, which researched into the entrepreneurial economy and its achievements in and for society during the last centuries. Only in the banking business there has been the Institut für bankhistorische Forschung in Frankfurt since 1969.

Nevertheless books on German business history can be traced back as far as 1811. We owe a lot of memorial publications to many economists, historians, journalists, archivists, and hobby historians from the economy. Most of them were ordered by entrepreneurs and managers interested in history. Even though economic history has been getting more and more important at German universities since the days of the historical school of national economy, and especially after World War II, business history hasn't been institutionalized, neither in a private nor in a public research institute. In marked contrast to the development in Germany, a special periodical, professors' chairs, and the Research Center for Business History in Harvard fostered by the Rockefeller Foundation came into being in the United States since the 1930s. Yet, we have to realize, that the business schools there with their empirical and theoretical teaching and researching concepts formed a much better platform.

Even the fact that there was no institutionalized business history in Germany didn't prevent some scholars from publishing important studies in business history, scholars like Richard Ehrenberg, Bruno Kuske, Walter Däbritz, Conrad Matschoss or Wilhelm Treue, who founded a periodical for business history and entrepreneurial biography back in 1956. That was only possible because of some entrepreneurs and enterprises being interested in history, following the example of Krupp, Siemens, and Deutsche Bank in keeping their records. Men from the entrepreneurial economy and German economic historians thus suggested to institutionalize business history by found-

ing a scientific society. The Gesellschaft für Unternehmensgeschichte e. V., which was founded in 1976, is
- "to do and to promote research in business history
- to make available the results of that research to science, the economy and the public
- to work for the preservation of historic sources in the economy".

The Gesellschaft für Unternehmensgeschichte and the Institut für
bankhistorische Forschung are striving for a close cooperation with
all those persons and institutions in Germany and abroad working on
the same subject. They endeavour to cope with these aims
- by editing the Zeitschrift für Unternehmensgeschichte and the
  Bankhistorisches Archiv
- by initiating research work, for instance studies of the image of the
  entrepreneurs' economy in schoolbooks or of the history of the
  German banking business
- by arranging public lecture and discussion meetings with representatives of various scientific disciplines, of the economy, of the administration, of the media for example on the concentration movement in the German economy, on co-determination law, on marketing strategies, or on the universal bank system, on the development of bank legislation (state superintendance of banks), or financing an adverse balance of payments
- by arranging scientific symposions, for example on entrepreneurial welfare policy, on professional education and on the job training, on the development of labor dispute legislation in an international comparison
- by providing material for scientific research, for instance by publishing two volumes of a guide to archives in the economy
- by counselling and helping German and foreign scholars in their
  research work
- by cooperating with scholars from abroad. In 1979 and 1981 there
  were symposions together with the Business History Society of Japan and in 1979 there was the first international symposion on
  bank history in Berlin.

This Yearbook is to help German research in keeping contact and in
cooperating with scholars and enterprises from abroad, by making
available some select articles on business history from German peri-
odicals to the English speaking world. Thus we want to promote
the international dialogue between business historians and want to
arouse more consciousness in history among representatives of the
economy around the world. We hope at the same time to contribute to
the strengthening and further development of our free economic and
social order, because only that person who is able to understand the
interdependence in the world economy that has developed in the past
centuries will feel sure to promote a free world economy.

WOLFRAM ENGELS   HANS POHL

Table of Contents

List of Contributors

Prof. Drs. HORST ALBACH
Institut für Gesellschafts- und Wirtschaftswissenschaften
der Universität Bonn, Adenauer-Allee 24–42
5300 Bonn

Priv.-Doz. Dr. WILFRIED FELDENKIRCHEN
Historisches Seminar der Universität Bonn, Konviktstraße 11
5300 Bonn

Prof. Drs. WOLFRAM FISCHER
Zentralinstitut für sozialwissenschaftliche Forschung der Freien
Universität Berlin, Hittorfstraße 2–4
1000 Berlin 33

Dr. WILFRIED GUTH
Member of the board of directors of the Deutsche Bank AG,
Große Gallusstraße 12–14
6000 Frankfurt am Main 1

Prof. Dr. HANSJOACHIM HENNING
Fachbereich 1 der Universität Duisburg – Gesamthochschule –
Lotharstraße 65
4100 Duisburg 1

Prof. Dr. JÜRGEN KOCKA
Fakultät für Geschichtswissenschaft der Universität Bielefeld,
Postfach 8640
4800 Bielefeld 1

The Change in Leadership and Continuity in an Enterprise*

Wilfried Guth

First of all, Herr von Siemens, let me offer you my very warmest congratulations on your 70th birthday, which we are celebrating here today.

These are my personal wishes but I also extend them to you on behalf of Deutsche Bank AG, which has followed faithfully the unparalleled rise of Siemens since the time of the "Gründerjahre" in Berlin to its present position as a world-wide electrical engineering concern. We feel very special ties both to the enterprise and to you personally, my dear Herr von Siemens. A relationship of trust and confidence binds our two institutions and this has developed over many decades, but precisely for this reason I suggest that there is no need for me to speak of it further and I can turn to the subject on which I have been asked to speak: "The Change in Leadership and Continuity in an Enterprise".

Actually, it is presumptuous for anyone who does not belong to this company to speak on one of its most important but at the same time most intimate events, the change at the top – and presumptuous bankers are certainly bad bankers. I am only protected from such a verdict – at least I hope I am – by Peter von Siemens' express birthday wish which I am delighted to fulfil today as a token of friendship and personal esteem.

A change in leadership – I am referring to the organic change which becomes necessary through the passage of time and not the abrupt change occasioned by particular circumstances – is an important milestone in the history of any enterprise. It is out of the long chain of such events that the company's destiny evolves. Certainly, I do not wish to overestimate the role of individuals or deny, particularly today, their integration in a confident management team, but basically I believe the old theory that personalities make history, or to put it more cautiously, that they very largely determine the style and direction in any given period. Of course the converse also applies. The chief editor of the "Börsenzeitung", Bernd Baehring, once put it very aptly: The great enterprises have for a long time been forming their leaders no less than their leaders have been forming them. The history of Siemens seems to me a particularly fine example of that.

Changes at the top – even if they are as well prepared and proceed with the same admirable smoothness and calm as the one we are experiencing here – are exciting moments in the life of the enterprise. Not only the general public but especially the news-hungry press will focus full attention on the event, and in the enterprise itself

---

* Speech given at a function of Siemens AG on the occasion of the 70th birthday of Dr. Peter von Siemens, January 29, 1981 in Munich.

there will scarcely be anyone not watching anxiously to see how the change goes and what it will mean to the firm.

It is hard to avoid the much-used image of handing over the baton. The smoothness of the change is at least as important as the ability of the individual runners, both of whom must concentrate all their strength – almost like the Zen Buddhists – on ensuring success. Neither may concentrate only on himself and his achievement – and certainly not his reputation.

The image of the baton leads me to another thought: despite the complexity of handing over the baton the relay team runs faster than a single athlete who has to run the whole distance alone. I do not want to draw the comparison, but it seems to me that handing over the baton in an enterprise at fixed points, i.e. at certain age limits, is the right method, although we human beings have very different constitutions and the degree of discipline in our life styles may keep one person efficient for longer than another. In family businesses especially we have often seen that the head of the firm tends rather to emulate the marathon than the relay runner. Peter von Siemens on the other hand is handing over to Herr Plettner two years before the end of his mandate, because corporate rationale makes this appear appropriate.

Or we can put it differently: is it not one of the most important human and at the same time entrepreneurial virtues to accept the process of growing older and its consequences – even or perhaps precisely when one still feels young enough to carry on? Different laws apply to enterprises: they may add year to year and proudly celebrate their jubilees but they must remain young and elastic. That is why they need a change in leadership from time to time.

I spoke just now of the risk involved in handing over the baton, and clearly an enterprise must try to eliminate this as far as possible. It is also clear how this can be done: through careful and early selection of the successor and ensuring his integration into the process of continuity in the firm. At once we see that a change in leadership and continuity are not opposites, they belong together.

But let me speak a little more on the subject of the choice of successor. Much has been said and written on the planning of succession and I do not imagine that I will be able to add anything new. But I would like to stress what we can all learn from Siemens especially. Firstly: the choice of successor at the top should not be an isolated individual process, it should be only a part, although it is the most important part, of a systematic selection, promotion and training of management staff throughout the enterprise. Siemens, as we all know, spends a great deal of time and money on these activities, in the last business year nearly DM 500 million were spent on training and further training of staff. This also includes engagement in management training outside the enterprise itself, for example within the framework of the "Baden-Baden Discussions". This concern for the able and the talented within the enterprise pays a hundredfold dividend, it creates a reservoir of well-trained and motivated people to whom loyalty and hard work for the firm come naturally.

I believe that there is a direct relationship between the quality of the managers in the various areas of an enterprise and the "quality at the top", if I may call it that. Quite simply: the standards are set higher. Or put more bluntly, (though I am afraid it doesn't necessarily always apply): the management gets the chief it deserves. At least when the middle and senior management are highly qualified it quickly becomes apparent if the necessary human or specialist qualifications are lacking at the top.

We do not need a long explanation to see that with such a consistent policy of promotion and training for leadership, choosing the successor at the top from within the company's own ranks is the best and surest way to success. Not only does the new leader know the company, its products and services, its style, its strengths and weaknesses, i. e. above all those of its staff, but also the converse is important: the staff know him and know that he has proved his ability in various posts; he does not have to win the trust which is essential for successful management in a long process of trial. This is not to say that the occasional much-quoted "infusion of new blood" is not welcome as well. We all know cases where this has proved a blessing or was even urgently necessary. But it should remain the exception to the rule, for it is the more difficult way both for the company and for the man who comes in.

In the history of Siemens, which now spans 133 years, the head of the firm has always come from within the company's own ranks. In 1934, at the age of 23, Peter von Siemens joined what was then Siemens & Halske AG in Berlin. He may have borne the family name but this did not bring him easy success. Like every other future manager he had to prove his worth in various management positions before his way led him to the top of the enterprise – a way he trod so successfully, with a seemingly natural self-possession, and with the self-confidence of someone who combines knowledge, a cosmopolitan outlook, a broad view of things and at the same time insight into detail.

Bernhard Plettner has also made his career at Siemens. He embodies in the best possible way the virtues which have helped the company to world standing and renown. During the last 10 years he has given repeated proof of his management ability and leadership qualities and so we all feel that his move yesterday to the chairmanship of the Supervisory Board is a logical step which we can confidently applaud.

And finally in Karlheinz Kaske, an experienced manager from the power engineering and energy technology divisions, another proven "Siemens man" is moving to the highest level of executive responsibility. To him in particular we wish good fortune and success for the great tasks ahead.

Can we deduce from the succession of leaders at Siemens general principles or instructions which we could all observe in finding the "right" man for the job out of the list of possible candidates? I hardly think so. But let me make one negative qualification and say that continuity, the continuance of a tradition and style do not require a succession of the same type of personality. On the contrary: a change in type of ability and professional experience at the top can be good for the company, it can harbour opportunities and give new impulses. Just consider the succession of commercial, organisational and technical talents which we have seen in the Siemens management in recent decades.

Indeed, I think that the argument that different phases of our economic and socio-political development require different types of entrepreneur is right to a certain extent; however, I would rather speak of different specific abilities for which, in each case, there is a specific need.

What does that mean for the man who is handing over? Concern for the correct successor is rightly seen as one of his most important management tasks, indeed it is perhaps the most important. It requires above all, as it seems to me, a little humility to let other talents have their due. Only those who cannot see their own limitations will want to create successors "in their own image". We should not measure others by our own strengths and abilities but recognise and encourage their ability to lead.

Ability to lead: a big concept. It has many components, and these have often been listed and analysed: strength of character, physical and mental stability, superior ability and a good number of other qualities. I shall restrict myself to one essential gift which has always been particularly valued, and rightly so, at Siemens: the ability to lead people – I deliberately say people, not subordinates. And to lead here certainly does not only mean to set them goals, direct or steer them, it means first and foremost inducing their critical participation, and arousing their enthusiasm for the task in hand. I believe that it is this quality of leadership which is today of decisive importance for the success or failure of an enterprise.

In speaking of the opportunities which a change in personality at the head of an enterprise may give rise to, I must of course add that this can also conceal a risk. If every new head of a firm saw his task only in developing his own personality – now generally referred to by the fashionable term "self-realisation" – the enterprise might find itself on a zig-zag course which, instead of generating new energy, would uselessly consume its strength and give rise to uncertainty among the staff.

This brings me to the question of continuity and I think it would be appropriate to dwell a little on this concept which also plays a great part at Siemens.

Continuity is firstly an appealing word: it inspires confidence. Not for nothing is it so frequently used particularly in connection with a change in leadership, in politics, too, incidentally (unless the government is changing!). We need only recall Adenauer's favourite slogan: "No experiments". The successor will also want to stress continuity, for without respect for his predecessor and the history of the enterprise he would be like a tree without roots exposed to the wind. Thomas Mann's Konsul Buddenbrook has given us a particularly sensitive formulation: ". . . for we are not unconnected, independent individual beings, each for himself, we are like links in a chain and we would not be conceivable as we are without the number of those who have gone before us and shown us the way by themselves . . . following a well-tried and honourable path".

But what can continuity mean in an age in which rapid adjustment to new world economic situations, structural change in other words, has become a matter of survival for many enterprises, and in which modern management has been described as "intelligent reaction to changes"? Continuity as a postulate for the beginning of the 1980s, when so much will have to change, on a small and on a large scale if we are to survive economically at all – continuity, then, in the age of discontinuity – will that not degenerate easily into a meaningless phrase? Even worse, can such a postulate not bring a risk of inflexibility and rigidity, of fear of all things new?

Of course we can all quote examples of the wrong kind of continuity in politics and business but we also know that these dangers are not relevant for us here today. This enterprise stands firm in its traditions but it is flexible as well, its gaze is firmly fixed on the future. The Siemens tradition is progress. That is how Peter von Siemens put it.

And so we can and must understand by continuity only the preservation and handing on of important basic virtues in an enterprise, which have proved their worth and grown stronger throughout the course of its history. That is easily said, and one hardly needs to ponder for long to enumerate some of these virtues which probably every enterprise would like to claim for itself.

But we should ask whether Siemens has particular virtues which in their sum create what one can call the style or "spirit" of the firm. I think it has, and only the fact that it has can probably explain the special sense of belonging and the pride the employees feel in their enterprise. A name can only acquire such force if certain very specific qualities are associated with it.

Let me attempt – as a friend but not as a member of your company, in other words then from outside – to list several what I think are important Siemens virtues. Perhaps I am idealising a little here – for of course like any other the firm has its weaknesses and it makes mistakes – and one or the other of the "Siemens men" may smile and be self-critical enough to see things a little differently, but virtues do not appear in a pure clear light in other areas of life either. And so I can leave it to the persons to whom these remarks are addressed to classify what I should like to call "Siemens virtues" as already achieved or worth achieving as their consciences and knowledge dictate.

First of all I think of Siemens' world-wide perspective and its knowledge of the world. These have conditioned its development right from the start. Today they are more than ever a maxim for its management. One might be tempted to say that the founders of the firm, Werner von Siemens and Johann Georg Halske, were simply making a virtue of necessity, for the domestic market as it was within the narrow confines of the Kingdom of Prussia in 1847 offered little scope to a new company which was devoted to technical progress. But there was more than this behind their decisions: expansion abroad was in keeping with Werner von Siemens' general attitude to life. In his youth he had modelled his work on that of the Fuggers and the Rothschilds, sending his brothers to London and Petersburg so that they could view the world from these places. This also shows that in speaking of a world-wide perspective I mean more than simply a consistent orientation to exports which has been characteristic of many German firms in the period since the Second World War and has brought us generally acknowledged success.

In the long history of the company Siemens was almost always headed by men who had themselves learned to look abroad and to use experience and knowledge gained in other countries in their own country as well wherever this seemed useful. Not "the German character", but sensitivity to and respect for other modes of thought and different ways of life. So it is not by chance that Peter von Siemens as well, true to tradition, spent many years of his long career abroad before taking over responsibility at home. He embodies the Siemens virtue of a world-wide perspective in a very special way. As the new President of the World Energy Conference he will be able to use this virtue in his company's original field in working towards a greater assimilation of views.

But I should not like to go on without mentioning all the Siemens leaders – too many to list by name – in the plants and companies all over the world. Their many contacts and high standing in their host countries are qualities I have often experienced personally. This is perhaps the best illustration of the fact that however much these qualities may be virtues in their own right, they also help the business. Today Siemens would be inconceivable without its world-wide network of sales and production facilities and without the knowledge of the world which has been acquired in generation after generation since the company was founded.

That is closely connected with another of the Siemens virtues. Even at a very early stage in its history the delegation of responsibility was practised, i.e. the company was managed decentrally. The head of the firm did not, and he does not today, desire to direct everything himself from the top. The wisdom of this policy can be seen in the many able, self-confident and active personalities which Siemens has in its head office and outside, as managers of factories or plants, heading distribution and production companies abroad. There is many a king within his own realm. Delegation is a consistent principle in the organisational structure: each of the altogether 24 divisions is responsible for its own world business.

There is a further factor which I regard as of major importance and it is particularly marked in Siemens: the spirit of invention and entrepreneurial courage. Certainly these are qualities which we can point to in many other German enterprises as well; but such close interrelation and so strong a continuity in the history of the enterprise are very much rarer. Again one immediately thinks of the founder of the firm.

It is Werner von Siemens to whom the world owes the discovery of the principle of the electric dynamo which is still today of immense importance for the construction of electrical machines from the smallest engine to the generators in modern power stations. It is perhaps not so well known that it was the firm of Siemens which in 1875 took on the full business risk of laying one of the first direct cable links between Europe and North America with its own cable ship, the Faraday. There was a great risk because of the time and costs involved in repairing a broken cable. I could quote any number of further instances. The pioneering technical innovations and far-reaching entrepreneurial decisions stretch like a link of pearls through the history of the firm.

I should just like to mention two such decisions from more recent times, in both of which Bernhard Plettner and Peter von Siemens played a crucial part: firstly the courageous and consistent engagement in nuclear power technology. This decision not only has business significance, it had a socio-political dimension as well. From the point of view of earnings it would certainly have been easier for Siemens to find a different partner for the AEG share in KWU, perhaps an American firm; but it would not have been Siemens' style to go just half-way towards facing the challenge. And so the management of KWU and Siemens are now not only working together for technical and commercial success, they are carrying out patient publicity work, engaged in a process of education and enlightenment, as it were, "against the current".

Let me add here that ever since the company was founded the men at the head of the firm have taken an active interest in public affairs. We expect the same engagement from them today. Company management – and this naturally applies not only to Siemens – cannot and must not restrict itself to managing, no matter how successfully, affairs in its own house. In the interest of the company its leading personalities must operate over a wider radius.

It is becoming increasingly important – and Peter von Siemens has always recognised this – for the private individual to understand the purpose and benefits, but also the problems involved in new technical developments. This requires the provision of a flow of factual and objective information and it also means taking a serious and patient look at his worries and fears. I see this as part of the more comprehensive task of management; entrepreneurial activity must be made understandable and acceptable in the full range of its obligations and aims. We all know that the time of the "Geheimräte" and hermetically sealed off, lonely top managers is over. Only a management which participates freely and openly in discussions and plays an active part in the dialogue will succeed in achieving credibility for itself, its firm and the market economy as a whole. In a time of lower growth rates, correspondingly smaller room for distribution and harder international competition we have a particular need of this credibility if we are not to waste our efforts in conflict over social and socio-political aims.

This also means that those with a wider view of things must help to define and realise the aims which go beyond the immediate concerns of their firm. They should perhaps also be able to issue warnings and be in a position to offer resistance if things take an undesirable turn. It is in this wider sense that I see the political responsibility of the entrepreneur. I should like to use the rather old-fashioned term "courage of one's convictions" in this connection and add that to my list of Siemens virtues.

My second contemporary example, data processing, is of a completely different kind, but it shows the same Siemens qualities: it took a great deal of business courage and above all confidence in the company's technical abilities to start developments in this field and stand up to the American giant already firmly established in the market. The battle for the market of the future was fought despite all setbacks – not least to avoid abandoning the domestic market to foreign suppliers. Of course the main expectation was and still is the achievement of profits in this sector as well.

There is something else which I must mention: a good portion of pride in the company and perseverance – let us say quite openly stubbornness – these are all qualities which we can easily identify among those concerned in the change in management today.

And the new top management will need all these qualities in future too. The ability to innovate and the successful commercial exploitation of inventions are more important than ever, both for the individual firm and the economy as a whole. (Professor Lüst will, I am sure, say more on this). Siemens cannot afford to rest on its laurels and rely on the attraction of its name. "What thou hast inherited from thy fathers, earn it to make it thine own" (Goethe).

Technical and entrepreneurial courage are certainly decisive components of success but they are not sufficient in themselves, indeed they may even be dangerous. They have taken many into risky and loss-bringing efforts at diversification and overstrained balance sheets and finances. In the case of Siemens there are two further factors: none of the Siemens heads ever aimed to create more than a flourishing electrical engineering firm and expand it – and there has been and still is more than enough room for expansion – and they all had a well-developed sense of financial caution and soundness. They always observed the principle which Werner von Siemens formulated nearly a hundred years ago in a letter to his brother: "I am not going to mortgage the future for a quick profit now!"

Ernst von Siemens, without whose personality and achievement the great recovery of the firm after the Second World War, its reorganisation and present unity would have been inconceivable, spoke in exactly the same tradition when he took over the chairmanship of the Supervisory Board in 1956: "Our house became great because tomorrow was more important to it than today, technical progress counted for more than a quick profit and because it always considered its most precious possession to be the people whose fates were bound up with its own".

Mutual respect between the commercial and technical staff is one of the oldest traditions of Siemens and if an engineer is again taking over the chairmanship of the

Board of Managing Directors no-one who knows Siemens will underestimate the strong position of the financial director and controller. In the care and foresight of its world-wide financial dispositions, its proximity to the market and knowledge of developments Siemens can hold its own with any well-managed bank. And I am convinced that Siemens' top executives, whether from the commercial or technical side of the business, are proud of this! They would probably feel less secure if the financial director or controller did not occasionally play the part of awkward colleague.

My attempt to list the traditional Siemens virtues would be one-sided and incomplete if I did not say something on the human relations within the firm, difficult as that is for anyone who is not a Siemens man. There are two aspects of the much and often ironically quoted "spirit of the enterprise" which seem to me particularly important: firstly, and this is also evident immediately to friends of Siemens like myself, the modesty and unpretentious dignity of its heads, a readiness to lead and bear responsibility which is by no means a "desire to dominate". We can quote other examples in Germany but a comparison is not what I am aiming for. Here too Werner von Siemens set standards more than 100 years ago against which all his successors had to measure themselves and all of them so far – however different their characters may have been – have stood the test. It is certainly not wrong to speak here of the Prussian tradition in the very best sense; self-discipline and devotion to duty are part of it, but the English "understatement" also comes to mind.

The second typical human aspect of the Siemens tradition is for me the care which has been devoted to the staff ever since the time of the founder, Werner von Siemens. In his day that was by no means usual. But even Bismarck derived many a stimulus for his social policy from this enterprise. Concern for the personal interests of the staff has always been coupled in Siemens with respect for the individual personality. Let me quote Ernst von Siemens: "Economic and technical progress are first and foremost the result of the untiring efforts of the individual, of belief in the possible success of his work. If individualism were to be eliminated from the business world, expansion and progress would be impossible". In a company which needs to weld a large number of highly gifted individuals into a team to ensure a lead over its competitors genuine human engagement on the part of the management is essential. False tones or merely simulated interest are quickly recognised.

I have been speaking of the Siemens virtues and the role they have played in ensuring continuity in the company's philosophy through all the changes from one head of the firm to another. There is something important to be added: the sum of these virtues has brought that which, more than anything else, creates a feeling of belonging and pride in the company's name: business success and international recognition! Siemens is not a Japanese "Zaibatsu" with an ethical and almost insoluble bond with its staff. Siemens cannot and should not emulate that. And yet, if I may put it quite simply, the cohesion in Siemens, which has contributed so much to its success, seems to me to be of quite a special kind. As a birthday wish and a comment on the change in leadership one should say: "May this never change!"

For the first time since the firm was converted into a joint stock company nearly 84 years ago the Chairman of the Supervisory Board will not bear the family name. Is this a caesura? Hardly. That there has always been someone bearing the family name available when there was a change at the head of the Supervisory Board is a happy coincidence, but not a natural law. As we might expect, the Siemens family is displaying its customary realism and not adhering strictly to an established custom. All the more reason – we can say this quite openly – to admire their strength and the unbroken line of forceful and imposing personalities they have produced. What still counts today as it has always done is the unshakable inner cohesion of the family and the destiny of the firm, its adherence to the principles I have just attempted to outline. This will never change. It also means that each person who takes over the highest office in the firm must have served in the ranks and proved his worth on every level of management. Only in this way can the principle of achievement be secured in a company with a great family tradition.

That brings me to the last remark I would like to make on my subject today. Continuity here can best be achieved through a name: Siemens. All the members of the firm – not only the members of the family – bear the name and are proud of it. The family will continue to see the preservation of this tradition as one of its most important tasks. That they have also secured to a certain extent their influence as shareholders can only underline this. But all the members of Siemens – the family and the workforce – will be bound by the same energy, stimulus, knowledge, spirit of invention and entrepreneurial imagination. They will use all their forces to ensure the continuance and further development of the great world-wide concern with the resonant family name.

In this sense Siemens is today still a family business but it is at the same time much more – it is one of the largest joint stock companies in the Federal Republic with more than 340,000 employees and more than 400,000 shareholders – ten times the number at the time of the Currency Reform – and more than 100,000 of them members of the staff.

We all owe this not least to the genius of those who recognised in good time the signs of the times and carried out the transformation into one of the greatest publicly-quoted companies equipped to meet the tasks of the future. They also preserved the family nature of the firm – should we not, to close, praise the older generation for this and wish their successors good luck and great success, for they are now responsible for the future of Siemens and will one day be handing on the baton themselves in the spirit of the tradition. Finally then, once again, my thanks, respects and warmest congratulations to Peter von Siemens on his birthday! He can look back with pride on a life of achievement.

On the Re-Discovery of the Entrepreneur in Economic Policy Discussion

Horst Albach

I. Introduction

In "Wilhelm Meisters Wanderjahre" Frau Susanne, the widow of a Swiss cotton manufacturer, says to Leonardo: "The ever-growing use of machines frightens me, it is creeping up on us like a thunderstorm, slowly; but it is on the move, it will surely come ... there are only two alternatives to choose between and one is as bad as the other: We can either join the new movement ourselves and hasten our downfall or move, take the best and worthiest with us and seek a better life beyond the seas. Each has its drawbacks. But who can help us weigh the reasons which should guide us?" (Goethe, 1976 edition, p. 453 f.)

This cry of anguish from the year 1797 is indicative of the problems brought by the structural changes in the Swiss economy resulting from technical developments in the British textile industry since 1760.[1] Frau Susanne sees two possible solutions to the dilemma:

1. "Set up machines ourselves and grab what we can" (Goethe, 1976 edition, p. 454) – this would be called an active policy of adjustment today, or
2. leave the firm in Switzerland to the staff and move to the USA – a passive policy of adjustment.

However, Frau Susanne did not see what a commission appointed by the British parliament was to establish a few years later: the structural change had by no means hastened the downfall of the Swiss – on the contrary, it had caused an "economic miracle". As a commentator remarked in the 1830s it should indeed have been "an object of attention for all serious observers, that the Swiss manufacturers, almost unnoticed and quite unprotected, had gradually made a victorious progression to almost every market on earth, however remote or apparently inaccessible these might be". None of their factories owed its success to protective or favourable legislation and yet it was a fact that without tariffs or the appropriate legal means to hinder or limit competition they had progressed to a success which was almost without parallel (Bowring, 1837, p. 1). (See also Biucchi, 1972, p. 1 f.).

How did it come about that Switzerland did not experience the crisis so feared by Frau Susanne but an "economic miracle"? The answer can be found in her own words:

1. "If they gain an advantage by making good use of these growing inventions we must do the same, as soon as we can" (Goethe, 1976, p. 455).

---

1 Cf. Mann, 1958, p. 277.

2. "They will have to move, sooner or later" (Goethe, 1976, p. 454).

She had quite rightly recognised that what mattered was to mechanise in good time or emigrate. She was for joining in and playing an active part in the new development instead of letting herself be driven and certainly not be driven away by it. Active adjustment, or perhaps better an active, anticipatory reaction to structural change in a spirit of entrepreneurial courage and adventure. It was indeed the magic formula which brought about the economic miracle in Switzerland at the beginning of the nineteenth century.

But emigration too became an entrepreneurial decision: persons who until then had been in paid employment left to go to America and made themselves independent: first the best, recognising the signs of coming unemployment, the others later when they were unemployed. What was at first a passive reaction finally became an instrument of active, indeed aggressive penetration of new markets overseas: on June 7, 1850 a certain G. Schaefly wrote from California: "You can have anything for money here. Goods come from all over the world, there is even *Swiss cheese*" (author's italics) (Schelbert and Rappolt, 1977, p. 284f.).

The emigrants, who had at first been the victims of passive adjustment, used their entrepreneurial ability and great geographical and occupational mobility to create a network of Swiss companies and branches abroad and increase sales of Swiss goods. They became the prototypes of the modern multinationals. We can see this from their letters. There is one from a Frank Bieler in Minnesota, which is a good illustration of their 'wanderlust': "I am inclined to head off to California or Chile. It is eight thousand miles from here. It is a long time before you make any money here" (loc. cit., p. 289). And we can see the great occupational mobility of the Swiss emigrant from G. Schaefly in a letter to his mother from 1850: "For the rest no-one can say in advance what he wants to do in California, for you see here doctors, who now drive donkeys and oxen, traders, who run restaurants, and professors who are hairdressers" (loc. cit., p. 285).

So the lesson we can derive from Goethe's account and that of the emigrants is that the innovative power and mobility of entrepreneurs are the factors which enable economic structural crises and unemployment to be overcome. The same conclusion was drawn at the time, and it helped the ideas on liberalism in trade, which Adam Smith had developed at the end of the eighteenth century, to their break-through in the economic policy of the nineteenth.

II. The Role of the Entrepreneur in Economic Policy

1. The State as Crisis Manager

The world economic crisis of 1929 destroyed the belief that the entrepreneur himself could cope with economic crises. "The depression attacked not only the economic structure but the central nervous system of the nation. The crisis brought to a head a long pent-up need for security. The speed with which the ideal of 'rugged individualism' was replaced by that of security for the individual shows that the creed of striving for success had been stretched to breaking point. The depression was more than an economic catastrophe – it was the bankruptcy of the philosophy on which a whole age had been built" (Heilbronner, 1956, p.219). The old classical prescriptions seemed useless. In such a situation the state appeared as crisis manager: demand management with the help of unemployment insurance benefits and state investment programmes on the one hand and protectionism on the other were the instruments with which the state sought to overcome the problems. The new prescription came not from Adam Smith but from Lord Keynes.

The role into which the state gradually moved may have corresponded, as Heilbronner suggests, to a latent desire for security on the part of the individual. On the other hand, however, the state certainly helped to strengthen this desire. Job security through a full employment policy and a close network of social security on the one hand and a de facto guarantee of existence with state subsidies and maintenance grants for enterprises on the other made a major contribution to changing the attitude of both employers and employees.

As a result of the experience of the world economic crisis and the general conclusions which were drawn entrepreneurs lost standing. They no longer appeared to people as institutions to secure and improve the welfare of all. At best they might be taken for willing pack-horses which, if brought to the water, might bend and drink, in other words invest as state cyclical policy required. From time to time they actually seemed to be the scapegoats of society rather than valuable members of it. In 1972 Scheuch examined the image of the entrepreneur in the mass media and came to the conclusion that in 15 out of 20 selected programmes the actions of entrepreneurs either appeared as bordering on the criminal or directly criminal (Scheuch, 1972, p.144). Röglin established in 1974 that 64% of the population believed that entrepreneurs lived on the work of others (Röglin, 1974, p.28f.). But entrepreneurs themselves, or a good part of them, namely 28%, believed that people thought of them as a superfluous social group (cf. also Faupel, 1975, p.64).

As the state has increasingly taken on the role of insurer against economic difficulties the desire for insurance on the part of employees has risen and at the same time brought a decline in the readiness of entrepreneurs to take a risk. Riesman believes that the shortage of entrepreneurs in the United States is due to greater fear of risk (Riesman, 1955, p.153). For the Federal Republic Prognos AG has diagnosed a decline in the readiness to take on liabilities (Wolf and Hofer, 1975, p.104ff.), while Kamp gives the high cost of entrepreneurial risk as a reason why the number of those who are prepared "to embark on the adventure of making themselves independent" has dropped (Kamp, 1978, p.1).

2. Doubts in State Demand Policy

The continued high level of unemployment in the Federal Republic and in the other Western countries together with the problems of economic structural change which became apparent in 1973 with the oil crisis and the transition to flexible exchange rates have in turn given rise to doubts concerning the validity of Keynes' ideas.

The academic battle is largely being fought over how unemployment should be interpreted and whether the unemployed are out of work in the classical sense or the

Keynesian. Should Dr. Smith or Dr. Keynes be asked to write out the prescription? Who will provide the correct remedy and aid the process of recovery?

One group wants to give the state not only the role of global steerer but of fine tuner as well. The state is to pursue an active structural policy. This group has discovered the state as major entrepreneur: with a massive investment programme it can actively encourage the development of regions and industries, securing people's future and at the same time, if its economic policy should run into difficulties, fall back on its citizens' solidarity and extract levies from them.

The others stress the dangers to an economy in which the state itself acts as entrepreneur. They believe that the advantages which accrue to a society from the concentration of risks in the state and the distribution of losses among all its citizens are less obvious in continuous crisis than the disadvantage which the loss of individual responsibility, mobility and creative imagination causes in a society's ability to cope with crises. If the loss of motivation resulting from the centralisation of the task of mastering structural change outweighs the advantages of collectivism it is better to tackle the problem of structural change de-centrally. So this group has re-discovered the entrepreneur, especially the founder or director of the medium-sized, innovative business.

3. The Schumpeter Entrepreneur as 'deus ex machina'

What matters is not the entrepreneur per se but the pioneer entrepreneur. He is the central figure in economic development. Schumpeter himself assigned this role to him. The call for the "Schumpeter entrepreneur" is part of the current repertoire of economic and financial policy. The reproach "passive guest" is used as justification for granting maintenance subsidies to companies in defective industries and attaching business conditions to them.

But as early as 1929 Erwin von Beckerath had already pointed out that the Schumpeter entrepreneur was a 'deus ex machina'.[2] It is therefore rather surprising that the paradigm is being produced again today as a justification for economic policy measures in the present economic situation.

The re-discovery of the dynamic entrepreneur as 'deus ex machina' who is going to solve all our economic problems requires a closer analysis of this figure. This will be done here in three sections:
– firstly, an examination of what Schumpeter really meant in using the term "pioneer entrepreneur",
– secondly acknowledgement of the criticism of Schumpeter's image of the entrepreneur and
– thirdly a development of the argument that what matters for economic policy is not the dynamic entrepreneur alone but a dynamic combination of the entrepreneur, his workers, consumers and politicians.

---

2 Von Beckerath, 1929, p. 537. Predöhl's attempt to undermine the concept that the Schumpeter entrepreneur is a 'deus ex machina' is not tenable, for Schumpeter may have later established an empirical relation between innovation and economic development but did not explain the process of the emergence of innovation. Cf. Predöhl, 1964, p. 312.

III. The Dynamic Entrepreneur

1. The Dynamic Entrepreneur in Schumpeter's Theory of Economic Development

For Schumpeter the essence of the entrepreneurial function was "the recognition and implementation of new possibilities in business" (Schumpeter, 1928, p. 483). He divided the entrepreneurial function into five categories (loc. cit.):[3]

1. the production and establishment of new products or new qualities of product,
2. the introduction of new production methods,
3. the creation of new industrial organisations,
4. opening new sales markets,
5. opening new sources of supply.

These functions can be found in any properly conducted large enterprise in the Federal Republic today. The provision of the appropriate techniques for the systematic exercise of these functions is on the curriculum of every course in management,[4] while the practice of them forms part of the post-experience courses of many a management institute. We can find comments on the success with which they have been performed in the annual reports of many German companies.[5] The complaint that there are not enough Schumpeterian entrepreneurs might therefore appear a little surprising.

The Schumpeterian entrepreneur, however, exercised these functions in a rather different way from what we generally find today. We can see this if we take a closer look at his image. These are the aqualities which make up the entrepreneur as Schumpeter understood the concept:

1. "He is a typical climber and without tradition . . . a revolutionary in business and the involuntary pioneer of social and political revolutions as well; his contemporaries deny him as soon as they have gone one step further so that he is often not accepted even among established industrialists" (Schumpeter, 1934, p. 130).
2. He is driven by the urge for action, the delight in independent and creative work but he is not motivated by the desire to satisfy needs".[6]
3. He does not decide by weighing marginal costs and benefits.[7]
4. In his decisions he does not weigh risks and opportunities against each other. "He

---

3 Cf. also Rexhausen, 1960, p. 14.
4 Admittedly in Hankel's words "modern education in business administration is simply transmuting Smith's and Schumpeter's fine images of the creative entrepreneur who gives rise to employment into a professional jargon which is only intelligible to candidates for senior management posts. All we hear of is 'operations research', 'linear programming', 'management decision by cost improvement', 'marketing' and so on. Let him study who can, especially if his company pays. For the educated man of our time it will suffice to know that society can count on its entrepreneurs, thanks to Smith and Schumpeter, now turned into managers" (Hankel, 1975, p. 28). However, the basic argument of this article is of course that it cannot be a matter of indifference to the educated person today if current economic policy is based on an image of the entrepreneur which may be very fine but is false or at least obsolete.
5 The 1978 Siemens AG annual report contains statistics showing that 45% of turnover was achieved with products which were not yet five years old.
6 Schumpeter, 1934, 1st edition, p. 145, 4th edition, p. 138.
7 Ibid. 1st edition, pp. 145, 150, 4th edition, pp. 135 ff.

is that type which despises hedonist balance and does not gaze fearfully at the risks involved."[8]

5. He does not carefully study every possible alternative combination, for then "he would never get around to acting"; on the contrary he unconsciously takes the right decisions.[9]

6. He uses 100% borrowed funds.[10]

7. He overcomes all external difficulties and these are many, for " the worker resists new methods, the consumer new products and public opinion new forms of enterprise, as do the authorities, the law and creditors."[11]

8. This type of entrepreneur is neither a profession nor a permanent state; it is "behaviour which can occasionally be observed in a small percentage of individuals".[12]

2. Criticism of the Schumpeterian Entrepreneur

It is doubtful whether any modern entrepreneur would recognise himself in Schumpeter's image of the pioneer. Indeed, the Company Constitution Act no longer permits a type of whom Schumpeter himself said: "The results of defeat for him and the question of whether all those who are dependent on him will lose the provision for their old age does not matter to him."[13]

But clearly such figures exercised a tremendous fascination in their contemporary society. Schumpeter said of them: "Their acts are the most grandiose, brilliant thing which business life can offer to the observer and any static or hedonist explanation will appear quite miserable beside it. Ninety-nine out of a hundred impartial observers will admit this without hesitation, even if we refrain from mentioning names."[14]

Ernst Kretschmer in his famous book "Körperbau und Charakter" had no hesitation in mentioning names: "From the group of great organisers and technicians we can take as example the great engineer and inventor Werner von Siemens, a magnificent head with a sharply curving nose, glittering eyes and broad, full pycnic features. A conqueror, full of spirit, joy in life and courage, unconcerned, fresh, masculine and elastic. He is a creator, pouring out new plans and ideas in precipitate abundance, almost to the point of fragmentation; a modern major industrialist of bold and imaginative business sense. With no inherited fortune to help him he conquered the world „in almost giddy flight", creating major enterprises in Russia and overseas almost out of empty earth. A powerful, fundamentally cheerful personality, a great optimist, honest, proud, courageous and totally unsentimental."[15] Emil du Bois-Reymond also

---

8 Ibid., 1st edition, p. 163, 4th edition p. 125.

9 Ibid. 1st edition p. 177. The 4th edition is rather more cautious: "Here success entirely depends on the "glimpse", the ability to see things in a way which later proves its worth even if at first no reasons can be given for this" (p. 125).

10 Ibid., 1st edition, p. 208, 4th edition, p. 104; (1929) p. 313; 1928 p. 485.

11 Ibid., 1928, p. 483; 1934 1st edition, p. 152; 4th edition, pp. 118, 126.

12 Ibid., 1934, 4th edition, pp. 116, 121.

13 Ibid., 1934, 1st edition, p. 163.

14 Ibid., 1934, 1st edition, p. 138.

15 Quoted from Moths and von Haselberg, 1978, p. 30.

broke into spasms of delight when he introduced Werner von Siemens into the Prussian Academy of Science in 1874 (Du Bois-Reymond, 1956, p. 281): "Now you are master of a world which you created. Your telegraph wires encircle the earth. Your cable steamers crown the ocean. Under the tents of nomads with their bows and arrows whose green meadows are traversed by your messages your name is spoken in superstitious awe." In addition to the national pride – "What German science and German industry can achieve" – comes admiration for the man who "has scaled the heights, a prince of science, holding in his hand the threads of innumerable combinations with a hundred plans going through his head."

We may take it that such hymns of praise were rather the expression of the exuberance of the age than a sober reflection of the nature of the entrepreneur in the nineteenth century. For we must not forget that the image of the entrepreneur at that time was not only formed by men like Werner von Siemens and Robert Bosch, who formulated the business principle "better to lose money than our clients confidence" but also by men like Jim Fisk, who dismissed his flight from a group of furious cheated shareholders with the laconic comment "lost nothing but honour."[16]

How critically dynamic entrepreneurs were regarded even at the time when Schumpeter was describing them can be seen from a letter from the Chairman of the Board of Managing Directors of Mannesmann AG, Eich, to the Chairman of his Supervisory Board, Steinthal, on 12.12.1918 (Strandmann, 1978, p. 146): "Rhenish-Westphalian industry has been characterised so far, I would say, by men like Kirdorf, Thyssen and Stinnes. They were born to command and their industrial beginning came at a time which should be seen as long past; they have certainly well understood how to use their enormous influence but not in such a way as to suggest that the workforce is also entitled to represent its interests." Four years earlier Eich had written to Steinthal: "The old captains of industry have not yet been able to get over the fact that during the last twenty years the old serfdom which dominated in industry as well has given way to a situation where the workers can have their own say. That industry has been through an exemplary development under the new conditions, in other words that it has fared better rather than worse, is something these gentlemen entirely overlook" (Strandmann, 1978, p. 132).

So Schumpeter's image of the pioneer entrepreneur was not correct even when he drew it. It is certainly right that entrepreneurs have to be obsessed by their work and need missionary fervour to convince potential and initially reserved customers that their new ideas are worthwhile. The intensity with which they do this is no less today than it was in the nineteenth century. Of Robert Wood, President of Sears & Roebuck up to 1954, it has been said that he was so intense in business discussions that he put sweets in his mouth and forgot to remove the paper and actually chewed cigarettes instead of lighting them (Ways, 1979, p. 45). But that does not affect the criticism of Schumpeter's image. Rexhausen has assembled it in a careful analysis (Rexhausen, 1960, p. 33) and summarises it in these words: "Economic development does not simply take the form of new combinations which become established. Sometime somewhere these have to be accepted and if they are not accepted no "forcefulness" will suffice. There will be neither an entrepreneur nor a successful enterprise nor economic development." So it is not only the dynamic entrepreneur who is the prerequisite

16 Boyd, 1972, p. 160 f., on Jim Fisk see also Kirkland, 1951, p. 365.

for development, – or this is my argument – but the dynamic combination of entrepreneur, staff and environment. Schumpeter himself was not totally unaware of this as we see from a remark in the first edition of his "Theorie der wirtschaftlichen Entwicklung:" "Certainly even the man of action has to come to terms with any particular given circumstances and equally certainly he can only do this if the time is right. Of course I do not mean by this that he can put up the latest blast furnace in an economy run by nomadic tribes" (p. 152). But Schumpeter did not devote enough attention to the conditions under which the pioneer entrepreneur may expect to awaken latent demand with his new product and satisfy this.[17] That is the reason for the foreshortened view of the dynamic entrepreneur in present economic policy discussion.

IV. The Innovative Combination

1. Social Conditions for Innovative Enterprises

Modern business research devotes particular attention to the social conditions under which innovative enterprises may emerge.[18] Here we can point to four main conditions:
1. A basic consensus on the functions of the enterprise in the economy,
2. Sufficient incentive for an adequate number of members of society to engage in business,
3. Sufficient purchasing power on the part of innovative and imitative customers,
4. Sufficient dynamic politicians.

ad 1. The Basic Consensus

The need for a basic consensus in society has been the particular concern of those authors who, standing in the tradition of Max Weber, have analysed modern industrial society. Among the most important are Müller-Armack, Heuss and McClelland.[19]

If a society places high value on independence and achievement, dynamic entrepreneurs are likely to emerge either directly or through the upbringing of children. Biucchi speaks of a "consensus populi"in Switzerland which produced these "notable figures from the cultural and economic background of the age" (Biucchi, 1972, p. 16). As surveys have shown this basic consensus would appear to have grown again in the Federal Republic in recent years (Noelle-Neumann, 1976). Between May 1965 and June 1976 the share of those who believe that the entrepreneur bears not only great responsibility but also has a wealth of ideas and progressive, far-reaching thinking has very greatly increased. The consensus is obviously much greater than the entrepreneurs themselves, still shocked from the wave of rejection of the early 1970s, suspect.

---

17 See also Dürr, 1977, p. 107.
18 See also Kamien and Schwartz, 1975, p. 1.
19 See Dürr, 1977, p. 105 ff.

But in the view of the Council of Economic Experts the "amount of entrepreneurial courage and social consensus necessary for a high level of employment" was not great enough in 1976 (Sachverständigenrat, 1976, Fig. 283).

ad 2. The Incentive to Entrepreneurial Activity

That adequate incentive is needed to motivate sufficient people in a society to engage in business activity is a platitude. It is more difficult to answer the question of what is adequate incentive. The Council of Economic Experts measures this by the number of new enterprises being founded and by how nearly investors "have their backs to the wall" (Sachverständigenrat, 1977, Fig. 281 and 309).

Schumpeter himself has compared the incentives which must be offered to the dynamic entrepreneur with a game: "The game is not so similar to roulette as it is to poker . . . extraordinary rewards, much greater than are really needed to stimulate a particular achievement, are loaded on to a small minority of happy winners, and this stimulates the great majority of entrepreneurs to much greater activity than a more even and "fairer" distribution could" (Rexhausen, 1960, p. 49). Our society does not appear to offer this condition and we may point to two reasons. Firstly considerable inequalities in distribution may be accepted in the football pools or lotteries but where the distribution of incomes is concerned high gains for pioneers often appear to be unacceptable both to the workforce and the Federal Cartel Office. On the other hand, however, the chances of being able to develop a new and successful product are not much better than of winning the football pools: "The chance of getting the right number in roulette is much greater than of finding a really effective new substance which will take us further in medical science" said Adolf Jann in 1978 in an interview.[20] He put it at one to ten thousand, and Büchel gives the same figure (Büchel, 1979, p. 2). We should add that today it takes ten years from the time a new substance is discovered to the time when it can be offered (as medicine) on the market. "If ten years ago documentation of between 200 and 500 pages was enough now a pile of between one and four metres high will be required, not counting the copies that have to be made. That is simply to register the product in the Federal Republic." (loc. cit.) Under these social conditions innovation is no longer the result of the imagination and forcefulness of one entrepreneur, it is a long and wearisome and extremely expensive process, needing detailed planning of means and careful coordination of many different people and bodies.

ad. 3. The Innovative Customers

There is no lack of the third condition, purchasing power on the part of innovative and imitative customers, in the Federal Republic.[21] There is rather a lack of innovative demand to try out new products or encourage the development of new products and procedures. But it is of decisive importance for the success of the Schumpeter en-

20 Reflections of a Corporate Autocrat, International Management, September, 1978, p. 15, here 17.
21 Von Hayek only saw this condition in justifying high incomes with their economic function of trying out new products. The equation of high incomes and a high readiness to experiment, however, is not justifiable. Purchasing power is a necessary but not adequate condition for an innovative purchaser. Cf. von Hayek, 1952–3, p. 508; p. 19, 1968.

trepreneur that he should find innovative demand to take up the new product. This sparks off a process of imitation by less risk-happy purchasers which helps to establish the new product on the market.

We can find a good example of the innovative customer in Chancellor Bismarck. In 1887 Wilhelm Maibach was arrested because he ignored a veto and used a boat with a Daimler-Benz petrol engine on the Main during the Frankfurt regatta. The authorities justified the veto by reasoning that a boat full of petrol would be bound to blow up and this would disturb the festivities (Rathke, 1953, p. 140). A year later Bismarck ordered a similar boat for pleasure use on lake Friedrichsruhe. After that the motor boat was established and its triumphal progress began.

For reinforced concrete it was not the public sector but private industrial customers who created the innovative demand. A building specialist (in the public sector) had reacted angrily in 1903: "Don't mention that latest swindle, reinforced concrete, to me." But between 1905 and 1908 the new product became increasingly popular in industry "because purchasers here proved more ready to accept innovations" (v. Klass, 1965, p. 38). Impressive examples of such innovative purchasers were the Zeiss works in Jena and the Opel works in Rüsselsheim, whose building of 1906 used the new procedure.

How dynamic the innovative demand which helped Thalysia Edelformer to establish itself at the beginning of this century proved to be can unfortunately no longer be established. Paul Garms, Schumpeterian entrepreneur, advertised the new product by announcing: "No stopping German victory in ladies' wear! The natural consequence of the rejection of foreign elements brings us this happy development, a product to rout the ruinous effects of French fashions in corsetry which have made invalids of our German women. This is the only true German product, a creation of pure and natural beauty giving no damage to health, with no imitation of French models. Thalysia-Edelformer has long been widely known and patented. Our noble model is not laced, does not hinder breathing or freedom of movement, it is not troublesome to wear or so fiendishly expensive as the Paris corset. Nor is it shameless like these but envelopes even the stronger figure in a tender and gently natural German shape."

ad. 4. Dynamic Politicians

The fourth condition for the success of the innovative entrepreneur is finally that he should find politicians who accept the new combinations and are prepared to create the necessary legal and political conditions for their establishment on the market. Schumpeter was too one-sided here and saw only the resistance which politicians can put up and which the pioneer entrepreneur has to combat. He rather overlooks the fact that the spread of business enterprise in the nineteenth century was not least due to the positive attitude on the part of the territorial rulers. But it should not be overlooked that the creation and establishment of free trade at the beginning of the nineteenth century and the removal of the need for concessions in the second half of the century created essential political prerequisites for the emergence and development of the dynamic entrepreneur.

The dynamic combination of entrepreneurs and politicians in the nineteenth century can be illustrated in a wide range of cases. Let us just take one from that sphere in which the state now appears rather in the role of supervisory office than of dynamic politician: insurance. Friedrich Adolph Brüggemann, of whom it was said that "he made the Aachener und Münchner Feuer-Versicherungs-Gesellschaft, which he headed, into one of the leading German insurance enterprises" (Koch, 1968, p. 265), was appointed by the founder of the company, David Hansemann, as agent because "he could pursue his insurance business in the town-hall in addition to his function as civic official." Later Brüggemann succeeded in establishing his enterprise in Bavaria as well as Prussia. In the royal resolution on the establishment of 10. 2. 1834 King Ludwig I pointed out "that it had long been his endeavour as sovereign of his people to acquire for them such an insurance enterprise; so far however there had neither been funds for a state institution nor sufficient interest from private backers." Now the sovereign's wishes had met and combined with Brüggemann's enterprising spirit, and the result was an unprecedented success for the company.

Nowadays such dynamic combinations of private enterprise and politics are perhaps even more important, but they are more rare. Sometimes one even has the impression that it is the dynamic city councillors who make good use of enterprises to create new combinations and achieve their aims in local politics. The significance of the dynamic local politician in combination with the dynamic entrepreneur would certainly appear to have received too little attention so far and it has not been sufficiently assessed in relation to economic policy. The resistance to the abolition of the pay-roll tax in the local authority areas concerned could be taken as an indication of the fact that the dynamic local politicians bitterly oppose any restriction on their entrepreneurial freedom, here their financial autonomy. Those who call for the dynamic entrepreneur should not overlook the dynamic local politician.

2. The Innovative Enterprise

2.1. Features of the Innovative Enterprise

These four conditions are the soil in which the modern innovative enterprise can flourish. But this has quite different features from Schumpeter's entrepreneur as can be seen from the following seven points:
1. The more established an enterprise is and the more successful it has been in the past, the stronger are its efforts at innovation. Only great enterprises are constantly active in innovation (Kamien and Schwartz, 1975, p. 16 f.)
2. Innovation processes are steered by the market. This can be either directly through pressure of competition, as is largely the case with smaller enterprises (innovation through demand pull) or it can be through recognition of market chances and a systematic search for innovation (innovation through supply pressure) (Albach, 1972, p. 11 f.).
3. A clear identification of need is an important prerequisite for the success of the innovation process.[22]
4. The decision on innovation projects follows on the basis of detailed business analyses. Project cost calculations and project direction on the basis of stopping rules

---

22 Kamien and Schwartz, 1975, p. 11. Mensch refers to the effect of external contacts in increasing innovation, 1979, p. 74.

are to ensure that the expected marginal benefit of the project exceeds its marginal costs.

5. The innovative enterprise is not obsessed by risk but it calculates this carefully. Many methods have been developed in recent years for doing this. On the basis of detailed historical examinations Kocka reaches the conclusion that "it is possible for the readiness to innovation at the head of major enterprises to increase – a direct contradiction of Josef Schumpeter's grim prognoses of increasing rigidity and slackening dynamic in modern bureaucratised large enterprises" (Kocka, 1978, p.581).

6. Especially enterprises which are research and innovation-intensive study every possible alternative combination very carefully. Computers and a great arsenal of "creative methods" are used to ensure that every possibility is considered and none overlooked in the innovation process.

7. Only the company's own funds are available for research and development. Asked why his enterprise only financed future development out of its own funds Jann answered: "As you know, I used to be a banker. So you needn't be surprised if I say that I do not want to be dependent on the banks."[23] Most companies do not even have a choice. They have no access to bank credit to finance innovation. The power to self-finance is decisive for the innovation process.

Hence the modern innovative enterprise varies on every point from the image of the dynamic entrepreneur as drawn by Schumpeter. The cry for the "Schumpeterian entrepreneur" in business is due both to a nostalgic view of the social conditions of the nineteenth century and lack of knowledge of the innovative processes in a modern enterprise.

Enterprises today have found organisational forms which see innovation as a continuous task and so organise change through innovation instead of leaving this to the chance interactions of Schumpeter's entrepreneurs.

2.2. New Forms of Organisation

For Schumpeter too the creation of new forms of organisation in industry was a major aspect of dynamic entrepreneurial action. But he overlooked the interdependence between the various forms of entrepreneurial dynamic. It was Chandler more than anyone who drew attention to this (1977). His argument is that the actual innovative achievement in industrial development is not so much the creation of new products and procedures but the coordination of the activities in the enterprise which these entail and which make innovation possible by the "visible hand of management."

The owner-entrepreneur with a medium-sized business generally controls his own staff and initiates innovation in his enterprise himself. He looks after his customers directly. The coordination of production and sales is through personal contact on the market. Coordination within the enterprise is not a serious problem. This type of enterprise comes closest to the picture drawn by Schumpeter of the dynamic entrepreneur.

The owner of a major enterprise faces different problems. For this type of busi-

---

23 Reflections of a Corporate Autocrat, International Management, September, 1978, p. 17.

ness the concept "entrepreneurial enterprise" has been coined in literature.[24] The need here is to coordinate mass production with mass sales. The owner can no longer do this himself. He needs the middle management. The techniques of production steering through scientific management and the coordination of distribution to production through a systematic stock and distribution policy is the innovative achievement of middle management.

As this innovative level became independent and professionalised within the enterprise it led to the separation of ownership and control and the development of the great manager enterprise or public company. It was only in this form of enterprise that the new management techniques of sales fore casting, long-range planning and diversification could develop. Methods of systematic search for new products were developed. Systematic research became an independent function in the enterprise. The divisional organisation form was the organisational innovation, making it possible to manage so complex a structure.

So major enterprises are not only themselves the carriers of important innovation processes, they also produce innovations which enable new forms of the innovation of products and procedures to be developed to a degree hitherto unknown. The modern big company is a major carrier of the functions which Schumpeter saw incorporated in the dynamic entrepreneur: it is not only the inflexible, bureaucratic power structure which has appeared in many critical analyses since Max Weber and which is recognisable in this later, more friendly approach: a baby is found in front of the gates to a large enterprise. No-one knows whose it is and a commission is formed to find out. After a considerable length of time the commission produces a report, in which it states that this cannot be the child of one of the workforce since in this enterprise a) nothing is produced which is perfectly in order b) nothing is produced with love and joy and c) nothing is ever finished within nine months.

For Schumpeter opening new markets for well-known products was also innovation. In the nineteenth century our Swiss emigrants opened up new sales markets overseas. Today many enterprises see it as their task to meet the material need in the developing countries and so contribute to reducing the prosperity gap between north and south. Many observers believe that multinational enterprises represent an organisational innovation and that under present social and business conditions they can best cope with this task. Others doubt this and see in the multinationals institutions of business exploitation. Clearly what is needed is an organisational innovation to effect a dynamic combination of multinational enterprises and dynamic politicians in developing countries.

V. Conclusions

As we see, it is no longer possible to build up a meaningful business or economic policy on the Schumpeterian concept of the enterpreneur. The "Schumpeter-entrepreneur" is, as a historical concept, a rather confusing abbreviation of what in the pres-

---

24 See i. a. J. Kocka, 1975, p. 203, esp. p . 218 ff.

ent economic situation would be a meaningful policy to improve production, investment and growth conditions for enterprises. It has little in common with what Schumpeter described as the dynamic enterprise. The abbreviation has led to many a misunderstanding, as we see in the discussion of the supply-oriented policy recommended by the Council of Economic Experts. For present economic policy it is not the dynamic entrepreneur but the dynamic combination of entrepreneur, politician, workers and consumers which matters. The emphasis on this dynamic combination is based on the recognition that there is inter-dependence between the rate of product and procedure innovation and the rate of organisational innovation. Measures to encourage new products and procedures within the framework of economic policy are only efficient if the interest of local politicians is considered and the business climate is such that it may be expected that the new products will be taken up; it is also necessary for an enterprise to be able to cope organisationally with the conflict of interests inside the plant. If a balance cannot be found in the development of the three factors, social consensus, rate of product innovation and rate of organisational development one-sided measures such as investment programmes to stimulate demand, wage restraint to encourage the entrepreneur to invest or innovation incentive programmes to lower the risk will achieve little. What we must strive for is the dynamic combination in which today's enterprises are prepared to take risks to cope with structural change and to create new jobs.

The alternatives mentioned at the beginning of this article, on which Frau Susanne sought Leonardo's advice, to "adopt the new methods or emigrate," no longer apply. Under present-day conditions Leonardo would have to advise her both to set up machines at home and to open a branch in the USA! With a combination of the two Frau Susanne would not have to fear that she was taking bread out of people's mouths, she would know that she was making more available to all of them. But the combination is now only possible through joint efforts by dynamic entrepreneurs and dynamic politicians. The expression "Japan Inc." is hardly fair. But there are increasing signs that particularly the smaller countries have recognised that the implementation of such a dynamic combination is a strategic task.[25] Perhaps we should think about this in the Federal Republic as well.

Bibliography

Albach H (1972) Fusionskontrolle und Preisbildung von Unternehmen. In: Bartholomeyczik H et al. (ed) Beiträge zum Wirtschaftsrecht. Festschrift for Heinz Kaufmann's 65th Birthday. Cologne-Marienburg, pp 1–12

Beckerath E von (1962) Einige Bemerkungen zu Schumpeters Theorie der wirtschaftlichen Entwicklung. Schmollers Jahrbuch 53, 1929, pp 537–555; reprinted in: Lynkeus: Gestalten und Probleme aus Wirtschaft und Politik. Tübingen

Boston Consulting Group (1979). En Rom for Svensk Industripolitik. Preliminary report.

Bowring J (1837) Bericht an das englische Parlament über den Handel, die Fabriken und Gewerbe in der Schweiz. Zürich

---

25 See e. g. Boston Consulting Group, 1978, Honko, 1979.

Boyd J (1972) Men of Distinction. In: Heilbronner R L (ed) In the Name of Profit. Garden City, NY pp 154–219

Biucchi B M (1972) Schweizerische Textilunternehmen im Zeitalter der industriellen Revolution 1800–1830. In: Blümle E B, Fleck F (ed) Festgabe für Professor Dr. Josef Schwarzfischer zu seinem 70. Geburtstag. Freiburg/Sw., pp 1 ff

Büchel K H (1979) Investitionen in die Zukunft, Bayer Berichte 41, pp 27 ff

Chandler A D Jr (1977) The visible hand – The managerial revolution in American business. Cambridge, London

Du Bois-Reymond E (1956) Erwiderung auf die Antrittsrede von Werner von Siemens. In: von der Leyen F: Das Buch deutscher Reden und Rufe. Passau, pp 279–282

Dürr E (1977) Wachstumspolitik. Bern, Stuttgart

Faupel M (1975) Tätigkeitsbilder und Persönlichkeiten des deutschen Managers. Thesis, Bonn

Goethe J W von (1976) Wilhelm Meisters Wanderjahre. Quoted from: Poetische Werke Berliner Ausgabe, vol 11, 3rd edition, Berlin, Weimar

Hankel W (1975) Heldensagen der Wirtschaft oder: schöne heile Wirtschaftswelt. Düsseldorf, Vienna

Hayek F A von (1968) Die Ungerechtigkeit der Steuerprogression, Schweizer Monatshefte 32, 1952-3, pp 508–17; ibid.: Grundtatsachen des Fortschritts, ORDO 9, 1957, pp 19–42; ibid.: Der Wettbewerb als Entdeckungsverfahren, Kiel

Heilbronner R (1956) The Quest for Wealth, New York

Honko J (1979) Suomalainen talousrooli, Helsinki

Kamien M I, Schwartz N L (1975) Market Structure and Innovation: A Survey. Journal of Economic Literature 13, pp 1–37

Kamp M E (1978) Probleme neugegründeter Unternehmen – Eine empirische Untersuchung. Beiträge zur Mittelstandsforschung. Heft 40, Göttingen

Kirkland E C (1951) A History of American Economic Life, 3rd edition, New York

Klass G von (1965) Weit spannt sich der Bogen 1865–1965. Die Geschichte der Bauunternehmung Dyckerhoff und Wiedmann. Wiesbaden

Koch P (1968) Pioniere des Versicherungsgedankens. Wiesbaden

Kocka J (1975) Expansion – Integration – Diversifikation. Wachstumsstrategien industrieller Großunternehmen in Deutschland vor 1914. In: Winkel H (ed) Vom Kleingewerbe zur Grossindustrie. Schriften des Vereins für Sozialpolitik. N F Vol 83, Berlin

Kocka J (1978) Entrepreneurs and Managers in German Industrialisation. In: Matthias P, Postan M M The Cambridge Economic History of Europe, Vol VII; pp 492–589

Mann J D (1967) The Textile Industry: Machinery for Cotton, Flax, Wool 1760–1850. In: The Oxford History of Technology, vol IV, 1958, Reprinted

Mensch G (1979) Beobachtungen zum Innovationsverhalten kleiner, mittlerer und mittelgrosser Unternehmen. Zeitschrift für Betriebswirtschaft, pp 72–78

Moths E, Haselberg P von (6th Ocotber 1978) Unternehmen – Das unbekannte Wesen. Die Zeit, p 30

Noelle-Neumann E (18. and 22. November 1976) Das Unternehmerbild 1976. Frankfurter Allgemeine Zeitung. Blick durch die Wirtschaft

Predöhl A (1964) Bemerkungen zu E.v. Beckeraths Gedanken zu Schumpeters Theorie der wirtschaftlichen Entwicklung. In: Kloten N et al. (ed) Systeme und Methoden in den Wirtschafts- und Sozialwissenschaften. Erwin von Beckerath zum 75. Geburtstag. Tübingen, pp 312–333

Rexhausen F (1960) Der Unternehmer und die wirtschaftliche Entwicklung. Berlin

Riesman D (1955) Selected Essays from Individualism Reconsidered. Garden City N Y

Röglin H C (1974) Unternehmer in Deutschland. Vivisektion einer Elite. Düsseldorf, Vienna

Rathke K (1953) Wilhelm Maibach. Friedrichshafen

Sachverständigenrat zur Begutachtung der Wirtschaftlichen Entwicklung: Zeit zum Investieren, Annual Report 1976/77, Stuttgart, Mainz; ibid.: Mehr Wachstum, mehr Beschäftigung. Annual Report 1977/78. Stuttgart, Mainz

Schelbert L, Rappolt H (1977) Alles ist ganz anders hier. Auswandererschicksale in zwei Jahrhunderten. Olten-Freiburg

Scheuch E (1972) Das Bild der Wirtschaft in nichtwirtschaftlichen Sendungen der Massenmedien. In: Veröffentlichungen der Walter-Reimann-Stiftung, vol 14: Wirtschaft und öffentliche Meinung, Cologne

Schumpeter J A (1928) Unternehmer, article in Handwörterbuch der Staatswissenschaften, 4th edition, vol VIII, Jena, pp 476–87

Schumpeter J A Der Unternehmer in der Volkswirtschaft von heute. In: Harms B (ed) Strukturwand-
    lungen in der deutschen Volkswirtschaft, vol 1. Berlin, 1929; Ibid.: Theorie der wirtschaftlichen
    Entwicklung. 4th edition, Berlin 1934. Reprint 1952.
Strandmann P von (1978) Unternehmenspolitik und Unternehmensführung. Düsseldorf, Vienna
Ways M (1979) The Hall of Fame for Business Leadership. Fortune, May
Wolff H, Hofer P (1975) Analyse und Prognose der Unternehmensgrößenstruktur. Gutachten der
    Prognos AG für das Bundeswirtschaftsministerium (report by Prognos AG for the Federal Minis-
    try of Economics), Basel

The Banks and the Steel Industry in the Ruhr

Developments in Relations from 1873 to 1914

Wilfried Feldenkirchen

I.

The growth of the iron and steel industry before the First World War is seen in literature as closely related to the development of the major German banks. Helmut
Böhme pointed out a few years ago, however, that modern research is largely based
on theoretical work as the factual basis is uncertain.[1] The difficulty of obtaining adequate source material raises a number of problems in an attempt to establish the significance of the banks for the development of enterprises in the iron and steel industry in the Ruhr. The records of the major banks for the period up to 1914 appear to be
lost. There are virtually no public records for this field. It is therefore only possible to
make statements concerning the relation between the banks and enterprises in the
iron and steel industry on the basis of the archives of the enterprises themselves.

This article is the result of an assessment of the archive material of Gutehoffnungshütte (GHH), Fried. Krupp, Hörder Bergwerks- und Hüttenverein (HV), Phoenix, Aktiengesellschaft für Bergbau und Hüttenbetrieb, Bochumer Verein für Bergbau und Gusstahlfabrikation (BV), Union Aktiengesellschaft für Bergbau, Eisen-
und Stahlindustrie, Rheinische Stahlwerke (RSW), Eisen- und Stahlwerk Hoesch,
Schalker Gruben- und Hüttenverein, Gewerkschaft Deutscher Kaiser (GDK) in regard to this question. At the end of the period concerned these companies accounted
for roughly 70% of pig iron production and about 64% of raw steel production in the
Ruhr. With regard to the date of establishment, their legal forms and activities the
choice of these companies would appear to enable statements to be made which are
representative at least for the big integrated concerns of the iron and steel industry in
the Ruhr.

---

1 Cf. Gerald D. Feldmann: Iron and Steel in the German Inflation, 1916–1923. Princeton, 1977, p.
   19; Karl Erich Born: Geld und Banken. Stuttgart, 1977, p. 151 ff. Richard Tilly: The Growth of
   Large-Scale Enterprise in Germany. In: The Rise of Managerial Capitalism. Ed. H. Daems and
   H. van der Wee. Leuven, 1974, p. 145 ff.; Jürgen Kocka: Unternehmer in der deutschen Industrialisierung. Göttingen, 1975, p. 100–105; H. Neuburger/H. Stokes: German Banks and German Growth. In: Journal of Economic History 34, 1974, p. 710 ff.; Helmut Böhme: Bankenkonzentration und Schwerindustrie 1873–1896. Bemerkungen zum Problem des "Organisierten Kapitalismus". In: Sozialgeschichte heute. Festschrift für Hans Rosenberg. Göttingen, 1974,
   p. 432–451; Böhme also gives a survey of the most important older literature on this subject.

II.

Until the middle of the last century the iron and steel industry in the Ruhr played only a relatively small role in the German iron industry as a whole. With a production of pig iron of 11,500 tons in 1850 the Ruhr accounted for a share of about 5% in total German pig iron production.[2] Its share of further processing was slightly higher as several puddling works and rolling mills had been established in the 1830s and 1840s. The general cyclical upswing at the beginning of the 1850s, the steady lowering of transport costs through the railways, the rise in the demand for iron to build railways and finally the possibility of using coke instead of charcoal as fuel brought the establishment of a number of iron works in the early 1850s. The works established in the east of the Ruhr were to mine and process the ore discovered there after 1849. Among the large number of companies founded between 1852 and about 1856 the most important were Phoenix, Aktiengesellschaft für Bergbau- und Hüttenbetrieb and Henrichshütte. Hermannshütte and Mayer & Kühne, which had existed since the 1840s, were changed into Hörder Bergwerks- und Hüttenverein and Bochumer Verein für Bergbau und Gusstahlfabrikation in 1852 and 1854 respectively. As few of the industrial enterprises had the necessary capital the existing banks played a large part in these establishments by acquiring shares in the reorganised or newly founded enterprises.

As there were at that time no banks in the Ruhr capable of business on such a scale it was mainly the Cologne banks which provided the funds for these new establishments in the 1850s.[3] The Schaaffhausen'sche Bankverein, the first German joint stock bank which had taken over the customers of the old private bank, provided considerable funds to the emergent Rhenish-Westphalian industry.[4] As the Cologne banks had maintained international relations, especially with France and Belgium, for a long time, they were also able to provide foreign capital. For Phoenix, founded in 1852, Franco-Belgian capital was used with Sal. Oppenheim acting as intermediary.[5] The Hörder Bergwerks- und Hüttenverein was changed into a joint stock company in

---

2 Wirtschaftliche Entwickelung des Niederrheinisch-Westfälischen Steinkohlen-Bergbaus in der zweiten Hälfte des 19. Jahrhunderts. Vol. III. Berlin, 1904, p. 22.

3 Cf. Jacob Riesser: Die deutschen Grossbanken und ihre Konzentration im Zusammenhang mit der Entwicklung der Gesamtwirtschaft in Deutschland. 3 rd completely revised and enlarged edition. Jena, 1910, p.379 ff.; Walther Däbritz: Entstehung und Aufbau des rheinisch-westfälischen Industriebezirks. In: Beiträge zur Geschichte der Technik und Industrie. Jahrbuch des Vereins deutscher Ingenieure. Ed. Conrad Matschoss. Vol. 15. Berlin, 1925, p. 43f.; Martin Gehr: Das Verhältnis zwischen Banken und Industrie in Deutschland seit der Mitte des 19. Jahrhunderts bis zur Bankenkrise von 1931 unter besonderer Berücksichtigung des industriellen Grosskredits. Thesis, Tübingen, 1959, p. 9ff. Albert Blumenberg: Die Konzentration im deutschen Bankwesen. Thesis Heidelberg, Leipzig, 1905, p. 36ff.; A. Schaaffhausen'sche Bankverein Köln (1848–1928). Cologne, 1928, p. 6f. Die Disconto-Gesellschaft 1851 bis 1901. Publication to mark the bank's fiftieth anniversary, Berlin 1901, p. 158.; Hellmut Gebhard: Die Berliner Börse – Von den Anfängen bis zum Jahre 1896. Thesis, Erlangen, 1928, p. 45; Kurt Bergmann: Die wirtschaftsgeschichtliche Entwicklung des Ruhrkohlenbergbaus seit Anfang des 19. Jahrhunderts. Thesis, Cologne, 1937, p. 125.

4 A. Schaaffhausen'sche Bankverein AG, Köln 1848–1928. Cologne, 1928, p. 6.

5 There were a number of banks in Cologne operating internationally long before the Ruhr acquired any great importance. In addition to Schaaffhausen Oppenheim and Deichmann & Co.

1852 through a group with which the Schaaffhausen'sche Bankverein maintained close relations.

The Bankverein generally limited its activities to the establishment of companies in close geographical proximity to itself, so as to be able to exercise better control. Generally it took only a small participation, seeing its task rather to make freely disposable funds available to the new companies than to tie up its own funds over the longer term. The fact that it largely restricted its engagement to the coal, iron and steel industry in the Ruhr, which fully utilised its financial capacity, secured the Schaaffhausen'sche Bankverein the leading position in this sector, which it was to retain until the end of the period we are concerned with here.

While the Cologne banks generally only provided aid for the establishment of an enterprise, prefering regular banking business after the successful establishment, the Disconto-Gesellschaft and the Berliner Handelsgesellschaft, which also played an important part in the establishment of the new enterprises, took larger direct participations in companies they established. The Disconto-Gesellschaft, however, had to pay for its readiness to involve large funds with heavy losses. The Henrichshütte, reorganised in 1857, was changed into a limited partnership in 1863 after causing the bank considerable loss. From 1860 to 1863 the Disconto-Gesellschaft participated in the successful financial reorganisation of the Phoenix enterprise, which had got into financial difficulties. The bank retained its close relations with the company and played a large part in the later capital increase.

By 1857 the first phase of establishments in the iron and steel industry in the Ruhr was over. The economic crisis lasted until 1859 and the subsequent only slow rise in demand could be satisfied by existing companies. In financing the expansion of the existing companies in the 1860s priority shares played the major part. These had a fixed interest rate and were often issued at a discount. The large number of newly founded companies and the expansion of existing enterprises brought the share of the Ruhr in pig iron production in the German "Reich" to around 26% by 1870.

The favourable economic situation after the mid-1860s, the removal of the approval requirement for joint stock companies and the successful conclusion to the war with France, which had to make heavy reparation payments, brought a huge economic upswing at the beginning of the 1870s. Large growth rates were registered in the production sphere and profits climbed. A number of new enterprises, such as Rheinische Stahlwerke, Thyssen & Co., Eisen- und Stahlwerk Hoesch and Schalker Gruben- und Hüttenverein came into being. The establishment in 1872 of Dortmunder Union, Aktiengesellschaft für Bergbau, Eisen- und Stahlindustrie brought several large and hitherto independent enterprises together into one giant concern. Beside the establishment of Dortmunder Union the Berliner Disconto-Gesellschaft also participated in the establishment of Gelsenkirchener Bergwerks-Ges. in 1873. As the

---

were institutions of importance. These banks mainly transacted business with Belgium and France. They were the channels through which French and Belgian capital flowed into the newly established companies in the Ruhr. Cf. Alfred Krüger: Das Kölner Bankiergewerbe vom Ende des 18. Jahrhunderts bis 1875. Essen, 1925, p. 151; Friedrich Wilhelm Klinker: Studien zur Entwicklung und Typenbildung von vier Rheinisch-Westfälischen Provinzialaktienbanken. Volkswirtschaftliche Abhandlungen der badischen Hochschulen, N.F. 22. Karlsruhe, 1913, p. 11; W. Däbritz: Entstehung . . . loc. cit. p. 47 f.

Bessemer process came to be more widely used Bessemer plants were erected at Phoenix and Jacobi, Haniel & Huyssen.

The unexpected cyclical downswing of 1873, the full extent of which was not at first recognised by companies, lasted until 1879 and brought a number of enterprises in the Ruhr into dependence on the banks. The plants which had been newly built or considerably enlarged during the "Gründerjahre" (the "foundation years", years of intense activity in industrial expansion), generally at very high prices, had brought an expansion of capacity which was no longer matched by sales chances.[6]

Firstly it was thought that the downswing would only be temporary. Prices for pig iron dropped from their peak of 125.20 Marks per ton in 1873 to 51.65 Marks in 1879 but it was thought better to produce at a loss than not to operate the new plant or to close it again, which would have resulted in a definite loss of value. In 1877 pig iron production in the superior mining district of Dortmund was therefore again higher than in 1873. That district achieved average annual growth in production of 3.1% for the years from 1873 to 1879, while prices during the same period dropped to about 40% of their 1873 level. With such a fall in prices companies were not in a position to write off the plant erected at excessive prices in keeping with its real depreciation and still make a profit. Of the older enterprises Gutehoffnungshütte and Hörder Berg-werks- und Hüttenverein had to reduce their capital. Krupp was forced in 1874 to take up a loan for 10 million thalers, the conditions of which must have been felt as more than oppressive.[7] Of the enterprises founded after 1870 Rheinische Stahlwerke and Dortmunder Union reduced their capital stock. Schalker Gruben- und Hütten-verein wrote off all its capital and was changed into a cost-book company ("Gewerk schaft").

The Bochumer Verein was able to avoid deficits but it undertook only very low depreciation, not in keeping with the real depreciation of the plant. The adjustment of the plant to its true value was only made in the 1880s through the profit and loss account.

The Hoesch iron and steel works, which was only able to commence operations when the cyclical situation had already changed, was at times considerably indebted to the Schaaffhausen'sche Bankverein. These credits were repaid at the beginning of the 1880s when the first profit was available for distribution. At the same time Hoesch could fall back on loans from Leopold Hoesch. In some years these accounted for more than 10% of the share capital.

The economic upswing in the Ruhr at the beginning of the 1870s brought the es-tablishment of a number of banks as well, again in some cases with participations by older existing institutions. In 1871 the Bergisch-Märkische Bank was set up with a large participation by the Disconto-Gesellschaft.[8] The Cologne banks Oppenheim, Stein and Merkens participated in the establishment of the Barmer Bankverein (first as a partnership limited by shares) in 1867. The Essener Credit-Anstalt established at the beginning of 1872 with the cooperation of F. Grillo came into being through the reorganisation of the Essen banking firm L. von Born. The Disconto-Gesellschaft al-

6 Zentrales Staatsarchiv Merseburg (ZSTA) Rep. 120, Ministerium für Handel und Gewerbe, C VIII 1 No. 65. Vol. 3, p. 1.
7 Krupp archives WA IV 1641; WA II 13.
8 F. W. Klinker: Studien . . . loc. cit. p. 16.

so took a participation here. In 1874 the Duisburg-Ruhrorter Bank was founded, the main interested parties being the families Haniel and Böninger.

The close relations between the banks and the coal, iron and steel industry meant that the capital reductions in the 1870s were not only among industrial enterprises. The provincial banks, some of which had only been established after 1870, were strongly affected. Many were forced to liquidate. The Essener Credit-Anstalt reduced its capital from 18 to 10.5 million Marks. The Barmer Bankverein reduced its capital in a ratio of 3:2 from 12 to 8 million Marks and the Bergisch-Märkische Bank reduced its from 8.1 million to 7.2 million. Even the Schaaffhausen'sche Bankverein eventually had to reduce its capital in a ratio of 4:3 from 48 to 36 million Marks.[9]

The after-effects of the events in the late 1870s meant that in the following years the capital market was largely closed to companies. The banks' readiness or lack of readiness to grant credit meant survival or disaster for many enterprises. The fact that all the companies which the major banks supported were able to survive the financial difficulties brought the banks growing direct influence in the business policy of these enterprises. The loan taken up by Krupp in 1874, to which he was forced as he had financed plant at short term and his credits had been terminated in view of the general cyclical situation, shows how the banks used the dependence of companies to further their influence. The loan, which was placed with the help of the Seehandlung and some of the Berlin banks, was for 10 million thalers. It was issued at 86 and repayable at 110 with an interest rate of 6%. The loan was to be repaid in 9 years. At the same time the banks sent a representative to the company's management to observe at first hand the course of business. That the company was supported at all was due to the fact that the banks themselves were interested in its survival.[10]

The introduction of the Thomas process by the Hörder Verein and Rheinische Stahlwerke in 1879[11] brought a fundamental change in the iron and steel industry in the Ruhr and made the consolidation that might have been possible in the brief and slight upswing between 1879 and 1882 more difficult as the plants which had been newly erected at the beginning of the 1870s became obsolete overnight.[12]

The funds to meet the cost of the construction of new plants or the conversion of existing facilities which the introduction of the new process entailed generally had to be provided by the banks as companies did not have sufficient means themselves. For many companies this meant continuing under the influence of the banks, especially as the economic situation deteriorated again after 1882 and although production

9 W. Däbritz: Entstehung . . . loc. cit. p. 62. F. W. Klinker: Studien . . . p. 18, p. 61, p. 93.
10 Krupp archive FAH IV C 28, p. 38: "The cardinal error was made of acquiring the sum needed for the purchases of fixed assets with the help of floating bank debts instead of using a fixed-interest amortisation loan at an early stage."
11 Dortmund-Hörder-Hüttenunion archives (DHHU) in the Hoesch archives: 51, 63, 752, 1605. Rheinische Stahlwerke archives (RSW) No. 64,000, 64,000 C 1 and 2.
12 See the minutes of the meeting of the Supervisory Board of the Schaaffhausen'sche Bankverein of November 12, 1879 (in the archives of the Deutsche Bank): "The success which has been achieved with the Thomas de-phosphorisation process in works in Germany as well has brought a new element of uncertainty into this sector of industry. Perhaps it must be feared that those of our customers who feel that their existence is threatened by this innovation, will prove of greater importance than those who are in a position to make use of it." Of the older enterprises the Hörder Verein, Gutehoffnungshütte and Phoenix had built new Bessemer plant.

continued to rise prices dropped to considerably below even the lowest point of the 1870s.[13]

Hence the establishment and issue business became less important for the banks, which concentrated on regular banking business. Current lending took the form of overdrafts, discounting bills, loans against collateral (lombard credit) and acceptance credits. Especially after 1883 companies tended to prefer acceptance credits as the discount rate was low. As this caused the banks losses in interest they were only prepared to agree to this form of lending with financially sound enterprises and for competitive reasons (examples were with the Bochumer Verein and Hoesch). The credits granted by the banks were used to prefinance the new plant and to finance operating expenses.

The way in which the banks used the influence which accrued to them from the dependence of industrial enterprises brought a certain mistrust of the major banks among companies whiel as time went on were no longer so dependent on direct bank aid as they had been in the 1870s. Particularly companies which were largely still in private hands, such as Krupp, GHH and Hoesch attempted to keep the influence of the banks as low as possible, as a result of their own or other enterprises' experience in the 1870s.[14] In some cases the managements preferred not to undertake possible expansion if this would have entailed strengthening the influence of the banks. In many cases this was the main reason for the disinclination to borrow larger funds.[15] The banks' influence and supervision was especially strong in Dortmunder Union[16] and the Hörder Verein[17] although other enterprises also found that they could not eliminate the influence of the banks altogether.[18] In enterprises which were highly indebted or in which the banks held large participations influence was exercised on the

---

13 On the development of prices see Emil Müssig: Eisen- und Kohlekonjunktur seit 1870. Preisentwicklung in der Montanindustrie unter Einwirkung von Technik, Wirtschaft und Politik. 2nd ed., Augsburg, 1919, p. 19ff.

14 Krupp archives FAH IV C 28, p. 45ff.; Hoesch archives A 3 b 2 p. 63; See also the Annual Report of the Bochumer Verein for 1877/78: "It must be seen as our most important task to improve our financial position and make the works independent of the will and ability of the banking institutions."

15 On the relation between the company's own and borrowed funds in enterprises in the iron and steel industry in the Ruhr see Wilfried Feldenkirchen: Kapitalbeschaffung in der Eisen- und Stahlindustrie des Ruhrgebiets. Zeitschrift für Unternehmensgeschichte, Vol. 24, 1979, p. 60/61 and the table on p. 70/71.

16 In 1872 the Disconto-Gesellschaft had brought the Henrichshütte and the Hütte Neu-Schottland into the newly established Union. The bank also maintained close relations with Phoenix, participating in its financial reorganisation and capital increase, and with Gelsenkirchener Bergwerks-AG, whose expansion the bank encouraged. Cf. W. Däbritz: Gründung Disconto, p. 165; H. Böhme: Bankenkonzentration, p. 436 f.; The Bochumer Verein, on the other hand, when its credit facilities were reduced at the end of the 1870s, broke off business relations with the Disconto-Gesellschaft at the earliest opportunity. In addition to its old bank, the Schaaffhausen'sche Bankverein, the Bochumer Verein took up relations with the Berliner Handels-Gesellschaft. After Carl Klönne joined the Deutsche Bank (he had been a member of the board of the Bochumer Verein since 1892) relations were also opened with the Deutsche Bank, Cf. the archives of the Bochumer Verein (BV archives) 129 00 No. 11; 142 04 No. 5.

17 DHHU archives 51, 818, 1193. It should be pointed out that the Hörder Verein made more than 3.4 million Marks out of the Thomas patent by 1894. The difficult financial situation was due to the very high investment in the 1880s, far higher than that of comparable companies.

18 BV archives 129 00/15, 129 00/22, 129 00/24, 142 04 No. 5.

management as the banks sent delegates to sit on the board of managing directors of the company.[19]

After the amendment to the joint stock legislation in 1884 had made the supervisory board of a joint stock company a more effective organ of control the banks preferred to be represented on this body.[20] Their attitude can be seen from a minute of the meeting of the Supervisory Board of the Schaaffhausen'sche Bankverein of 16. 6. 1886: "Under such circumstances a large number of our customers need special supervision, especially since there is a greater tendency than usual to draw upon our services."[21]

In some companies it was only particular business developments which brought greater representation by the banks on the supervisory board. In the Bochumer Verein this was the failure of the foreign interests in Italy and Spain which caused the banks involved, the Berliner Handelsgesellschaft and the Schaaffhausen'sche Bankverein, to send two delegates, Hermann Rosenberg and Carl Klönne, to join the board of this company in 1892.[22] More frequently in the 1880s the banks tended to ask for exclusive banking relations with a company they were supporting as this made it easier for them to assess the company's borrowing. It was possible for the banks to ask for exclusive relations as investment generally was low and the sum required did not overstrain the capacity of a single bank. In 1891 the Hörder Verein had to agree at a creditors' meeting not to enter into any business relations with any other bank. On this basis the Schaaffhausen'sche Bankverein and the Bankhaus Deichmann & Co. which had already provided considerable sums in credit in the 1880s[23] to finance investment by the Hörder Verein, agreed to undertake a thorough financial reorganisation of the company and so save it from bankruptcy. The director of the Schaaffhausen'sche Bankverein, H. Schröder, was also delegated to the Board of Managing Directors of Hörder Verein until the successful conclusion of the work.[24] The old Board of Managing Directors was dissolved.

The banks generally tried to avoid direct capital participation in enterprises in the coal, iron and steel industry in the 1880s. This was probably the result of their experience in the 1870s, when they had had to make considerable value adjustments as prices of shares in these enterprises fell. If a bank still held a major participation, this was because the shares could not be placed at all or only at very unfavourable rates, or because for general reasons the bank wanted to maintain its influence in this sector. The Schaaffhausen'sche Bankverein, which generally only took small participations, remained a large shareholder of the Hörder Verein.[25] The Disconto-Gesellschaft was

---

19 DHHU archives 113.
20 After 1884 the supervisory board elected the board of managing directors and could summon an extraordinary general meeting in the case of important decisions which were in the interest of the company.
21 Minutes of the meeting of the Supervisory Board of the Schaaffhausen'sche Bankverein on 16. 6. 1886.
22 BV archives 142 0 4 No. 5.
23 Cf. minutes of the Supervisory Board meeting of the Schaaffhausen'sche Bankverein and DHHU archives 1193. The credits had at first been secured by mortgages. But the banks also provided considerable funds later which could not be secured. It was then generally believed that the Hörder Verein had got into difficulties through an excessive investment programme. The new plant had not proved very profitable owing to technical difficulties and to the drop in prices.
24 DHHU archives 113 and 818.
25 DHHU archives 51; Riesser Grossbanken, p. 56.

at first unable to place its shares owing to the catastrophic situation of the Union but was later less interested in selling, perhaps at least at times for the sake of being able to exercise a direct interest in the cartel questions.

Of the banks which were strongly engaged in the iron and steel industry the Schaaffhausen'sche Bankverein and the Disconto-Gesellschaft, although it was more strongly engaged in coal, were most important for the Ruhr. The Bankverein was particularly closely related to the Hörder Verein, the Bochumer Verein, Phoenix and Hoesch. The Disconto-Gesellschaft was closely related with Dortmunder Union. It also maintained business relations with Phoenix, GHH, the Bochumer Verein (until the end of the 1870s) and a large number of companies in mining (especially Gelsenkirchener Bergwerks-Gesellschaft.[26] In addition to these two banks the Berliner Handels-Gesellschaft played an important part in the issue business in the Ruhr.[27] Of the provincial banks the Bergisch-Märkische Bank[28] and the Essener Credit-Anstalt were of importance for the heavy iron industry, although the latter bank put the main focus of its business on coal mining.[29]

Altogether the period up to 1895 is not a uniform picture as far as the relations between the banks and heavy industry are concerned. On the one hand there were companies which could hardly take a major decision without the approval of interested banks, while on the other there were companies in a relatively good financial position and free to operate as they wished. The share of financing contributed by the banks on enterprise level varied considerably particularly in the 1880s and early 1890s. The higher the degree of indebtedness the greater grew the influence of the banks and this was generally reflected in stronger representation on the supervisory bodies.

III.

In the years after the turn of the century the banks were more strongly represented on the supervisory boards of all the enterprises. However, it would not appear to be justifiable to conclude from this that enterprises generally were more strongly dependent on the banks. In many cases this was certainly not so. The better financial position of enterprises can be seen for instance from the negotiations on new issues. Now it was the banks who tended to woo enterprises, while before 1895 companies were financially so dependent that there was hardly room for negotiation on conditions, which

---

26 H. Böhme: Bankenkonzentration p. 439; W. Däbritz: Disconto, p. 164f.
27 The importance of the Berliner Handelsgesellschaft increased considerably after Carl Fürstenberg became owner in 1883. One of its major customers was the Bochumer Verein, another Rheinische Stahlwerke; in mining Harpener Bergbau-Gesellschaft.
28 Up to 1896 the textile industry accounted for an important share of the bank's customers. In its Annual Report for 1889 the bank outlined its business principles: "As hitherto the main part of our business will be current account business with merchants and industrialists. We believe that an expansion on the one hand through various industries and on the other over a wider transport area will offer the best guarantees of a certain evenness and balance." Quoted from: F. W. Klinker: Studien . . . p. 31.
29 Walter Däbritz: Denkschrift zum fünfzigjährigen Bestehen der Essener Credit-Anstalt in Essen. Essen, 1922, p. 72f.

were imposed by the banks. The initiative in the concentration process tended to come from industry itself while in the 1880s the banks had exercised a decisive influence on this, certainly in coal mining.[30] After 1895 the banks generally only handled the financial transactions. So the beginning of the twentieth century brought a growing emancipation of the major enterprises in the iron and steel industry from the banks.[31] The concentration process, which was greatly strengthened by the formation of cartels,[32] further limited the influence any one bank could exercise on industrial enterprises. The mergers often brought several major banks on to the supervisory boards and the competition and rivalry between the banks also ultimately limited their influence when several were represented on the same body.[33] At the same time the investment sums needed by the new huge concerns grew to such proportions that they were beyond the financing power of any one bank. The issues almost always had to be handled by a consortium. Emil Kirdorf, General Director of Gelsenkirchener Bergwerks-Gesellschaft, was able to state at the meeting of the Verein für Socialpolitik (Social Policy Association) in 1905, and no doubt rightly: "It has been argued that there is already something like a state monopoly as the great finance houses dominate our industry, but I can say with all emphasis that that is not the case. The influence of the major banks on heavy industry in the Rhineland and Westphalia has never been as low as it is at present."[34] It was the increasing concentration process, which the

---

30 H. Böhme: Bankenkonzentration, p. 438; Otto Jeidels: Das Verhältnis der deutschen Grossbanken zu Industrie mit besonderer Berücksichtigung der Eisenindustrie. Leipzig, 1905, p. 105f.
31 M. Gehr: Verhältnis, p. 53. P. Barret Whale: Joint Stock Banking in Germany. New York, 1968, p. 55.
32 The regulations of the main cartels and syndicates greatly furthered the establishment and expansion of mixed concerns. Around the mid-1890s a number of companies acquired blast furnace works or built the necessary plant. Shortly before the turn of the century almost all the iron and steel enterprises in the Ruhr bought pits to counteract the price and supply policy of the Rhenish-Westfalian Coal Syndicate. There was another wave of acquisitions after 1903 resulting from the privileges granted to the collieries. The regulations of the steel works' association mainly helped companies to penetrate refinement work.
33 Plans to take up a loan by the Deutscher Kaiser mining company which was to be managed by the Deutsche Bank led to differences of opinion with the Disconto-Gesellschaft, which felt that "an old tradition was being infringed" and the Deutsche Bank. In a letter to Carl Klönne on 12. 11. 1903 August Thyssen pointed out that in addition to the Deutsche Bank, the Disconto-Gesellschaft, the Dresdner Bank and the Rheinische Bank the Schaaffhausen'sche Verein must certainly join in. "As you know, the Dresdner Bank and Schaaffhausen have always shown the greatest confidence in me. Neither of the banks has ever kept us short of credit, although in our most difficult period we, that is Thyssen & Co., owed up to 3 million and more." Cf. GDK archives: Personenarchiv August Thyssen No. 1.
The rivalry of the banks also became apparent over the 50 million loan for Krupp in 1908. A. Gwinner of the Deutsche Bank first declared: "The Deutsche Bank cannot join in a transaction which is being managed by the Dresdner Bank." Then on 11. 6. 1908 Gwinner withdrew his objections to working under the Dresdner Bank's management "in view of the close relations maintained with Krupp". The consortium finally consisted of: the Dresdner Bank, the Bank für Handel und Industrie, the Berliner Handelsgesellschaft, the Deutsche Bank, the Disconto-Gesellschaft and Delbrück & Co. The Seehandlung, which had managed the big loan of 1874, was not to participate owing to doubts on the part of the Finance Ministry.
Cf. Krupp archives WA IV 1264; FAH IV C 116. For the views of the contemporary press on the relations between the banks and heavy industry see: ZSTA Merseburg, Ministerium für Handel und Gewerbe, Rep. 120 C VIII 1 No. 72, Adh. 8, p. 205f.
34 Quoted from: F. A. Freundt: Emil Kirdorf, Essen 1922, p. 48.

banks had encouraged and helped to finance, which kept their influence down.[35] The Dresdener Bank commented in its Annual Report for 1908 that the wave of concentration and the formation of associations in industry, especially in heavy industry, had undeniably made these enterprises less dependent on the banks.[36] Like Krupp, August Thyssen aimed to keep the influence of any one bank to a minimum by drawing on the help of several banks for this larger loans.[37]

In this connection a memorandum from the Deutsche Bank (undated) which has been preserved in the correspondence between August Thyssen and Carl Klönne, is interesting: "It would not be advantageous to sell Mannesmann to Schalke. If Thyssen owns the Mannesmann works he will be dominating there as he is in all his enterprises and the little influence we have with Thyssen will have to be shared with four or five other banks and bankers."[38]

The increasing size of enterprises made it more difficult for the banks to obtain a clear picture of their technical and financial position, so that their General Directors were largely free to take their own decisions. From a report by the General Director of the Rheinische Stahlwerke, Hasslacher, to his colleague Beukenberg of Phoenix of 1910 we see that Hasslacher had already taken several hundred thousand Marks out of the profits before announcing these to the Supervisory Board to stock up the reserves, which in his view had been neglected.[39] In this connection we should also mention the purchase of the coal fields on the left bank of the Rhine by Rheinische Stahlwerke. Both the representative of the Disconto-Gesellschaft, Salomonsohn, and Carl Fürstenberg of the Berliner Handelsgesellschaft advised against the purchase on the grounds that it would prove too great a burden to the company. Instead in 1908 Fürstenberg suggested that refinement works should be acquired. But the Board of Managing Directors of Rheinische Stahlwerke got its way, only at Fürstenberg's suggestion cutting down the size of the land it was to buy on the left bank of the Rhine. On 2. 8. 1910 Carl Fürstenberg wrote on the matter to the new General Director of the company, Hasslacher: "I should like to tell you that during the omnipotent reign of Herr Dr. Feodor Goecke I greatly opposed the acquisition of the left bank fields, regarding this as an excessive purchase of ground space, but I was not successful."[40]

The influence of the banks was certainly latent after 1900 as well, but it was generally less apparent. An indirect influence was exerted through strong personalities

---

35 See contemporary press reports in ZSTA Merseburg, Ministerium für Handel und Gewerbe, Rep. 120 C VIII 1 No. 72 Adh. 45, Vol. 2, p. 87 f.

36 Dresdner Bank: Geschäftsbericht 1908. Quoted from: Wilhelm Hagemann: Das Verhältnis der Deutschen Grossbanken zur Industrie. Thesis, Berlin, 1930, p. 19.

37 See the Handelszeitung (financial journal) of the Berliner Tageblatt for 20. 9. 1904: "It was particularly astute of Thyssen not to let himself be nailed to any of the dominant financial groups. He has just floated the first big loans on his works in Bruckhausen with the Disconto-Gesellschaft and Schaaffhausen. Later the Deutsche Bank took the lead in business with GDK. Thyssen worked together with the Dresdner Bank to reorganise his problem child, the Rheinische Bank, and to finance the Saar- und Moselbergwerke. So the banks generally served Thyssen's interests, only in the Deutsche Bank, in the industry specialist Director Klönne, did he find a personality equal to his own." Cf. GDK archives: August Thyssen im Spiegel der Presse, A/869; 512.

38 Cf. GDK archives: Personenarchiv August Thyssen No. 1.

39 RSW archives 166 B 1.

40 RSW archives 166 B 2.

who had valuable specialised knowledge and whose advice was eagerly sought. The correspondence between August Thyssen and Carl Klönne for the period 1900 to 1905, which has been preserved, will serve as an example of this.[41]

Carl Klönne, who had been a director of the Schaaffhausen'sche Bankverein and represented the bank on the Supervisory Board of the Bochumer Verein before joining the Deutsche Bank in 1900, gave and received impulses for possible transactions which went far beyond the actual business relations between Thyssen and the Deutsche Bank. August Thyssen tried on various occasions to use his close relations with Klönne to induce the Deutsche Bank or the banks generally to influence enterprises or certain persons at his suggestion. On 31. 12. 1901 he wrote regarding the tube syndicate to Klönne, pointing out that concessions had been made on all sides except by Mannesmann. Thyssen himself had met all wishes, although this had made the Dinslaken plant exclusively dependent on orders from abroad.[42] When the Rheinische Stahlwerke decided not to join the syndicate Thyssen wrote to Klönne on 10. 9. 1903, urging the banks to exert pressure to induce it to do so. "It is absolutely essential for Commercial Councillor Goecke to be instructed to join the association under the given conditions." Klönne wrote back the following day: "I have suggested off the record to some of the banks – I cannot do so officially if I want to draw any benefit from it – that they should exert their influence with Goecke in the way you desire. I hope this will be effective."[43]

When the Union, after selling Henrichshütte, was not prepared to reduce its quota in the steel works' association August Thyssen approached Emil Kirdorf, asking the Disconto-Gesellschaft to exercise its influence with the Union.[44] For the extraordinary general meeting of Phoenix, which decided on joining the steel works' association, Thyssen at his own request was given sole power to represent the Deutsche Bank and some of the smaller banks. At Rheinische Stahlwerke it was Carl Fürstenberg who enjoyed the closest relations with the General Director, Hasslacher. But Fürstenberg by no means always took the same stand as the representative of the Disconto-Gesellschaft, Salomonsohn. Especially over the question of securing coal supplies for Rheinische Stahlwerke, which had to buy roughly one third of the coal it needed in 1910, there were intense discussions with Fürstenberg. When the Rheinische Stahlwerke proposed buying the Concordia pit in 1910 Salomonsohn as representative of the Disconto-Gesellschaft opposed the idea. He regarded it as more advisable to exploit the coal fields on the left bank of the Rhine which had been acquired in 1908 and were still unopened, although Hasslacher impressed upon him how difficult it would be to sink the shafts and how much time this would cost. In a letter to Hasslacher Fürstenberg supported his plan to buy a pit which was already

41 GDK archives: Personenarchiv August Thyssen No.1.
42 GDK archives: Personenarchiv August Thyssen No. 1. The Deutsche Bank maintained close relations with Mannesmann.
43 But the Rheinische Stahlwerke did not join the pig iron syndicate. Cf. Arthur Klotzbach: Der Roheisenverband. Düsseldorf, 1926, p. 119.
44 August Thyssen was at that time on the Supervisory Board of Gelsenkirchener Bergwerks-AG, of which Emil Kirdorf was General Director. He in turn was on the Supervisory Board of the Disconto-Gesellschaft. Since its establishment GBAG had maintained close relations with the Disconto-Gesellschaft; Cf. Walter Däbritz: Geschichte der August-Thyssen-Hütte, unpublished manuscript, Heft 6, p. 15 ff.

working so that its coal would be available straightaway to the Rheinische Stahl-werke.[45]

In 1911 there were negotiations on a merger between Rheinische Stahlwerke and Harpener Bergbau-Gesellschaft. The Berliner Handelsgesellschaft, which was interested in both companies exerted a decisive influence on the plans. The Disconto-Gesellschaft, largely no doubt in view of its close relations with Gelsenkirchener Bergwerks-Gesellschaft, opposed the merger with Harpener Bergbau, then the largest purely coal mining company in the Ruhr.[46]

The bank's influence can clearly be traced in mergers and acquisitions. The higher the share of external growth in the overall growth of an enterprise, the more easily could the banks influence the extent and direction as greater sums of money were involved. In many cases it was the banks which suggested mergers or acquisitions or at least facilitated these, when the same bank or group of banks were interested in the two companies concerned. In 1898 the Schaaffhausen'sche Bankverein sold its participation in the Hütten-AG vorm. Carl von Born, which it had established in 1896, to Hörder Verein.[47] In the boom just before the turn of the century the Hörder Verein had had to buy considerable quantities of pig iron and the Carl von Born smelting works, which were favourably positioned as far as freight was concerned, would form a welcome addition to its facilities. In another transaction the Schaaffhausen'sche Bankverein succeeded in selling a major participation. The merger of Phoenix with the Hörder Verein in 1906 was furthered by the bank as the two enterprises could supplement each other. Before the steel works' association was founded Hörde had always had to sell part of its semi-manufactures abroad, while Phoenix had had to buy. As Hörder Verein was working at rather below-average profitability after 1900 as well, Schaaffhausen was concerned to see the merger go through.[48]

The representatives of the banks on the supervisory boards of these companies were with their wide-ranging business contacts in a position to see which firms might prove candidates for mergers or acquisitions. In the merger of Phoenix with the Westfälische Union in 1898 it is striking that the major shareholders of the Westfälische Union, A. von Oppenheim, the bank director Michelet, the banker Franz Gaedecke and Baron von Thielemann, also a banker, were all at the time on the Supervisory Board of Phoenix.

The merger of Phoenix with the Düsseldorfer Röhren- und Eisenwalzwerke AG in 1910 was also due to the impetus of the Schaaffhausen'sche Bankverein. The bank was only prepared to grant the Düsseldorf enterprise new credits on condition that it

---

45 On 23. 11. 1910 negotiations took place in Cologne between members of the Supervisory Boards of Concordia and Rheinische Stahlwerke (Salomonsohn and Fürstenberg) but it did not prove possible to reach agreement on the price or the other conditions. Cf. RSW archives 166 B 1.

46 RSW archives 166 B 2. In 1913 there were once more rumours of a merger but Hasslacher denied this when challenged by the representative of the Dresdner Bank on the Supervisory Board, Henry Nathan. Hasslacher believed that in such a good economic situation it was hardly likely that any of the pits which might have proved candidates would agree to a merger at acceptable conditions. Cf. RSW archives 20001/7.

47 Cf. Annual Report of the Schaaffhausen'sche Bankverein for 1896. DHHU archives 51.

48 Cf. ZSTA Merseburg, Ministerium für Handel und Gewerbe, Rep. 120 C VII 1 No. 65, Vol. 4, p. 169; DHHU archives 1043; Phoenix archives P 125 361; Walther Kunze: Der Aufbau des Phoenix-Konzerns. Thesis, Frankfurt a. M., 1926, p. 74.

agreed to the merger with Phoenix. But the banks' proposals did not always meet with the approval, or not the immediate approval of the company managements. The Schaaffhausen'sche Bankverein had proposed a merger between Phoenix, the Hörder Verein and the Lothringer Hüttenverein Aumetz-Friede as early as 1904 but the Phoenix management refused. As the bank had interests, although of different magnitude, in all three enterprises, it had worked out detailed plans of how the three firms could be made into one huge concern. Particularly after the steel works' association was founded the bank saw great advantages in such a concern.[49] But the proposal to merge Phoenix with the Lothringer Hüttenverein Aumetz-Friede also shows that the banks certainly on some occasions also acted in their own interests in exercising their influence. The Schaaffhausen'sche Bankverein had had to carry out a financial reorganisation of the Lothringer Hüttenverein in 1901 and in 1904, contrary to its usual policy, it still held considerable shares in the company. Had the merger proved possible Schaaffhausen would have been able to unload its participation in a company which was working with rather uncertain prospects for the future. At the same time funds would have become available which could have been used more profitably with the reawakening interest in mergers in other enterprises in 1904.

The Disconto-Gesellschaft had founded the Dortmunder Union in 1872 by merging Henrichshütte, for which it had already carried out one financial reorganisation in 1863 and in which it still held the majority of the shares, and the Werk Neu-Schottland, which was also not on a very profitable basis, with the Dortmunder Hütte. Most of the shares in the Union were placed during the boom. In its Annual Report for 1875 the Disconto-Gesellschaft maintained that "the establishment of the Union was one of our most correct and faithful transactions" but it can hardly be denied that the bank was glad to be able to place its holdings in the new concern. Throughout its existence and right up to 1910 the Union suffered from the over-valuation of the plant at its establishment. In 1874/75, 1877/78, 1896/97 and 1901/02 reductions in the capital had to be made, which cost the shareholders altogether 73 million Marks.[50]

In 1899 the Union acquired 501 registered shares in the A. von Hansemann pit near Mengede from the Disconto-Gesellschaft. But considerable amounts were first called for contribution. At the beginning of 1901 one shaft flooded when it was attempted to sink another shaft. The same had happened a few years previously. Ultimately the Disconto-Gesellschaft provided the funds for the clearance work, which amounted to 700,000 M. However, in the following years as well production remained well below the estimated 2,000 tons a day and the company actually considered re-selling the pit.

In 1904, when the Board of Managing Directors of Phoenix was not prepared to join the steel works' association at the conditions then prevailing, the Schaaffhausen'sche Bankverein succeeded in having an extraordinary general meeting called on 26. 4. 1904 in Cologne. The banks, using their own votes and those of the shares deposited with them, decided on joining the association although the Board was able

---

49 Phoenix archives P 125 243, meeting of the Board of Managing Directors of 19. 5. 1904.
50 Paul Kehrein: Konjunktureinflüsse in der Grossindustrie. Eine Untersuchung der Bilanzen von 9 Unternehmen der Grosseisenindustrie von 1880 bis 1914 unter dem Einfluss der Scheingewinnverteilung. Thesis, Frankfurt a. M., 1928(1930), p. 121.

to produce good reasons why this should not be done.[51] The decisive factor for the banks was that they were expecting other companies in which they held interests to operate on a more profitable basis through the greater price stability which was one of the association's aims.

In most companies the banks at least gave advice to the management on major decisions. But it is not always possible to see clearly how strong their influence really was. No doubt the personalities of both the company directors and the banks' representatives were the decisive factors here.

IV.

The rapid growth of the iron and steel industry in the Ruhr and the high rate of investment required considerable borrowed funds although profits were rising and companies could take on an increasing amount of financing themselves. Often considerable amounts of credit were needed at short term. Financing through issues of new shares was generally postponed for more favourable phases of the capital market and a greater tendency to use loan issues came to be a sign of declining economic activity. Of the domestic financing institutions the banks provided the shortterm credits and could most easily be elastic in reaction to the demand from companies. So it was recourse to short-term credit and the provision of this which became the major feature of business relations between enterprises and the banks.[52] The fact that the role played by the capital market during this phase declined slightly or remained constant would appear to suggest that it did not prove possible at first to make greater use of this means of financing.[53]

In addition to financing current expenditure, which was growing both absolutely and in some cases relatively with the growing size of companies, the short-term credits, which were generally made available in the form of an overdraft on current account, were used to finance investment. In almost every company there is a very high degree of correlation between the amount of short-term borrowed funds and addi-

51 The Board of Managing Directors of Phoenix gave the following reasons:
    – the participation was too low as in the view of the Board the plant on which work had begun but which was not yet finished had not been adequately taken into account
    – With its A products the steel works association accounted for only 37.4% of the Phoenix production
    – If it joined the association Phoenix would have to bear part of the export costs for girders and semi-manufactures, although the company itself did not export these. But it would have to bear all the costs alone for its large exports of wire goods.
    Beside the banks the Rhenish-Westphalian Coal Syndicate also exercised pressure on Phoenix by threatening to cease export payments. The steel works' association refused to supply the quantities ordered by Phoenix, which was a heavy purchaser of semi-manufactures. Cf. Phoenix archives P 5 2566, 1. Cf. also ZSTA Merseburg, Ministerium für Handel und Gewerbe, Rep. 120 C VIII 1 No. 72 Adh. 53, Vol. 1, p. 17 ff.
52 G. von Schulz-Gavernitz: Die Deutsche Kreditbank. Tübingen, 1922, p. 121; Ekkehard Eistert: Die Beeinflussung des Wirtschaftswachstums in Deutschland durch das Bankensystem. Thesis, Berlin, 1970, p. 177.
53 R. Tilly: Growth, p. 161 f.

Table 1. First Degree Liquidity

company \ period	1878/79–1894/95		1895/96–1913/14		1878/79–1913/14	
	A	B	A	B	A	B
GHH	10,5	8,1	47,2	20,1	29,9	24,1
Krupp	56,1	26,0	51,3	13,7	53,5	20,3
Hörder Verein[1]	4,6	3,0	42,9	35,9	19,6	29,1
Phönix	18,5	18,7	47,0	19,3	33,6	23,7
Bochumer Verein	64,7	54,0	56,0	18,4	60,1	39,1
Union[2]	18,5	20,6				
RSW	82,1	79,1	54,1	49,2	67,3	65,6
Hoesch	64,1	69,5	95,0	42,8	80,6	58,2
DT-LUX[3]					35,9	29,3

[1] 1878/79–1905/06 A = Average.
[2] 1878/79–1896/97 B = Standard deviation
[3] 1901/02–1913/14

Please pay attention to the fact that Tables 1 to 5 are reprint of the original source. There for the Comma has to be read as a point (for surtance 10,5 mean 10.5).

tions to fixed assets. The major additions to fixed assets always came before the increase in the share capital or long-term borrowed funds.[54] The banks' expectation that a conversion or loan issue might follow from the short-term loan made them more ready to provide this type of credit.

Companies preferred to finance plant at short or medium term and were able to do this because the current account credits were constantly renewed, and thus were virtually available at long term. In view of the very much greater flexibility of this mode of financing over any other the interest rate played only a subordinate role in greater recourse to short-term credit.[55]

The desire of companies to be able to react as quickly and flexibly as possible to the constantly changing investment requirements can also be seen from the strong growth in liquid assets in almost every enterprise after 1895. This did not reach the level regarded as necessary today but it was a very considerable rise over the period 1870 to 1894 (Table 1).

As the General Director of the Bochumer Verein, Baare, commented at several annual general meetings, a company should always have highly liquid funds available to the amount of its reserves, so as to be able to react with the necessary speed to every requirement. Tables 2 and 3 give surveys on the amount of bank balances and holdings of securities and clearly show how companies aimed to do this, laying the greater emphasis on bank balances or securities according to their circumstances.

---

54 Wilfried Feldenkirchen: Kapitalbeschaffung in der Eisen- und Stahlindustrie des Ruhrgebiets 1879–1914. In: Zeitschrift für Unternehmensgeschichte, Vol. 24, 1979, p. 54.

55 Ekkehard Eistert/Johannes Ringel: Die Finanzierung des wirtschaftlichen Wachstums durch die Banken. Eine quantitativ-empirische Untersuchung für Deutschland 1850–1913. In: Untersuchungen zum Wachstum der deutschen Wirtschaft, ed. Walther G. Hoffmann. Tübingen, 1971, p. 118.

Table 2. Securities Holdings in M

Year	GHH	KRUPP	HÖRDE	PHÖNIX	BV	UNION	RSW	HOESCH	SCHALKE	DT-LUX
1878/79	75824	4769883	68723	93750	78649	13996	240000	2098	–	–
1879/80	16773	3518133	84210	51000	78648	30178	240000	11817	–	–
1880/81	13324	5861601	1084210	51000	35022	31882	240000	6599	–	–
1881/82	13560	5897740	93871	23550	35022	32566	180000	921358	–	–
1882/83	6031	6066121	93895	23550	35022	54457	240000	853925	–	–
1883/84	9500	9493492	107395	23550	3020478	28550	740000	483839	–	–
1884/85	7600	7918349	107395	23550	3017 8/5	5982	912000	262126	–	–
1885/86	12400	15094998	107486	0	3017976	5882	1061200	262128	–	–
1886/87	2000	14904721	108597	0	3732270[1]	136626[3]	1034192	24814	–	–
1887/88	6350	13941919	108213	0	2703112[1]	181049[3]	595760	24614	–	–
1888/89	4950	16884929	108213	0	2636814[1]	275885[3]	3037623	24614	–	–
1889/90	12600	15408159	107213	0	2635059[1]	0	698100	24614	809600	–
1890/91	279113	5302062	120890	0	2619330[1]	0	696100	24614	859300	–
1891/92	298813	8546227	109380	995220	2591212	964739	698100	26419	848800	–
1892/93	290900	5365547	116425	1665220	3401333	3185237	349050	27224	881300	–
1893/94	399465	9937340	118425	1803220	5368479[2]	3173797	87263	30115	881300	–
1894/95	403309	14901400	135625	994960	5342859	3182754	87264	30115	889500	–
1895/96	1065399	12608982	1942719	1298000	6339016	3182754	87264	530115	1126700	–
1896/97	1584643	11581268	1930969	7750	7489060[1]	3965990	56721	30115	1504463	–
1897/98	3640516	14402297	1930969	150130	7559248[1]	3979231[4]	43631	30115	4615958	–
1898/99	4485195	13963462	1954069	143648	7361032[1]	5576838	43631	30115	13087731	–
1899/00	4385539	10428546	1890353	167969	7124270[1]	218802	43631	72037	14605079	–
1900/01	4385639	13878760	1312112[5]	386732	7124270[1]	242055	114309	72040	14708250	–
1901/02	5902236	28684489	302956	372933	5239620[1]	250199	131768	22720	2408421	1643806
1902/03	5990237	43918257	348437	373437	5239520[1]	254649	109914	22726[1]	6536740	1715805
1903/04	5997937	54674893	397459	562080	5239520[1]	263849	109914	35726	14531855	1098961
1904/05	4332693	55527794	375892	872670	5239520[1]	287849	86682	34926	3693839*	2885181
1905/06	2326083	61569239	1127560	614851	5239214[1]	382851	86448	34927	3272896**	2552848
1906/07	3881349	56868606	–	5549677	3846107[1]	396486	103504	34800	3221047**	2042999
1907/08	3083110	52795324	–	5447857	3674769[1]	383855	103263	74587	–	1581237
1908/09	3124047	53620595	–	4043034	3742328[1]	383868	103712	74587	–	423533
1909/10	3130635	59962707	–	3997758	3393000	417305	109723	74587	–	1303272
1910/11	2863733	66887607	–	4385168	8118400[1]	–	126313	1215813	–	3784921
1911/12	2607986	83980182	–	4202707	5868000[1]	–	14969	907506	–	5929260
1912/13	4157037	88009522	–	4202639	5635800[1]	–	5900	594647	–	5296524
1913/14	4098287	88257217	–	4239607	5360366	–	6323	1235047	–	5756385

[1] Bochumer Verein without the securities of the Baare Foundation
[2] Bochumer Verein after 1893/4 including the shares of "Stahlindustrie"
[3] Union including bills
[4] Union after 1898/8 securities were shown under "Participations"
[5] Hörde after 1900/1 securities were shown under "Participations"
* rump accounting year July 1 to Dec. 31, 1904
** financial year Jan. 1 to Dec. 31, 1905 and 1906

While during what was known as the "slack phase" up to 1894 almost all the enterprises had considerable short-term debts with the banks, in the "upswing phase" after 1895[56] most of them often maintained very considerable bank balances. As Table 4 shows, in some cases in the last years before the First World War the share of bank balances to current assets was just on 50%.[57] The fluctuations in bank balances during these years were due to the investment behaviour of firms. If there was heavy investment the amount of balances maintained with the banks dropped in the following year; if investment was low the amount rose again.[58]

56 Arthur Spiethoff: Die wirtschaftlichen Wechsellagen, Vol. I: Erklärende Beschreibungen. Tübingen and Zurich, 1955, p. 124 and 130.
57 For most companies the relation between fixed and current assets remained relatively stable. In Krupp the share of current assets rose but the balance sheets do not reflect the general situation as each year just before balance sheet date large pre-payments came in.
58 See the Annual Report of the Bochumer Verein for 1913/14: "A comparison of debtors and creditors as per June 30, 1913 will show a shift to the disadvantage of our own funds, which is due to the

Table 3. Bank Balances and Bank Debts

Year	GHH	KRUPP	HÖRDE	PHÖNIX	BV	UNION	RSW	HOESCH	SCHALKE	DT-LUX
1878/79	−1289754	877735	·	−2381306	−2760936	·	·	·	−	−
1879/80	−1429123	221346	·	−2138230	−2650653	·	·	·	−	−
1880/81	−1375141	97251	·	−2392092	−2369528	·	·	·	−	−
1881/82	−1714557	190687	·	−1519774	−2091865	·	·	·	−	−
1882/83	−982908	1018560	·	−379880	−746854	·	284492	·	−	−
1883/84	−1397466	1246116	·	−1538085	146058	·	1065174	·	−	−
1884/85	−1143340	2646937	·	−933008	1599022	·	1286084	·	−	−
1885/86	−1544484	1241766	·	249174	1850158	·	731071	·	−	−
1886/87	−2305054	1029710	·	−135436	1980277	·	334262	·	−	−
1887/88	−2539608	714844	·	−624867	304470	·	870808	·	−	−
1888/89	−1659695	621369	·	−1518038	·	·	28650	·	−	−
1889/90	−1744205	198681	·	123688	·	·	34001	·	·	−
1890/91	505052	152115	·	1544941	·	·	·	·	·	−
1891/92	891152	318615	·	1604217	·	·	33517	·	·	−
1892/93	2119206	1377523	·	826811	·	·	94484	·	·	−
1893/94	1160902	2727881	·	381731	·	·	169132	·	·	−
1894/95	644967	984654	·	844793	·	·	14124	·	·	−
1895/96	1444552	6350380	922808	2428194	·	·	29904	·	·	−
1896/97	818594	371700	2819356	1667353	·	·	157036	·	·	−
1897/98	1662040	3632887	5515163	7699950	·	·	56156	·	·	−
1898/99	3736034	5451176	2859191	6543436	·	·	1912137	2721340	·	−
1899/00	3642731	10650112	·	4610224	·	·	8309271	3475818	·	−
1900/01	3830302	10548396	·	241000	·	·	·	1600097	·	−
1901/02	8492416	14510021	·	2144000	·	·	233227	788109	·	·
1902/03	6058167	15336252	·	2687901	·	·	·	4905503	·	·
1903/04	1573274	10361316	846882	8369719	·	·	1296654	5880120	·	·
1904/05	1399519	9362477	2081207	5645547	·	·	·	6552475	·	·
1905/06	1561876	10323608	3451699	7415122	·	·	4520672	5934317	·	·
1906/07	3960148	10403646	−	20001445	·	·	4527346	7000377	·	·
1907/08	11900540	10939610	−	15487143	5712596	·	3100061	8505277	−	·
1908/09	8787652	17826596	−	10339280	6208679	·	·	8910441	−	1094962
1909/10	6141328	33187574	−	26028487	8880511	·	10500442	11507687	−	12324113
1910/11	6956914	53459719	−	27161867	3006634	−	11083943	14161868	−	5937862
1911/12	7139989	68361020	−	27445632	1048294	−	10780880	20254375	−	·
1912/13	11039562	63823887	−	25759958	4459440	−	9741250	13858907	−	1775760
1913/14	3208293	44396050	−	23725338	·	−	11752547	12087944	−	10221581

* For these years neither bank balances nor debts could be ascertained from the balance sheets and other archive material. Larger bank balances were generally mentioned in balance sheets, balance sheet material and annual reports

The highly liquid assets accumulated by firms further reduced their dependence on the banks. These funds could be used as the company management desired without the knowledge of the banks or even against their will if necessary. The change in the position of enterprises with regard to the banks can also be seen in the negotiations on interest rates for short or medium-term deposits of company funds with the banks.[59]

V.

Up to the mid-1890s the big issue and loan business for the industrial enterprises in the Ruhr had largely been handled with the help of the major Berlin banks and the Schaaffhausen'sche Bankverein. The regular banking business was largely transact-

fact that the new plant in the cast steel factory and the pits . . . cost around 9,200,000 million Marks and were financed from existing company funds."

59 Hoesch archives A 3 b 5; BV archives 129 00/24; RSW archives 12300/15.

Table 4. Share of Bank Balances in Current Assets

Year	GHH	KRUPP	HÖRDE	PHÖNIX	BV	DT-LUX	RSW	HOESCH
1878/79	·	2,7	·	·	·	—	·	·
1879/80	·	0,6	·	·	·	—	·	·
1880/81	·	0,3	·	·	·	—	·	·
1881/82	·	0,5	·	·	·	—	·	·
1882/83	·	6,2	·	·	·	—	6,7	·
1883/84	·	2,6	·	·	1,4	—	21,5	·
1884/85	·	6,6	·	·	14,9	—	24,0	·
1885/86	·	3,0	·	·	16,3	—	13,7	·
1886/87	·	2,4	·	·	15,8	—	7,2	·
1887/88	·	1,6	·	·	2,0	—	17,2	·
1888/89	·	1,4	·	·	·	—	0,7	·
1889/90	·	0,4	·	1,1	·	—	0,7	·
1890/91	4,6	0,3	·	14,1	·	—	0,7	·
1891/92	7,7	0,6	·	12,9	·	—	0,7	·
1892/93	16,6	2,3	·	7,5	·	—	2,2	·
1893/94	10,6	5,0	·	3,2	·	—	3,9	·
1894/95	5,9	1,7	·	7,3	·	—	0,3	·
1895/96	11,4	10,8	7,9	17,9	·	—	0,7	·
1896/97	5,4	0,6	19,7	12,4	·	—	3,1	·
1897/98	8,5	4,6	33,1	30,8	·	—	1,2	·
1898/99	16,7	6,2	16,8	26,0	·	—	23,7	32,8
1899/00	13,9	10,2	·	17,1	·	—	44,2	36,1
1900/01	14,0	9,8	·	·	·	—	·	21,6
1901/02	22,0	11,5	·	·	·	·	2,7	11,9
1902/03	22,7	11,5	·	12,4	·	·	25,3	46,2
1903/04	0,6	5,6	8,9	24,0	·	·	12,4	49,9
1904/05	6,7	4,5	17,2	23,0	·	·	·	55,2
1905/06	6,8	4,4	23,4	27,2	·	·	30,4	45,5
1906/07	12,9	4,5	—	32,2	·	·	29,8	47,9
1907/08	29,8	4,8	—	27,3	19,5	·	19,3	51,8
1908/09	24,4	7,0	—	29,6	22,0	7,8	·	51,0
1909/10	17,0	11,7	—	40,0	30,4	29,0	44,8	59,8
1910/11	16,1	16,7	—	35,7	11,1	11,1	48,9	58,4
1911/12	18,5	18,5	—	33,9	6,9	·	45,2	64,6
1912/13	23,7	17,2	—	30,7	15,8	2,5	38,0	54,7
1913/14	8,1	12,4	—	29,0	·	12,4	43,3	30,4

* No bank balances available

ed by the Bankverein and the banks in the Ruhr. After the end of the 1890s the Berlin banks began to penetrate the regular banking business in the Ruhr as well. In the 1880s and early 1890s the Deutsche Bank, for example, had had only few connections with the coal, iron and steel industry. When in 1880 the bank was asked to join in the 4 million mark loan for Hörder Verein, the bank's Board of Management declined (September 1880), on the grounds that "under prevailing circumstances it would not be advisable for the bank to enter into engagements which in the nature of things can only be at long term".[60]

---

60 DHHU archives 1137.

After the Deutsche Bank had formed an interest pooling agreement with the Bergisch-Märkische Bank in 1897 and entered into closer relations with the Essener Credit-Anstalt in 1900[61] the Ruhr quickly began to gain in importance for the bank. Carl Klönne's move to the Board of Managing Directors in 1900 was external evidence of this. In 1902 the Duisburg-Ruhrorter Bank was taken over. This, together with the interest which the Deutsche Bank acquired in the Essener Bankverein greatly expanded the position it was building up with the coal pits in the Ruhr. The Duisburg-Ruhrorter Bank brought close relations with the Haniels, who owned the Rheinpreussen pit and Gutehoffnungshütte.[62] In its Annual Report for 1903 the Deutsche Bank commented: "We have further expanded our relations with the industrial enterprises in the Rhineland and Westphalia and this has brought us opportunities for a number of new business transactions."[63] Some of the Deutsche Bank's business relations with companies in the coal, iron and steel industry in the Ruhr were, as can be shown in the case of the Bochumer Verein and the Gewerkschaft Deutscher Kaiser, directly due to the influence of Carl Klönne.[64] Beside the business he brought the bank penetrated the iron and steel industry largely through its connections in hard coal mining,[65] but it did not acquire the importance or influence of the banks which had older established relations with this branch of the industry.[66] At the end of the period we are concerned with the Deutsche Bank was represented on the supervisory boards of the Bochumer Verein, Gelsenkirchener Bergwerks AG, Harpener Bergbau AG and Phoenix, to name only the most important enterprises. It also maintained close business relations with Thyssen, Gutehoffnungshütte and Krupp.

The Bank für Handel und Industrie refrained for a long time from taking up closer business relations with industry in the Ruhr. When Bernhard Dernburg joined the Board of Managing Directors of the bank and the financial reorganisation of the Deutsch-Luxemburgische Bergwerks- und Hütten AG was successfully carried out in 1901 business policy became more strongly oriented to the coal, iron and steel industry. The bank remained closely connected with the Deutsch-Luxemburger and always managed its many issues. The merger of Deutsch-Luxemburg with the pit Friedlicher Nachbar was initiated by the bank, which had interests in both enterprises.[67] The merger of Phoenix with Nordstern in 1906 also brought the Bank für Handel und Industrie relations with this enterprise. In 1913 the bank was represented on the supervisory boards of nine coal, iron and steel companies, including Deutsch-Luxemburg, Harpener Bergbau-Gesellschaft, Phoenix and the Saar- und Mosel Bergwerks-Gesellschaft, which was under the influence of Thyssen and Stinnes.

---

61 F. W. Klinker: Studien, p. 21.
62 GHH archives 30071/34. F. W. Klinker: Studien, p. 65.
63 Cf. ZSTA Merseburg, Ministerium für Handel und Gewerbe, Rep. 120 A XI 2 No. 24, Vol I.
64 Carl Klönne had already sat on the Supervisory Board of the Bochumer Verein as a representative of the Schaaffhausen'sche Bankverein. The close relations between the Bochumer Verein and the Deutsche Bank developed after his move to the Deutsche Bank.
65 The Deutsche Bank was one of the main banks used by Bergwerks-Gesellschaft Nordstern, which merged with Phoenix in 1906/7. After the merger the Deutsche Bank also participated in the Phoenix issues.
66 J. Riesser: Grossbanken, p. 285.
67 DHHU archives 1352, 2582, 2592.

Up to the end of the nineteenth century the Dresdner Bank maintained few relations to the coal, iron and steel industry in the Ruhr. It was not until the Deutsche Bank began to strengthen its interests here that the Dresdner Bank felt bound to take similar steps. In 1897 together with the Aachener Disconto-Gesellschaft the Dresdner Bank cooperated in the conversion of the Bankhaus Hüttemann & Korte in Bochum into a joint stock company, the Bochumer Bankverein. After 1900 the Dresdner Bank pursued the policy of acquiring existing smaller banks in the industrial area of the Ruhr. Where these had formerly been completely taken over, it now followed the policy of the Deutsche Bank in leaving its new subsidiaries their formal independence. In 1902 and 1903 the Dresdner Bank formed interest agreements with the Düsseldorfer Bankverein, the Westdeutsche Bank in Bonn and the Wechsler- und Kommissionsbank in Cologne. At the same time it took a participation in the Märkische Bank in Bochum, which maintained branches in Gelsenkirchen and Recklinghausen. In the same year it cooperated in the financial reorganisation of the Rheinische Bank in Mülheim, and this brought closer relations with Thyssen and Stinnes.[68]

Of greater importance, however, was the interest agreement concluded in 1903 with the Schaaffhausen'sche Bankverein.[69] This was no doubt desired by both banks to counteract the influence the Deutsche Bank had been able to build up within a very few years in the Ruhr with the capital at its disposal. The interest agreement gave the Schaaffhausen'sche Bankverein, which until 1891 did not have a branch in Berlin, better access to the Berlin issue market, while the Dresdner Bank was able to open up business relations with the coal, iron and steel industry on the basis of the old and extensive relations maintained by the Cologne bank. Although the competition from the Deutsche Bank was certainly a primary motivating factor in the agreement, the growing concentration in the iron and steel industry in the Ruhr will have been a further decisive factor. When the agreement was concluded the preparations were well under way for the formation of the steel works' association. In view of the increasing tendency to form associations in industry it was assumed that the new and stricter cartels in Germany would lead to greater concentration in German industry. But this also meant that a greater need for capital might be expected and the banks felt in a better position to meet these demands when acting in consort. Although the expectations which the institutions placed in the interest agreement were not fulfilled and the agreement only lasted a few years, it did enable the Dresdner Bank to take up relations with major enterprises in the iron and steel industry. The interest agreements with the Mülheimer Bank and the Rheinische Bank helped it to expand its relations with Stinnes and Thyssen, which became apparent particularly in the Saar- und Mosel-Bergwerks-Gesellschaft zu Karlingen. At the end of our period the Dresdner Bank was represented on the supervisory boards of 11 companies in the coal, iron and steel industry, among them Deutsch-Luxemburg, Gelsenkirchener Bergwerks-AG, Mülheimer Bergwerks-Verein, Phoenix and Rheinische Stahlwerke.

The traditionally close links which the Schaaffhausen'sche Bankverein, the Disconto-Gesellschaft and the Berliner Handels-Gesellschaft maintained with the

---

68 A. Blumenberg: Konzentration, p. 38. There was closer cooperation with Stinnes and Thyssen in the Saar- und Mosel-Bergwerks-Gesellschaft in Karlingen. Cf. GHH archives 300 193000/13.

69 A. Blumenberg: Konzentrationen, p. 68 ff.

coal, iron and steel industry in the Ruhr continued after 1895 and were further extended.

But in view of growing competition from the Bergisch-Märkische Bank, The Essener Credit-Anstalt and especially the Berlin banks the Bankverein had to adjust its organisation to the changing circumstances. Up to 1901 the Bankverein had not opened branches of its own except for those in Cologne and Berlin. Then in 1901 a branch was opened in Essen, followed by one in Düsseldorf in 1902. In 1903 the Schaaffhausen'sche Bankverein entered into an interest agreement with the Mittelrheinische Bank in Koblenz, which was a major shareholder of the Mülheimer Bank. This enabled the Schaaffhausen'sche Bankverein indirectly to strengthen its position in the Ruhr yet once again. In 1905 the Rheinische Bank, which had been founded in 1897 in Mülheim, moved its headquarters to Essen, taking over the office of the Schaaffhausen'sche Bankverein there. This was possible because the Dresdner Bank held a participation in the Rheinische Bank as the result of a financial reorganisation in 1903 and the Schaaffhausen'sche Bankverein took over the Dresdner Bank's holding.[70]

At the end of the period under review the Bankverein was still the bank most strongly represented in the coal, iron and steel industry in the Ruhr with more than 20 supervisory board seats. Of the great integrated concerns the Bankverein maintained particularly close relations with the Hörder Verein, the Bochumer Verein, Phoenix, Hoesch and at times the Gewerkschaft Deutscher Kaiser.[71] "The Bankverein was godfather to most of the great companies in the coal, iron and steel industry and with its many business contacts was able to make a valuable contribution to the development of these companies, even if there were some disappointments. It would be difficult to name one of the major enterprises now operating in heavy industry in Rhineland-Westphalia in whose history the Schaaffhausen'sche Bankverein has not at some time played a part. The institute always has been and still is very closely related with the heavy industry in the West".[72] Yet in comparison with the major Berlin banks the Bankverein dropped behind both relatively and absolutely in its development in the last years before the war. The unsatisfactory profit trend was one of the reasons why the Dresdner Bank in 1908 instigated the dissolution of the interest agreement which had existed since 1903.[73] As the Bankverein did not succeed in halting the negative trend it had to reduce its capital in 1914 after some unsuccessful transactions from 145 to 100 million Marks and was taken over by the Disconto-Gesellschaft.[74]

The Disconto-Gesellschaft was mainly active in the issue business after 1895 as well. It participated in almost all the issues for the coal, iron and steel industry, always managing the loans for the Gelsenkirchener Bergwerks-Gesellschaft and the Dortmunder Union. It also maintained close relations with Phoenix, Deutsch-Luxemburg, the Rheinische Stahlwerke, Schalker Gruben- und Hüttenverein and at times to Thyssen, Gutehoffnungshütte and Krupp.[75]

In 1911 the Disconto-Gesellschaft, which had for a long time been centrally or-

70 P. Wiel: Wirtschaftsgeschichte, p. 345.
71 A. Blumenberg: Konzentration, p. 26.
72 A. Schaaffhausen'sche Bankverein, p. 6.
73 J. Riesser: Grossbanken, p. 369.
74 P. Wiel: Wirtschaftsgeschichte, p. 345; W. Däbritz: Essener Credit-Anstalt, p. 187.
75 J. Riesser: Grossbanken, p. 286.

ganised, opened its first branch in the Ruhr.[76] By then it had already fallen behind the Deutsche Bank in the overall scope and size of its business. After the death of von Hansemann August Thyssen actually suggested to Carl Klönne that the Deutsche Bank should form an interest agreement with the Disconto-Gesellschaft, in which "the Deutsche Bank should naturally take the lead."[77] In 1913 the Disconto-Gesellschaft had roughly 20 seats on supervisory boards in the coal, iron and steel industry. When it took over the Schaaffhausen'sche Bankverein in 1914 it was able to strengthen its position in the Ruhr even further. However, the takeover should be seen in relation to the takeover of the Bergisch-Märkische Bank by the Deutsche Bank.

The Berliner Handelsgesellschaft retained its centralised structure right up to the end of the period we are considering. But as it had direct access to the main stock market centre, Berlin, it continued to act as issue bank for most of the major enterprises in the coal, iron and steel industry. It was also strongly represented in coal mining through Harpener Bergbau-AG and after 1904 through Hibernia. Among the integrated concerns it maintained particularly close relations with the Bochumer Verein and the Rheinische Stahlwerke, being also represented on their supervisory boards.

Altogether the provincial banks lost ground after 1895. The increasing concentration in the iron and steel industry brought many small and medium-sized enterprises under the influence of the major concerns. In this way the provincial banks lost customers, on some of whom they had been able to exercise a considerable influence. When the companies were incorporated into the huge concerns they had to share this influence with other, generally very much larger banks and accept a reduction in their power.[78] The provincial banks generally retained their legal independence but almost all of them came more strongly under the influence of the major banks. The Bergisch-Märkische Bank, which the Disconto-Gesellschaft had helped to found, formed an interest agreement with the Deutsche Bank in 1897 and was formally taken over by the Deutsche Bank in 1914. In the case of the Essener Credit-Anstalt the Deutsche Bank had already formally acquired the foundation rights in 1876 through the liquidation of the Deutsche Union Bank, but the Essener Credit-Anstalt continued to use the help of the Disconto-Gesellschaft up to 1900 and the branch of the Schaaffhausen'sche Bankverein which had been opened in Berlin in 1891 for issues.[79] It entered into closer relations with the Deutsche Bank in 1900 and this enabled it to take a subsidiary participation in a number of transactions.[80]

None of the other provincial banks was of anything approaching this importance. The Barmer Bankverein did have a share capital which was nearly as large as that of the Schaaffhausen'sche Bankverein but up to 1914 its relations with the coal, iron and steel industry were of little importance in comparison with its involvement in the processing industry.[81] The private bankers, who had played such an important part in the

76 P. Wiel: Wirtschaftsgeschichte, p. 345; W. Däbritz: Essener Credit-Anstalt, p. 187.
77 GDK archives: Personenarchiv August Thyssen, No. 1.
78 J. Riesser: Grossbanken, p. 213.
79 Wilhelm Lindsiepe: Die Essener Credit-Anstalt im Zusammenhang mit der wirtschaftlichen Entwicklung des niederrheinisch-westfälischen Industriebezirks. Thesis, Bonn, Essen, 1914, p. 72.
80 W. Lindsiepe: Essener Credit-Anstalt, p. 89; F. W. Klinker: Studien, p. 64f.
81 Barmer Bank-Verein, Hinsberg, Fischer & Co. 1867–1917. Essen, 1918, p. 195ff.; F. W. Klinker: Studien, p. 113.

early years in the Ruhr, were now of little significance if they had not taken up close links with one of the big banks. Foreign capital was only of importance up to the end of the 1870s.[82].

The increasing involvement of all the major banks in the industrial area in Rhineland-Westphalia after the second half of the 1890s must be seen in connection with the increased tendency to concentration in industry at the time. The development of the integrated concerns was mainly furthered by the Rhenish-Westphalian Coal Syndicate founded in 1893 and prolonged in 1903. In 1895 only seven smelters were able to meet all or part of their need for coal from their own pits but by the time the syndicate was due for prolongation this figure had risen to 18 and it increased further after 1903 through the granting of the pit privilege. The establishment of the steel works' association in 1904 and its prolongation in 1907 and 1912 helped the mixed concerns to penetrate the refinement business. While around the turn of the century only the Dortmunder Union had a share capital of over 30 million Marks,[83] at the end of our period all the companies examined here had more than this. Gelsenkirchener Bergwerks-AG, Krupp, Deutsch-Luxemburg and Phoenix each had a share capital of more than 100 million Marks.

The concentration movement can also be seen from an examination of the development in the balance sheet totals of the three largest companies at any one time.[84] The huge need for capital which the concentration movement gave rise to in turn affected the banks, causing an increasing tendency to concentration here too.

The attitude of the banks to the concentration movement in industry in the 1890s varied according to the bank's own interests. While the Berliner Handelsgesellschaft and the Schaaffhausen'sche Bankverein took a neutral stand on the foundation of the coal syndicate, having important customers both among the pits and among the steel works which needed coal, the Disconto-Gesellschaft, whose major holding in the steel industry was Dortmunder Union, which had coal pits of its own, was a strong supporter of the syndicate in its role as representative of the Gelsenkirchener Bergwerks-Gesellschaft. When around 1900 the tendency to form integrated concerns became general the banks, as can be seen in the case of the steel works' association, began to take an active role in the establishment of important cartels and syndicates. However, before the First World War concentration in the iron and steel industry in the Ruhr had reached such proportions that the continuance of the cartels, and indeed the influence of the banks, was jeopardised.

To summarise we can say that in the relations between the banks and heavy industry two main phases can be recognised which are similar to those in the cyclical development of the iron and steel industry in the Ruhr. In the 1870s and 1880s the bad

82 H. Böhme: Grossmacht, p. 328ff; Karl-Josef Ehlen: Die Filialgrossbanken. Entwicklung und Stellung im deutschen Kreditsystem. Beiträge zur Erforschung der wirtschaftlichen Entwicklung. Heft 6. Stuttgart, 1960, p. 6; Leo Kluitmann: Der gewerbliche Geld- und Kapitalverkehr im Ruhrgebiet im 19. Jahrhundert. Bonn, 1931, p. 64.
83 It was not until 1903 that the firm of Krupp was turned into a joint stock company. However, the capital held by the various members of the family amounted to between 80 and 90 million Marks before this date.
84 See the table in the Appendix. On concentration generally: Hans Pohl: Die Konzentration in der deutschen Wirtschaft seit dem 19. Jahrhundert. Supplement 11 to the Zeitschrift für Unternehmensgeschichte, ed. Wilhelm Treue and Hans Pohl. Wiesbaden, 1978, p. 4ff.

Table 5

Year	Balance sheet total of the three largest iron and steel enterprises in the Ruhr	Three largest iron and steel enterprises in the Ruhr (by balance sheet total)	Share of the three largest pig iron producers in total production in the Ruhr	The three largest pig iron producers in the Ruhr
1878/79	211 337 568	Krupp, Union, GHH		Krupp, GHH, Phoenix
1879/80	208 199 288	Krupp, Union, BV		Krupp, GHH, Union
1880/81	214 712 682	Krupp, Union, BV		Krupp, GHH, Union
1881/82	215 492 182	Krupp, Union, BV	28,8	Krupp, GHH, Union
1882/83	213 062 743	Krupp, Union, BV	32,3	Krupp, GHH, Union
1883/84	218 122 277	Krupp, Union, BV	30,7	Krupp, GHH, Union
1884/85	208 070 185	Krupp, Union, BV	28,7	Krupp, GHH, Union
1885/86	203 129 544	Krupp, Union, BV	28,5	Krupp, GHH, Union
1886/87	204 112 885	Krupp, Union, BV	27,6	Krupp, GHH, Union
1887/88	209 138 554	Krupp, Union, GHH	28,6	GHH, Krupp, Union
1888/89	213 010 613	Krupp, Union, Bv	30,6	GHH, Union, Krupp
1889/90	238 866 256	Krupp, Union, Bv	29,9	GHH, Krupp, Union
1890/91	232 648 963	Krupp, Union, BV	31,1	GHH, Krupp, Union
1891/92	240 943 356	Krupp, Union, BV	30,9	GHH, Krupp, Phoenix
1892/93	280 007 171	Krupp, Union, Hörde	32,0	GHH, Krupp, Phoenix
1893/94	261 130 237	Krupp, Union, BV	30,0	GHH, Krupp, Union
1894/95	268 211 510	Krupp, Union, BV	28,0	GHH, Krupp, Union
1895/96	271 622 695	Krupp, Union, Hörde	29,7	GHH, Krupp, Union
1896/97	263 545 536	Krupp, Union, Hörde	31,3	GHH, Krupp, Union
1897/98	296 020 267	Krupp, Union, Phoenix	32,7	GHH, Krupp, Union
1898/99	320 165 958	Krupp, Union, Phoenix	31,9	GHH, Krupp, Union
1899/00	366 974 822	Krupp, Union, GDK	32,9	GHH, Krupp, Hörde
1900/01	388 572 428	Krupp, Union, GDK	33,7	Krupp, GHH, Hörde
1901/02	408 406 444	Krupp, Union, GDK	31,7	GHH, Krupp, Phoenix
1902/03	425 723 414	Krupp, Union, GDK	32,0	GHH, Union, Krupp
1903/04	480 831 089	Krupp, GDK Union	31,4	GHH, Hörde, Union
1904/05	549 801 538	Krupp, GDK, Union	31,1	GHH, Krupp, Hörde
1905/06	597 703 754	Krupp, GDK, Union	32,9	Krupp, GHH, Hörde
1906/07	824 280 471	Krupp, GBAG, Phoenix	49,0	GBAG, Phoenix, Krupp
1907/08	895 230 589	Krupp, GBAG, Phoenix	48,3	Phoenix, GBAG, Krupp
1908/09	914 486 411	Krupp, GBAG, Phoenix	46,9	Phoenix, GBAG, Krupp
1909/10	990 811 404	Krupp, GBAG, Phoenix	46,6	GBAG, Phoenix, Krupp
1910/11	1 054 931 703	Krupp, GBAG, DT-LUX	46,1	GBAG, Krupp, Phoenix
1911/12	1 223 903 548	Krupp, GBAG, DT-LUX	46,9	Krupp, GBAG, Phoenix
1912/13	1 255 976 277	Krupp, GBAG, DT-LUX	51,4	GBAG, Krupp, Phoenix
1913/14	1 297 529 155	Krupp, GBAG, DT-LUX	50,1	GBAG, Krupp, Phoenix

* Up to 1896 North-western group of the Association of German Iron and Steel Producers. After 1897/8 Ruhr = Rhineland-Westphalia

economic situation and the need for bank funds to pre-finance plant made companies strongly dependent on the banks. After 1895 enterprises were increasingly able to free themselves of the influence of the banks, largely as a result of the trend to concentration in industry. The resultant huge concerns needed credits which were almost always too big for one bank to handle, so that consortia were formed. The cooperation of several banks over one issue brought stronger representation by the banks on the supervisory boards of these enterprises, but this should not, as has occasionally been the case, be taken as proof that the iron and steel industry in the Ruhr was dependent on the banks.

The Entrepreneur, the Family and Capitalism

Some Examples from the Early Phase of Industrialisation in Germany

Jürgen Kocka

The spirit and practice of capitalism emerged from non-capitalist structures and processes and were nourished by them for a long time. Max Weber illustrated this i. a. in his discussion of the relation between the Protestant ethic and the spirit of capitalism; Joseph Schumpeter generalised it and stressed the importance of pre-capitalist élites for the emergence and maintenance of the bourgeois capitalist economic and social systems. Many others have taken up the same idea, developed it further, differentiated and supplemented it. It would seem appropriate to examine it in terms of the relation between the family and (industrial) capitalism.[1]

There can be no doubt that the basic principles of family life were in crass contrast to those of the capitalist market economy and the competitive society which became fully established in the course of the process of industrialisation in the nineteenth century. The relations between members of a family were not or hardly regulated according to criteria of supply and demand, exchange and competition. On the contrary, the family was held together by ties which differed greatly from the principles of a market economy: personal dominance of one personality and loyalty, partly due to natural differences or inequalities and ties, partly to tradition and partly to emotional relations of the most complex kind. The claim of the bourgeois capitalist system to offer its members equal rights and opportunities, to secure individual freedom and distribute opportunities according to individual performance was not parallelled by any similar claim on the part of the family. Market processes were based on contracts much more than family life, which tended to be informal, generally very personal and transparent, while the market economy was highly formalised, quite impersonal and not very transparent. The family also differed from the market in the multi-dimensional and comprehensive nature of its functions and the greater diffusion of its internal structure. The market was characterised by the primacy of economic considerations and greater specification. Considered in terms of their basic features and typical examples the family and the market, the family and the capitalist economic order can be seen to have been and to be very different.

Although these characteristics appear most clearly in the middle class family which began to emerge in the eighteenth century and became fully established in the

---

1 M. Weber: Die protestantische Ethik und der Geist des Kapitalismus. Here quoted from ibid.: Die protestantische Ethik, ed. J. Winckelmann. Siebenstern Taschenbuch 53, Munich, Hamburg, 1965, pp. 29–114; J. A. Schumpeter: Kapitalismus, Sozialismus und Demokratie. Munich, 1972[3]; E. J. Hobsbawm: Die Blütezeit des Kapitals. Eine Kulturgeschichte der Jahre 1848–1875. Munich, 1977, pp. 284–299. – The basic idea is developed in: J. Kocka: Family and Bureaucracy in German Industrial Management, 1850–1914: Siemens in Comparative Perspective, in: Business History Review, Vol. 45 (1971), pp. 133–156.

nineteenth, some of them are also observable, occasionally in a weaker form, in families of an earlier age or other social groups, for instance the nobility and the crafts in the early modern age. But I do not wish to go into that, or the genesis of this family structure, in more detail here.[2] We can take it that the middle class family preceded industrial capitalism, which with its main characteristics – private ownership of the means of production, private enterprise, de-central investment decisions oriented to market conditions, competition and profit considerations, wage-work and the concentration of production in factories, in mechanical processes – did not become fully established in Germany until the second third of the nineteenth century.

The main argument of this article is that family structures, processes and resources furthered the break-through of industrial capitalism and helped to solve problems of (capitalist) industrialisation which could hardly have been solved otherwise.[3] This can be seen particularly clearly with problems during the first half or perhaps the first two thirds of the nineteenth century. How the family helped to solve many of these problems will be discussed in sections 1 to 5; section 6 considers what qualities made the family capable of fulfilling economic functions of this kind. Section 7 discusses some of the tensions which arose as the families became involved in the development of industrial capitalism. It also, conversely, dicusses some of the frictions which arose in enterprises through their family ties. The conclusion outlines some of the results and sketches some of the changes which can be traced in the relation between the family and industrial capitalism after the first phase of industrialisation from the 1830s to the 1870s (the "Industrial Revolution"), which, with its precursors, is the main focus of attention here.

I. Motivation and Legitimation

It is not a matter of course but for a successful process of industrialisation it is necessary that a considerable number of persons who are capable of doing so should want to become entrepreneurs. There are certain objective conditions which will greatly facilitate this: the availability of economic opportunities, a shortage of alternative ways of achieving social and economic success, the weakness of legal barriers, acknow-

---

2 For an introduction see M. Mitterauer and R. Sieder: Vom Patriarchat zur Partnerschaft. Zum Strukturwandel der Familie. Munich, 1977. D. Schwab: Art "Familie", in: O. Brunner et al. (ed.): Geschichtliche Grundbegriffe. Historisches Lexikon zur politisch-sozialen Sprache in Deutschland, Vol. 2, Stuttgart, 1975, pp. 253–301. On the family in the nobility: H.-G. Reif: Westfälischer Adel 1770–1860. Vom Herrschaftsstand zur regionalen Elite. Göttingen, 1979. On the older craft families especially: H. Möller: Die kleinbürgerliche Familie im 18. Jahrhundert. Verhalten und Gruppenkultur. Berlin 1969. See also material in: H. Rosenbaum (ed.): Familie und Gesellschaftsstruktur (seminar). Frankfurt 1978.

3 The opposite argument predominates in some of the literature on the history of enterprises and modernisation, e. g. Th. C. Cochran: The Entrepreneur in Economic Change, in: Explorations in Entrepreneurial History, Vol. 3, 1965/66, pp. 25–38, esp. pp. 26 f., 28, 36 (on the dis-functional role of the family in economic growth); D. S. Landes: French Business and the Businessman (1951), in: H. G. Aitkens (ed.): Exploration in Enterprise, Cambridge/Mass., 1965, pp. 184–200. Generally on the negative assessment of ascriptive and traditional elements in economic growth: B. F. Hoselitz: Wirtschaftliches Wachstum und sozialer Wandel. Berlin, 1969, esp. pp. 16 ff., 114 ff.

ledgement or at least tolerance of independent, profitoriented commercial activity in the dominant scale of values. There was no lack of these conditions in Germany. A wide range of subjective motives can be established for the decision to found an enterprise or take one over in the early phase of industrialisation: the desire for growing or regular profits to ward off current or threatening need or improve one's living, the desire to work independently, be one's own master, to be able to create something or exercise power, and the intention to lead a righteous and proper life, one which would be pleasing in the eyes of God.

Here I want to stress another motive which occurs frequently in the sources, although it is often interwoven with others: the desire to succeed as an entrepreneur, despite many obstacles, in order to help the family or needy relations. When – as frequently happened – a bourgeois or petty bourgeois family was threatened with poverty or decline after the early death of the head of the household or both parents, the elder son often justified his decision to go into business by the need to care for his younger brothers and sisters who were not yet old enough to work, indeed altogether by the desire to establish the family name. Alfred Krupp and Werner Siemens in the 1820s and 1840s are the most prominent examples of this. In other constellations a sense of identity with the family had a similar motivating effect.[4]

It is even more significant that after the firm was successfully established and material prosperity assured, the need for personal security well covered and social recognition achieved most entrepreneurs still continued to work; they strove for expansion, struggled, fought, made sacrifices, generally until their heirs took over or until their death, in other words they did what a quickly growing, industrial capitalist economy needed them to do. Of course there were objective conditions which favoured this but – from the point of view of the individual entrepreneur – there was no compulsion. A very pleasant "rentier" existence was one of many alternatives available during those decades to a man who had some property or state securities. Why did most of the entrepreneurs go on working, struggling, investing to expand? One motive occurs again and again in the sources: it was not primarily for themselves but for the family that the enterprise was to continue and expand. The family gave an added dimension and significance to the work. It was for the good of their children and grandchildren or – more fundamental and more abstract – for the family name, a collective identity which stretched through several generations and on into the future. This not only justified the efforts the entrepreneur himself put into the business, it also justified his demanding that others – members of the family or employees – should subordinate their individual interests to those of the firm, at least to a certain extent. Orientation to the family and its future development also enabled the entrepreneur to take a long-term view of things and made it easier for him to renounce short-term speculative advantages. He could organise his business in such a way that it probably would survive his death (making it more "objective" through the appropriate business regulations, changes in the legal form and the appropriate provisions in the will). The family united past, present and future. It provided an important ideological base for the gradual emancipation of the business from the current needs of the founder and head of the firm, a process frequently observed in the literature on later manage-

---

4 See J. Kocka: Entrepreneurs and Managers in German Industrialization, in: CEHE, Vol. VII/I, Cambridge 1978, pp. 527–536.

rial enterprises. As we see it also occurred, even though for different reasons, in large family businesses in the first phase of industrialisation. There can be no doubt of the economic efficiency of such a family orientation. Among other things, it served as an incentive and a legitimation for the reinvestment of a large part of the profit instead of distributing it for the sustenance of various members of the family.[5]

II. Motivation and Qualification

Even if family advantage was not an explicit aim of the entrepreneur, and the desire for profit, ambition or love of power and independence were the main driving forces, this motivation was itself a product of the family background. Insofar, the upbringing and education provided by the family must be seen as a contribution to the emergence of the business. For a closer analysis of this we should concentrate on the types of family from which the early entrepreneurs – nearly all male – came: first on craftsmen's and artisans' families, second on those of merchants and putters-out, and thirdly, slowly increasing, on the families of factory entrepreneurs themselves.[6] The lower middle class families (of master artisans and small retailers) were still often characterised, during the period under review (the first half of the nineteenth century), by the integration of household and business. The children were brought up in the context of production and selling. Experience of real or threatening need, in his own family or among relations, was a formative experience for many a later entrepreneur who grew up under these circumstances, as was the experience of uncertainty, dependence on market conditions and changing circumstances. These were the decades when the guilds were being dissolved or loosened, when pauperism was on the increase and capitalist principles gained influence on production as well. In these families with their potential poverty or modest prosperity – good examples are the knife-maker, Henckel, in Solingen and the miller, Bienert, in Eschdorf in Saxony – the children were brought up in the intimate family circle, by their father (if he did not die early), by their mother, who was a strong influence and often took independent family decisions alongside the father, and, very important, by elder brothers and sisters. Grandparents living in the house are rarely mentioned. School, which a boy often left early to help in the business, played a smaller part. The influence of the family was intensive and it lasted for a long time, at any rate in the artisans' families which still followed the old tradition. Even the apprenticeship, which a boy might begin at the age of 12 or 14, was sometimes in his father's workshop, though more generally he was sent to another master. Even so, his education and training until he qualified as a journeyman would be in a family: that of the new master simply replaced that of his parents.

---

5 On principle issues: Schumpeter: Kapitalismus, loc. cit., p. 258 ff.; see also: H. Schelsky: Wandlungen der Familie in der Gegenwart. 2nd edition, 1954, p. 154; F. Oeter: Familie und Gesellschaft unter dem Einfluß des Industriekapitalismus, in: Schmollers Jahrbuch, Vol. 77, 1957, pp. 513–546, esp. p. 519. For Siemens cf. below p. 75. On Krupp: H. Witt: Die Triebkräfte des industriellen Unternehmertums vor hundert Jahren und heute. Hamburg, 1929, p. 97.

6 For a summary of the origin of the first generation of industrial entrepreneurs see Kocka: Entrepreneurs and Managers, loc. cit. pp. 510–11, 516–527.

Still, it is clear that only a small percentage of these families produced entrepreneurs (although conversely nearly half of the first generation of industrial entrepreneurs came from the families of master-artisans). And we may take it that the chance to rise to the position of entrepreneur and move beyond the traditional patterns of living and working of the artisan milieu, still oriented largely to pre-industrial principles such as the honour of the "Stand" and "sustenance" ("Nahrung"), came for those sons whose up-bringing had not exactly followed the traditional mode but had been driven somewhat off course by factors such as want, reversals of fortune, unfavourable market influences, sickness or the death of one or both parents or simply through unusual contacts. There is much to suggest that in times of change or want craftsmen's families may have produced many who slid down the social scale but they produced many entrepreneurs as well.[7]

The situation was different in the wealthy merchant and trading families like the Schramms in Hamburg or already established entrepreneurs' families like the Schoellers or Carstanjens in the Rhineland. Here parents and brothers and sisters handed on much of the up-bringing of the children to the nurse, the governess and later the tutor. But again the family influence was strong and intense in the early years, especially since, as it appears, uncles, aunts and grandparents also played a part. School did not begin to compete with family influence until the later stages and it was only after this that apprenticeship took the boy to a business associate's firm, that is further away from the parental sphere. Education for independence, for the search for new paths, the expansive achievement and vision was something which could be expected in the sons of more wealthy merchants and in the early entrepreneurs' families – together with an equally strong obligation to the traditional sense of honour, middle class solidarity and the proven forms of work. So the sons of these rising bourgeois families hardly needed to loosen family ties or break away from what they had been taught in order to achieve later success as an entrepreneur, as was sometimes the case in the artisan's world. In the biographies of the better-off bourgeois families we also find attention focussed on the education of the girls, most of whom later married into commercial families. They were given a thorough training in household skills, often a certain literary education and accustomed to their role of supporting their brothers and menfolk while taking a subsidiary position. They also helped in the office or with the accounts – before they married or if they remained single.[8]

So the field from which the first generation of industrial entrepreneurs were re-

---

7 Particularly Möller: Kleinbürgerliche Familie, loc. cit., R. Stadelmann and W. Fischer: Die Bildungswelt des deutschen Handwerkers um 1800, Berlin, 1955. H. Kelleter: Geschichte der Familie J. A. Henckels in Verbindung mit einer Geschichte der Solinger Industrie. Solingen, 1924, p. 125 ff.; on G. T. Bienert (1813–1894) see E. Dittrich (ed.): Lebensbilder Sächsischer Wirtschaftsführer. Leipzig, 1941, pp. 58–73. On education also: H. Beau: Das Leistungswissen des frühindustriellen Unternehmertums in Rheinland und Westfalen, Cologne, 1959, pp. 25 ff.; see also G. Tietz, Hermann Tietz: Geschichte einer Familie und ihrer Warenhäuser. Stuttgart, 1965, p. 20 f., on the great importance of the family of a small Jewish carter for the education and training of the son, the later founder of a department store, Oscar Tietz.

8 Cf. P. E. Schramm: Neun Generationen 1648–1948. Dreihundert Jahre deutscher Kulturgeschichte im Lichte der Schicksale einer Hamburger Bürgerfamilie (1648–1948). Vol. I, Göttingen, 1963. Esp. p. 206 ff., p. 238 ff.; R. v. Carstanjen: Geschichte der Duisburger Familie Carstanjen, Cologne, 1934; B. Nadolny: Felix Heinrich Schoeller und die Papiermacherkunst in Düren. Ein

cruited – the petty bourgeois or bourgeois families, most of them Protestant and engaged in small and medium-sized businesses, was actually highly differentiated. But in every case the family was the strongest influence in childhood and early youth; this was the major factor in the later choice of occupation. There was always a strong integration of education and work; these children were indoctrinated at a very early age with a respect for independent work which was quite un-feudal and often had a religious dimension, independent work either as a means of earning an honourable living or as a satisfactory means of individual achievement in competition with others and in the battle against circumstances. The stress on the fulfilment of duty, on order and punctuality was common to all these families; the dominant position of the father was hardly questioned and the children were expected to be obedient, if necessary this was strictly enforced. At least in the commercial families of the middle and upper bourgeoisie this was combined, though often not without contradictions, with education to a sense of responsibility and independence. Permissive or indifferent, hedonistic or playful, culturally refined or intellectual, impinged with doubt or uncertainty, pessimistic or sceptical – family education for the first generation of industrial entrepreneurs was none of these. It was oriented right from the start and quite wholeheartedly to the sons' later economic activity. This was taken as a matter of course and generally desired. Certainly, in the merchant and entrepreneurial families it was assumed that one of the sons, generally the oldest, would take over the business. But it was not only the oldest who was seen as a future entrepreneur and appropriately motivated, the younger sons as well, though perhaps to a lesser extent and certainly in the early bourgeois families, were expected to go into business. They may have become partners in the family firm or – using their share of the inheritance and other help from the family – joined another firm or opened their own business.

On the one hand these early craft, commercial and entrepreneurial families did not see themselves as a transitional phase which the children would soon leave to move into a non-commercial sphere. It was a rising class, optimistic, increasingly self-confident. On the other hand, there was still a considerable objective and subjective gap separating them from the leading groups in agriculture, the bureaucracy, the army and cultural life. Unfortunately we do not have good quantitative studies of what occupations the offspring of these groups took up. Stahl established that 67% of the sons of a selection of successful founders of enterprises worked as entrepreneurs themselves, about three quarters of these had inherited their father's business or a share in it and the others worked elsewhere.[9]

This inheritance rate can certainly be regarded as high and it was the result not only of the successful motivation of the male progeny but also other factors which were due to the family background and up-bringing: specific skills and qualifications, for

Lebensbild aus der Gründerzeit. Baden-Baden, 1957. F. Zunkel: Der rheinisch-westfälische Unternehmer 1834–1879. Ein Beitrag zur Geschichte des deutschen Bürgertums im 19. Jahrhundert. Cologne-Opladen, 1962, esp. pp. 69 ff., 111 ff.; and F. Decker: Die betriebliche Sozialordnung der Dürener Industrie im 19. Jahrhundert. Cologne, 1964, esp. pp. 115 ff.; L. Beutin: Die märkische Unternehmerschaft in der frühindustriellen Zeit, in: Westfälische Forschungen. Vol. 10, 1957, pp. 64–74, esp. p. 69; W. Köllmann: Sozialgeschichte der Stadt Barmen im 19. Jahrhundert. Tübingen, 1960, p. 111 ff.

9 W. Stahl: Der Elitekreislauf in der Unternehmerschaft. Eine empirische Untersuchung für den deutschsprachigen Raum. Frankfurt/Zurich, 1973, p. 287 f.

example. It is difficult here to separate the role of motivation from the role of qualification. Neither before nor after this period did the family ever make such a decisive contribution to the professional qualification of entrepreneurs as in the first decades of the nineteenth century. For the traditional means of acquiring qualifications outside the family – on the basis of the guilds and corporations – had been weakened by the liberal economic reforms of the turn of the century. State provision of commercial education and training in schools was developing only slowly and markets for special skills and knowledge had hardly developed. It was still hardly possible to generalise qualifications and even less to build up theories about them – in the extreme case they were still closely guarded secrets – and hence they had to be handed on personally, through demonstration and imitation. All this goes far to explain the dominant role of the family in handing on qualification and training and hence in qualifying the first generation of industrial entrepreneurs.

The role of the family was particularly important in the provision of *technical* skills; this was especially the case for the sons of craftsmen who, when they became entrepreneurs, generally worked in industries which were the same or closely related to that in which their fathers (had) worked.[10] But the sons of great merchants also derived from their background the commercial qualifications which they needed most: they absolved their apprenticeship in the offices of one of their relations, were sent on trips abroad and enabled to build up contacts; their first job was in the enterprise of a business associate or friend, or they went into their father's firm, at first as a privileged employee and later as co-owners. The influence of the family was even stronger in the case of the sons of manufacturers or factory owners, especially where they were regarded as future heirs. Their education was often specifically designed with the later function in mind, carefully planned and varied to provide experience in many different departments of their father's business or in that of a relative or associate.[11]

So what the early entrepreneurs learned from their fathers' generation – mainly from their fathers themselves – in other words, what they acquired through family channels and not market mechanisms gave them a tremendous advantage over other members of their generation when they had to compete – now generally according to market criteria – for access to enterprises or resources to found a business.

III. Capital Formation

If the laws of inheritance or provisions in a will did not introduce modifications the same applied as to money and property: what the fathers' generation had achieved through work, performance and favourable circumstances – often in market pro-

---

10 See Beau: Leistungswissen, loc. cit., pp. 13–15.
11 In addition to the works by Beau already mentioned (esp. pp. 13–27), Beutin (p. 70f.), Decker (p. 114f.), Köllmann (p. 112), Schramm (p. 177, 238f.) and Zunkel (p. 72ff.) see also F. Hellwig: Unternehmer und Unternehmungsform im saarländischen Industriegebiet, in: Jahrbücher für Nationalökonomie und Statistik, Vol. 158, 1943, pp. 402–430, esp. p. 408; A. Eyberg: Umwelt und Verhalten der Unternehmer des Oberbergischen Kreises im 19. Jahrhundert. Thesis, Cologne, 1955, p. 125f.; Witt: Triebkräfte, loc. cit., p. 103ff.; F. Redlich: Der Unternehmer. Göttingen, 1964, p. 328.

cesses – was handed on to the children through non-market mechanisms, i. e. within the family, and became an *ascribed* advantage for the new generations, to be used in market and competition processes of very varying kinds.[12]

The most obvious cases of inherited advantages are those of the heirs to enterprises. As however industrial enterprises during the Industrial Revolution rarely developed in a continuous process from pre-industrial craft shops or manufactories, these heirs constituted a very small minority, albeit a rapidly growing one, among the entrepreneurs of the Industrial Revolution. Kaelble has counted them in Berlin: among persons who had founded an enterprise in Berlin or taken one over up to 1835 they accounted for 14%; of those who joined this category between 1836 and 1850 28%; but 57% of those who joined the ranks of the entrepreneurs in Berlin from 1851 to 1873 had inherited. Altogether in Berlin as in Thuringia from 1830/40 to 1870/80 every third entrepreneur had inherited his business.[13]

But inheritance also played a large part in the establishment of new businesses, most of which were founded by the sons of master craftsmen or merchants. These persons could generally draw at least on a small inheritance – or they received a payment from their fathers out of the future patrimony to help them acquire the initial capital they needed.[14] This is one of the main reasons why if not the heirs to enterprises, certainly the sons of independent craftsmen and merchants so clearly predominated in the early generation of industrial entrepreneurs. It is also one of the reasons why individual "dynasties" in the commercial middle class proved so prosperous, lasting from the pre-industrial age through the first decades of industrialisation and in some cases on into the twentieth century, even if they sometimes had to change enterprises, location and occasionally even industry.[15]

Which was the most important, the inheritance of money and property or the inheritance of qualifications and motivation can hardly be answered in general terms. The situation was different in the case of a smelting works, which cost between 200,000 and 300,000 Thalers around 1850, or a combined blast furnace and puddling works which cost 1 million, than for the 60,000 Thalers which a medium-sized mechanical engineering factory cost or the 15,000 to 50,000 needed to start a mechanised spinning works or weaving shed or a paper mill.[16] However, we know from a sample

---

12 Generally J. Kocka: Stand – Klasse – Organisation. Strukturen sozialer Ungleichheit in Deutschland vom späten 18. bis zum frühen 20. Jahrhundert im Aufriss, in: H.-U. Wehler (ed.): Klassen in der europäischen Sozialgeschichte. Göttingen, 1979, p. 140 f.

13 See H. Kaelble: Berliner Unternehmer während der frühen Industrialisierung. Herkunft, sozialer Status und politischer Einfluß. Berlin, New York, 1972. p. 55, 123 (the figures on Thuringia are from W. Huschke).

14 Examples in P. Coym: Unternehmensfinanzierung im frühen 19. Jahrhundert. – dargestellt am Beispiel der Rheinprovinz und Westfalen. Thesis, Hamburg, 1971, p. 37 f.; L. Baar: Die Berliner Industrie in der industriellen Revolution, Berlin, 1966, p. 144 f. and in most entrepreneurial histories.

15 See e. g. H. Mönnich: Aufbruch ins Revier. Aufbruch nach Europa. Hoesch 1875–1971. Munich, 1971, p. 61 ff., 91 ff.; H. Kelleter and E. Poensgen: Die Geschichte der Familie Poensgen. Düsseldorf, 1908, p. 119 (the move by old entrepreneurial families from the Eifel or Düren to Dortmund and Düsseldorf in the middle of the nineteenth century).

16 Figures from W. Herrmann: Entwicklungslinien montanindustrieller Unternehmungen im rheinisch-westfälischen Industriegebiet. Dortmund, 1954, p. 15; A. Schröter and W. Becker: Die deutsche Maschinenbauindustrie in der industriellen Revolution. Berlin, 1962, p. 72; E. Klein: Zur Frage der Industriefinanzierung im frühen 19. Jahrhundert, in: H. Kellenbenz (ed.): Öffent-

of nineteenth and twentieth century entrepreneurs that over the longer term the sons and sons-in-law of owner-entrepreneurs very much more frequently (in 89% of the cases) became entrepreneurs than did the sons and sons-in-law of manager-entrepreneurs (only 21%). The majority of the sons of owner-entrepreneurs were heading the business which their fathers had owned or headed, while only the minority of the managers' sons were doing so.[17] Both of these categories of entrepreneurs' families must have passed on very similar kinds of qualification or the access to qualifications and "connections", style of living and so on but only the sons of owners will have inherited larger amounts of funds or property, the sons of managers will hardly have done this. We do not know for certain what occupations those young men who did not follow in their fathers' footsteps and go into industrial management took up, the results are only provisional as yet and not limited to the period of the Industrial Revolution. However this example suggests that the inheritance of property and fixed assets was of relatively greater importance in the assumption of an entrepreneurial position than the mere inheritance of qualifications and motivations.

Capital to found an enterprise, to operate one or expand it was often acquired through marriage with the daughter of a wealthy family who brought a dowry and access to further credit facilities or – less frequent – through marriage of one's daughter to a man who had capital at his disposal and would perhaps come into the business as a partner. The social endogamy rate was high among the sons and daughters of entrepreneurs and there were many and intricate marriage ties between the great entrepreneurial families. Indeed marriage ties can be seen as family mechanisms of capital retention in wealthy families before joint stock companies became generally established and modern company law developed. They counteracted the tendency to divide the accumulated wealth inherent in the inheritance laws and practice.[18]

Even where there was no inheritance or dowry, or where these were inadequate or already used up, members of the family would often make payments to make up the capital needed to start a business or finance the investment which became needed as it developed or to bridge the occasional bottleneck. That applied in the first instance of course to the families of the owners or shareholders of firms who used their other income, their reserves and savings and if necessary were prepared to make sacrifices in their personal lives to enable the business to go on. It also applied to loans and deposits by brothers and sisters, parents and grandparents, brothers-in-law, uncles and aunts and cousins of all kinds. The literature and sources contain plenty of evidence of this. An American study has quantified: in Poughkeepsie in New York, a medium-sized trading town, of 249 enterprises between 1850 and 1880 (to the value of at least 1000 dollars) 153 (61%) had acquired their capital entirely or partly from relations of

---

liche Finanzen und privates Kapital im späten Mittelalter und in der ersten Hälfte des 19. Jahrhunderts. Stuttgart, 1971, p. 118–128, esp. 119f.

17 From figures and calculations by Stahl: Elitenkreislauf, loc. cit., p. 309f.

18 On the marriage ties between great entrepreneurial families see below. On the accumulation of capital through marriage generally see the study of Boston merchants in the 18th century: P. D. Hall: Family Structure and Economic Organization. Massachusetts Merchants, 1700–1850, in: T. K. Hareven (ed.): Family and Kin in Urban Communities 1700–1930. New York/London, 1977, p. 38–61, here p. 41 ff. More detailed studies on the marriage and investment policy of the great commercial families and the practices and effects of inheritance which go beyond studies of indiviual cases are urgently needed for Germany as well.

the owner(s), not including inheritances. It can be taken that members of families in comparable German cases were no less involved.[19]

The forms of financial involvement varied, ranging from fixed-interest credits to deposits with a share of the profits. Sometimes a guarantee was enough. Generally the credit was granted without a claim to co-direction or a share in the management being requested. Financial help from the family generally came without recourse to market criteria, or this did not play a primary role: the main motive was non-economic, family solidarity. Indeed, help from the family came even or because normal cover was not available, it was given on the basis of personal trust. Nor was the money withdrawn as soon as the business outlook worsened; close relations were prepared to help even when things seemed virtually hopeless. Many an enterprise only survived the initial turbulent period because it could rely on help like this, finance provided independent, indeed often in direct contravention, of capitalist rationality. As a whole, however, and over the longer term credits from relatives were not given contrary to market rationale. They were rarely given without financial considerations, certainly not by distant relatives. If the recipient was persistently unsuccessful there were requests for the money to be returned, sometimes justified by family considerations, too.[20] Nevertheless, loans and deposits from relatives were of inestimable value as there were hardly any alternative sources of funds – there was no developed capital market, for example, nor were there a powerful banking system or joint stock companies, and often the risk did appear to be too great for money to be lent according to purely economic considerations. Trust and loyalty were a necessary basis, from a non-capitalist source.[21] If he were not a member of a large family the early industrial entrepreneur had a hard time of it.

IV. Management

In the same way family resources were used to solve problems of industrial management which could not have been satisfactorily solved in any other way. The recruitment, motivation and control of senior staff was a real problem for German entrepreneurs around 1850, especially in large companies with several plants which may well have been far apart. The career and occupation of senior employees in industry were not yet clearly profiled. There was no developed market for managerial staff. The

---

19 S. and C. Griffen: Family and Business in a Small City: Poughkeepsie, New York, 1850–1880, in: Hareven (ed.): Family and Kin, p. 144–163, here p. 150. A few German cases in Coym: Unternehmensfinanzierung, loc. cit., p. 38 ff.
20 See the examples in W. Berdrow: Die Familie Krupp in Essen 1587–1887. Essen, 1932, p. 247 f. (Retraction of a contract handing over property to Friedrich Krupp by his mother and grandmother); pp. 296, 313. When Friedrich Krupp, aged 61, quite unexpectedly married a 21-year old girl considerable sums which had been lent by his in-laws were demanded back, completely ruining him. On this problem generally and on lawsuits between members of families see Griffen: Family and Business, loc. cit., p. 153 f.
21 Whether state credits could have helped here is doubtful. In practice they played a very minor role. See Coym: Unternehmensfinanzierung, loc. cit. p. 113 ff.; H. Winkel: Kapitalquellen und Kapitalverwendung am Vorabend des industriellen Aufschwungs in Deutschland, in: Schmollers Jahrbuch, Vol. 90/I (1970), p. 275–301, here p. 286 ff. (with a rather more favourable verdict).

work which the senior "official" in an enterprise had to do was complex, subject to rapid change, hard to standardise and hence difficult to control with bureaucratic methods. It could only be mastered with a certain independence. Particularly during the years when an enterprise was being built up the owner was often away on long business trips. If there was no other shareholder in the business the senior official had control. The employees who were in charge of a section which may have been a long way away from the centre, perhaps even abroad, were particularly hard to supervise: the post took a long time, there was no telephone and travelling was difficult.[22] All this goes to explain why the entrepreneurs of the Industrial Revolution esteemed the loyalty and honesty of their staff as highly as their technical qualification.

As far as possible posts which entailed decisionmaking functions were given to relatives. Often the first person to be appointed and paid a salary in an enterprise was a brother or nephew of the founder and the first manager his brother-in-law or cousin. When the diversification of the production programme created new management problems the entrepreneur may have reacted by building up a legally independent enterprise to produce the new article and putting a trustworthy (and not exactly inefficient) nephew or son at the head of it. Special work such as difficult business or discovery trips were, as far as possible, entrusted to the son. In all these cases business cohesion was intensified by family loyalty.[23] This helped to make constant control and regulation at least partly superfluous and achieve the necessary de-centralisation of responsibility and authority. In addition to contractual ties, financial interest and the authority of the head of the factory this form of extra-economic solidarity helped to ensure a measure of cohesion and cooperation in the management of the enterprise and largely contributed to the success which would otherwise have been hard to achieve in the initial period.

This applied to a particular degree to the management of the early "multinationals". The coordination of the three branches of the electrical concern Siemens & Halske in Germany, Russia and England was largely achieved through private correspondence and the trust between the three Siemens brothers, Werner (in Berlin), Carl

---

22 Around 1820 the Solingen knife-manufacturer Henckels needed between two and three weeks for his trip to Berlin, where he had set up a sales branch which was soon taken over by his son (Kelleter: Henckels, p. 127). In 1854 a letter from Berlin to St. Petersburg took a fortnight. The head office of Siemens & Halske was in Berlin and the company had set up a branch in St. Petersburg, which was soon taken over by the brother of the founder. See the letter from Werner Siemens, 16.6.1854, in: F. Heintzenberg (ed.): Aus einem reichen Leben. Werner von Siemens in Briefen an seine Familie und an Freunde. Stuttgart, 1953, p. 90.

23 See J. Kocka: Unternehmensverwaltung und Angestelltenschaft am Beispiel Siemens 1847–1914. Stuttgart 1969, p. 82 f.; Decker: Betriebliche Sozialordnung, loc. cit. p. 19 (on cases in Düren); an impressive account of the establishment of a department store "concern" on a family basis is in Tietz: Hermann Tietz, loc. cit., p. 19–33; Kaelble: Berliner Unternehmer, loc. cit., p. 57 f.; G. Goldbeck: Kraft für die Welt, 1864–1964. Klöckner-Humboldt-Deutz AG. Düsseldorf/Vienna, 1964 (cases of relatives travelling for the firm); for similar material: H. Kelleter and E. Poensgen: Geschichte, loc. cit., p. 110. And: Mönnich: Aufbruch ins Revier, loc. cit., pp. 62 and 91 (on Hoesch); Kelleter,: Henckels, loc. cit., p. 129 ff.; Berdrow: Familie Krupp, loc. cit., pp. 296, 306 f., 310, 349 ff. – see Schramm: Neun Generationen, loc. cit., p. 272, 365 – the de-centralisation of a business into two legally independent units in 1805/6 and its re-unification soon after on a family basis. On management organisation on family lines in British industry see S. Pollard: The Genesis of Modern Management. London, 1965, p. 145 ff.; in general: W. A. Lewis: Die Theorie des wirtschaftlichen Wachstums, Tübingen 1956, p. 125 f.; A. Marshall: Industry and Trade. London, 1959, p. 326.

(in St. Petersburg) and William (in London). Each directed his branch without over-frequent reference to the others. The loyalty of the brothers to each other was the most important base which held the business together. Conflict broke out when one of the brothers left his branch or lost his influence for some other reason. These personal methods of coordination achieved only a loose connection between the individual parts of the enterprise, which remained largely autonomous. But as long as it sufficed, family loyalty was a very fine tool with which to achieve the goal – it was cheap and accessible.[24] Most of the early enterprises were partnerships. Relations were preferred for partnership required trust and cooperation which was most likely between relatives. In Poughkeepsie, New York, between 1850 and 1880 48% of partnerships were between relatives.[25] There is nothing to suggest that comparable figures for German cities would be lower if we knew them. We do know that German entrepreneurs made their sons or sons-in-law partners in their business at a very early age.[26]

Family relationships also facilitated cooperation between enterprises. They provided a basis for early cartel-type agreements. Carefully planned marriages between the sons and daughters of the great entrepreneurial families created a complex network of connections, making the businesses like great concerns, links which could have been neither created nor maintained in those days in any other way.[27]

V. Connections and the Formation of a Class

It would be wrong to interpret the many marriage ties between the great entrepreneurial families exclusively with regard to their direct economic functions, the formation of capital and concerns. They also, like the family relations of the early entrepre-

---

24 See Kocka: Unternehmensverwaltung, loc. cit., pp. 76, 82, 132f., 207, 253; S. v. Weiher: Die Entwicklung der englischen Siemens-Werke und des Siemens-Überseegeschäftes in der zweiten Hälfte des 19. Jahrhunderts. Thesis, Freiburg, 1959; ibid.: Carl von Siemens 1829–1906. Ein deutscher Unternehmer in Russland und England, in: Tradition, Vol. I, 1956, pp. 13–25.
25 Griffen: Family and the Kin, loc. cit., p. 156f. According to Beau: Leistungswissen, loc. cit., p. 69, of 400 enterprises in North Rhine-Westphalia between 1790 and 1870 266 were headed by a technician and a merchant (partnerships) together.
26 In the sample given by Stahl (Elitenkreislauf, loc. cit., p. 241), owner-entrepreneurs of the second or a later generation became shareholders in a family business on average at the age of 24. See below and Note 62.
27 See Hellwig: Unternehmer, loc. cit., p. 429 for cartel-like agreements in the Saarland. See also Decker: Betriebliche Sozialordnung der Dürener Industrie, loc. cit., p. 113f.: "In 1754 Anna Katharina Deutgen, daughter of the iron manufacturer Eberhard Deutgen, married Hugo Ludolf Hoesch, the head of the Düren Hoesch family. The Deutgen family was also linked by marriage with the Schüll and Wergifosse families. There were also many links between the Hoesch and Schüller families. Marriages between the Düren industrialists' families had become so frequent in the course of the centuries that industry in Düren in the nineteenth century can be described as one huge family concern. Indeed family relations worked like business relations, and in many cases they gave rise to groups of companies which functioned like concerns and included plants both in the same and different industries. One of these groups was formed by the marriages of the five daughters of Hugo Ludolf Hoesch, all of whom married leading industrialists in the metal industry. In the second half of the nineteenth century further families joined the network. Often these were young technicians and merchants, like Gustav Renker, Ernst Grebel, Richard Rhodius and so on who obtained work in Düren and then married the daughters of industrialists."

neurs in general, fulfilled important social functions as well, although these were certainly of relevance for the business. It is sometimes overlooked[28] that the entrepreneur could not as a rule act as an isolated individualist or achieve his success as a lonely genius. Of course a streak of individualism was needed, a desire for independence, an ability to look beyond what the majority thought, felt and desired – in other words a little distance. But more than anything the entrepreneur needed contacts. With no highly developed school or publication system he needed relations, friends and acquaintances for an exchange of experience. Without a very well developed communications system, without a specialised press or special correspondents, without the experts who later did nothing in the business but collect information, the early entrepreneur needed personal contracts if he was ever to recognise business opportunities of various kinds at all.[29] The low degree of insitutionalisation in the commercial and trading sphere, the weight placed on the person and his known and acknowledged qualities in the granting of credit, the attraction of qualified staff and obtaining major contracts – all this meant that the entrepreneur had to be known: not necessarily to the public at large but in not too small a circle of persons who were engaged in business, and to whom he had to be known as trustworthy and reliable.

The entrepreneur of the Industrial Revolution had also to rely on other entrepreneurs in order to implement interests which could only be represented collectively, with regard to state legislation and administration and increasingly in relations with the workforce. We need only recall the customs legislation of the "Vormärz" and the early strikes, which by the 1840s at the latest had provoked collective answers from the employers. But the means for collective interest representation were not well developed: older forms of the organisation of joint interests (guilds, corporations) had weakened since the reforms of the turn of the century. New forms of organisation (industry associations, employers' associations) only slowly emerged and they took some time to grow in influence; it was not until the second half of the nineteenth century and particularly after the 1870s that they were really effective. There were of course no special schools for entrepreneurs. Up to the 1870s/1880s very few went to the universities with their student fraternities. Only the mining sector, which had been in state ownership for a long time, had its own academies. Nor did military experience count for much, in the Rhineland military service was avoided as far as possible up to the time of the foundation of the Reich.

Beside church and communal organisations – and more than these – it was the family in the widest sense, the relations or "class" who provided the social contacts necessary to fulfil these various needs. Networks of family relationships provided contacts which went beyond the individual entrepreneur and enterprise, loyalties

---

28 See A. Gerschenkron: Social Attitudes, Entrepreneurship and Economic Development, in: Explorations in Entrepreneurial History, Vol. 6, 1953/4, pp. 1–19, here p. 13: the view of the entrepreneur as particularly lacking in tradition and relations.

29 See Redlich: Der Unternehmer, loc. cit., p. 186; R. Engelsing: Bremisches Unternehmertum, in: Schriften der Wittheit zu Bremen II, Bremen, Hannover, 1958, pp. 7–112, here p. 49. This is the great economic significance of belonging to religious minorities which were socially closely linked but geographically widely distributed. Cf. on the Jewish case D. S. Landes: The Bleichröder Bank: An Interim Report, in: Publications of the Leo Baeck Institute. Year Book 5, 1960, pp. 201–220 and a major study by Werner E. Mosse on the German-Jewish bourgeoisie in the nineteenth and early twentieth centuries to be finished shortly. See also below Note 50.

and a sense of belonging together which the business could not adequately supply but which it needed.

A large number of children and a high endogamy rate were the most important prerequisites for the emergence of this family network. The great majority of entrepreneurs' sons married daughters of the middle and upper commercial classes and a large minority or even a majority of entrepreneurs' daughters married sons of the same group. Five out of seven leading entrepreneurs in Leipzig in the 1840s had mothers who came from entrepreneurs' families; five of them in turn married entrepreneurs' daughters. Of 17 leading businessmen's sons who married in Bielefeld between 1830 and 1910 (a random sample), twelve, i. e. a good 70%, married the daughters of businessmen. Four out of the 17 brides were the daughters of public servants, one, in the Wilhelmine Reich, was the daughter of a land-owner. Conversely, of the daughters of Berlin entrepreneurs in the 1850s and 1860s 65% married into commercial families, most of them the sons of merchants, factory owners and bankers. Here too public servants, ministers of the church, officers and independent scholars formed the second largest group of origin.[30]

As marriage may have loosened ties to the parental family but hardly dissolved them, networks of relationships and loyalties were built up and could be mobilised when needed (to provide information, testimonies of character, for help in presenting a petition, in the formation of busines ties, when an employee was needed or help to acquire capital), especially since the help did not entail too much in the way of input or sacrifice on the part of the "son-in-law", "cousin" or "uncle" – the terms were very generally used. In any case the looser relationships would hardly have offered an adequate base for more.[31]

The marriage patterns also show how the middle and upper commercial classes cut themselves off from the lower classes or groups – manual workers and the lower classes altogether, those engaged in agriculture and small craftsmen or traders. On the other hand they had, at least at first, little contact with the aristocracy or the major land-owners. Their marriage ties reflected and encouraged the formation of the bourgeoisie as a class. A more frequent move was into the educated middle classes. It was only in the later decades, in the Rhineland after about 1870, that more mobility developed in marriage between the major entrepreneurs and the aristocracy or major land-owners, in keeping with the process of assimilation between the bourgeoisie and the old ruling class.[32]

The marriage patterns of the commercial bourgeoisie would need a closer examination. Here I can only point out that with the geographical expansion of markets

30 See H. Zwahr: Zur Klassenkonstituierung der deutschen Bourgeoisie, in: Jahrbuch für Geschichte, Vol. 18, 1978, pp. 21–83, here p. 28 (figures on Leipzig); the Bielefeld figures are calculated by K. Ditt; also cf. J. Kocka et al.: Familie und soziale Plazierung, Opladen 1980, Berlin figures from Kaelble: Berliner Unternehmer, loc. cit., p. 185.
31 The history of every enterprise, which does not completely ignore family relations, contains a large number of such cases. Cf. B. Berdrow: Familie Krupp, on the 7th and 8th generation (Friedrich und Alfred Krupp), esp. pp. 240, 245f., 276f., 282ff., 287f., 290, 293f., 296f. (for a crisis in these relations), 299, 300f., 305f., 309ff., 316ff., 349ff., 352.
32 See Zunkel: Der rheinisch-westfälische Unternehmer, pp. 110ff.; Zwahr: Klassenkonstituierung, loc. cit., pp. 41f. (on Saxony); M. Barkhausen: Der Aufstieg der rheinischen Industrie im 18. Jahrhundert und die Entstehung eines industriellen Großbürgertums, in: Rheinische Vierteljahrsblätter, Vol. 19, 1954, pp. 135–178, esp. p. 174.

and commercial activities the geographical range of the potential marriage market also expanded. The rather local limits of the seventeenth and eighteenth centuries widened, however strong regional accents remained even in the nineteenth century.[33]

The mutual preference of two or three commercial families in marrying their offspring has frequently been shown, especially in the eighteenth century. P. E. Schramm has described how three wholesale firms in Hamburg grew together in this way to a "business clan", continuing to put chances in each other's way. Between the Krefeld silk manufacturers, von der Leyen, and the Cologne bankers Herstatt there were five marriages in two generations in the late eighteenth and early nineteenth centuries and of course intensive business relations.[34] These strong inter-relations suggest a careful marriage strategy observing economic considerations as well as family interests. They seem to have become less frequent in the nineteenth century. In the same way it can be seen that, especially in the textile industry, what had been a frequent conjunction of marriage and industry[35] became rarer. Both suggest that the social and only indirectly economic ends and functions of these networks of relations moved into the foreground – contacts, loyalties, information, collective interests, the emergence of supraregional groups or class cohesion – and the direct economic aims (capital concentration, the formation of "concerns" on family bases) became less important in the course of the 19th century.

These family networks were not sharply delineated. They were relatively unstructured and flexible. In the case of the Krupps, for instance, the contact with the big families with whom there had been close ties in the eighteenth century were largely broken off by the 1820s but an important new network was being created through new marriages.[36] Business clans of this kind and prominent groups linked by many inter-marriages and relationships on the local level could take in "new blood" if it appeared economically and socially necessary. Often cooptation into a family (sometimes the way was prepared by acting as godfather) was followed by economic suc-

---

33 The expansion beyond local areas is stressed by Zunkel after the second half of the nineteenth century. Der rheinisch-westfälische Unternehmer, loc. cit., p. 19 f., P. 13–22 contain a survey of important dynasties in the West German commercial bourgeoisie after the early modern age and shows that these generally successfully survived the first phase of industrialisation. One example of a close marriage network which extended beyond one industry but was geographically limited (for Hamburg up to the 1770s) is in Schramm: Neue Generationen, esp. p. 296 and pp. 252 f., 272 and 365. A case extending beyond regional boundaries from the same period is in Barkhausen: Aufstieg, loc. cit., p. 174, Note 27. For the marriage patterns of leading Leipzig industrialists, which went beyond regional limits but were concentrated in Saxony see Zwahr: Klassenkonstituierung, loc. cit., pp. 36–42. Hellwig: Unternehmer, loc. cit., p. 408–13, esp. p. 409 concentrates on the expansion of the marriage policy of industrialists in the Saar to the whole of the south west of Germany.

34 See Schramm: Neun Generationen, loc. cit., pp. 176, 255 ff.; Zunkel: Der rheinisch-westfälische Unternehmer, p. 21; similarly for the Saarland Hellwig: Unternehmer, p. 408.

35 See G. Adelmann: Die wirtschaftlichen Führungsschichten der rheinisch-westfälischen Baumwoll- und Leinenindustrie von 1850 bis zum Ersten Weltkrieg, in: H. Helbig (ed.): Führungskräfte der Wirtschaft im neunzehnten Jahrhundert 1790–1914, Part II, Limburg/Lahn, 1977, pp. 177–99, here p. 183; E. Dittrich: Vom Wesen sächsischen Wirtschaftsführertums in: ibid. (ed.): Lebensbilder sächsischer Wirtschaftsführer. Leipzig, 1941, p. 1–56, here p. 48 f. (on the textile industry). In Bielefeld they used to say "Linen to linen".

36 See Berdrow: Familie Krupp, pp. 284, 308. Generally on this social phenomenon see also Mitterauer/Sieder: Vom Patriarchat, loc. cit., p. 27.

cess.[37] On the other hand the family dimension meant that it was not possible to be fully accepted only on the grounds of economic success and that generally economic success and social standing – in cities like Hamburg and Barmen political power as well – went hand in hand.[38]

It was more difficult to get rid of members of the clan who were not pulling their weight. In this respect, the market mechanism, if left to itself, might have been more effective. Not even major Hamburg merchants always succeeded in getting rid of a ne'er-do-well son by despatching him to Surinam. It would appear that these families were very reluctant to disinherit. It was occasionally done and then justified with reference to the grandson.[39] But generally they went no further than threats. Clearly such a step, had it been taken more often, would have caused uncertainty and rancour, jeopardising family solidarity and perhaps the basis of the whole system.

VI. The Particular Qualities of Entrepreneurs' Families

It has been argued so far that mechanisms which were inherent to capitalism were clearly not enough for the solution of early industrial entrepreneurial problems and hence the establishment of industrial capitalism. In addition to other pre-capitalist structures, processes and resources the family played a considerable part in solving the business problems of the early industrial age. In many respects family loyalty, energy and resources functioned if not as a motor then as a vehicle of early industrial capitalist development.

The next paragraphs are meant to demonstrate that the families of the early industrial entrepreneurs which fulfilled these functions in part consciously and deliberately, but in part unconsciously and unintentionally, were a *form of transition* between the traditional "household" with the business and family under one roof and the later "middle class family".[40]

On the one hand they differed from the traditional farmers' and master artisans' families or those of the cottage workers in that the household and business were largely separate, a necessary consequence of the centralisation of production which became established with the breakthrough of industrialisation. For the family this brought a certain relief: there was no pressure, for instance, to fill all the family roles: the widow or widower could afford, if they wished, not to marry again.[41] The separa-

---

37 See Schramm: Neun Generationen, loc. cit., p. 264; Köllmann, Barmen, loc. cit., p. 112.

38 See Kocka: Stand – Klasse – Organisation, loc. cit., p. 138 f.

39 See Schramm: Neun Generationen loc. cit., pp. 248, 253; see also J. V. Bredt: Haus Bredt-Rübel: Geschichte des Hauses und seiner Bewohner. Wuppertal-Elberfeld, 1937. p. 43 ff.: the exclusion of two ne'er-do-well nephews from an inheritance, a decision which was to be re-examined and if possible revoked after six years.

40 The German concepts are "ganzes Haus" and "Hausgemeinschaft", translated here by "household", resp. "bürgerliche Familie", translated by "middle class family". On the choice of concepts see Mitterauer/Sieder, pp. 18–23, esp. p. 22 f.; O. Brunner: Das "Ganze Haus" und die alteuropäische "Ökonomik" in ibid.: Neue Wege der Verfassungs- und Sozialgeschichte, 2nd edition, Göttingen, 1968, pp. 103 ff.

41 An example of a widow who carried on the business until her son could take it over in R. L. Mehmke: Entstehung der Industrie und Unternehmertum in Württemberg, in: Deutsche

tion between household and business brought new chances and created qualities which had not been so strongly marked in the old farming or petty bourgeois households. Marriage and the family created for the entrepreneurs of the Industrial Revolution a protected, private sphere, in which moral self-realisation and emotional satisfaction were possible and "homely" pleasures could be enjoyed because the family was at a distance from the struggles of the business world and the storms of public life. Generally the young couple set up home immediately after marrying, even if the parents of one of them were in the vicinity and could have housed them. And if the son who married last and his wife did not leave the parental home and the widowed mother, the rooms and floors were carefully divided: the young family needed and were given their private quarters. The home was to be a secure refuge, where the "pains of the knocks and blows could be forgotten", a nest, from which the husband was repeatedly torn by "the inexorable demands of business" but to which he regularly returned to gather new strength.[42] However idealised and romantic this concept may have been the reality for the factory owner around 1850 was less of a contradiction to it than for the master artisan family as it had traditionally been and still was. The wife of the entrepreneur usually did not take part in her husband's business life as the farmer's wife, the master artisan's wife or the cottage worker's wife often did. Nor did the children have to work in the business, they grew up in the home and not in the workshop, even if in the first decades the factory owner's home was near the workshop, often on its site and only later, when the villa became attainable, in another quarter of the town and a better position. The people the husband worked with did not belong to the household nor to the family. When housekeeping books were kept they were clearly separate from the firm's accounts.

On the other hand, as we have seen, these families fulfilled many economic functions, their separation from the production and business sphere was not so marked as that of the public servant's family and certainly not that of the modern, twentieth century family which serves primarily reproductive, socialisation, consumption and leisure functions. A family could however only fulfil these economic functions if it had certain qualities inherited from the past. These have hardly been systematically researched and I can give here only some impressions and assumptions:

a) Only larger families could make the contributions to the management of enterprises and the formation of a social network as outlined here. In capital formation larger families were more likely to be able to help than smaller – and the families of most entrepreneurs were large. Four to eight children was the norm among seven leading entrepreneurs in Leipzig in 1840s.[43] Johann Gottfried Henckel, knife-maker and merchant in Solingen (1735–1811), was one of nine children of a father who himself had five brothers and sisters. Johann Gottfried founded his business, a supra-regional trade in metal goods and, although he married again a year after the death of

---

Zeitschrift für Wirtschaftskunde, Vol. 4, 1939, p. 113. See also E. Schmieder: Die wirtschaftliche Führungsschicht in Berlin 1790–1850, in: Helbig (ed.): Führungskräfte, pp. 1–58, here p. 57.

42 Quotations from letters by Werner Siemens to his fiancée and later wife in the 1850s, in: Heintzenberg (ed.): Aus einem reichen Leben, pp. 50, 77. On the way the "middle class family" of the nineteenth century saw itself see Schwab: Art "Familie", loc. cit., p. 293 ff. See Bredt: Haus Bredt-Rübel, p. 77 for a case in which the family of the younger son shared the same house but not the same household as the mother.

43 From Zwahr: Klassenkonstituierung, p. 28.

his first wife, had "only" four children. Of the two sons who carried on the business, one remained unmarried and childless – a rarity among entrepreneurs to the present day,[44] while the other, Johann Abraham Henckel (1771–1850), had eight children, among them three sons, one of whom died as a boy. The main heir, Johann Abraham (1813–1870) had fifteen children. Ten of them, some still living in the twentieth century, produced off-spring, altogether 31.[45] In a study of the "Deutsches Geschlechterbuch" (genealogy records) for Lower Saxony A. von Nell has shown that between 1750 and 1849 the families[46] of major entrepreneurs and merchants had on average 5.9 children and hence clearly surpassed the average family in the educated classes and the commercial petty bourgeoisie. It was not until c. 1850 that this figure declined, slowly at first and then rapidly after 1900.

b) Loosely tied and unstable families could hardly have fulfilled the functions we have outlined. The early industrial entrepreneurs' families in the narrower sense, the family which lived together under one roof, held together firmly. We can recognise four major reasons, four characteristics of these families, three of which are traditional and only one modern. First, one should stress the dominance of the father. These families had a clear centre of will and this was also the centre of direction of the firm. It was a dual role, the two aspects mutually supporting. As his family ties helped the entrepreneur in directing his firm, so his business influence helped the father in governing the family. He decided on the appointment of staff, the allocation of shares, he gave recommendations and made careers. Above all he also decided – within the broad legal limits – on the distribution of the patrimony. Tradition and custom supported his authority, as did ideology. And as long as political power in the public sphere was largely limited to the heads of household this also furthered the patriarchal, autocratic structure of the family. The head of the household and director of the firm was hence powerful enough to determine the use of family resources – within the limits set by law, tradition and custom. Certainly he decided on the education of the children, on whether relatives should live in the house and what servants should be appointed. He influenced the choice of occupation and marriage partner in the younger generation within limits which admittedly were shifting. He kept the family together; he brought up his children in this attitude of mind; he was generally powerful enough to enforce conformity to these ideals even against opposition. He did this from firm conviction and probably because he knew how well a properly functioning family served his dual role as head of the household and of the firm. The family was far too important an element in this complicated structure of personal, business and social relations to be left to itself. If necessary it was held together with pressure. The scope for individual members was very limited, and there was little room for non-conformism. The family as a unit ranked before its individual members, who of

44 Of 148 entrepreneurs in employment examined by Stahl (Elitenkreislauf, loc. cit., p. 302) in the 19th and 20th centuries only 7 were unmarried. On the present over-representation of married persons among entrepreneurs see B. Biermann: Die Sozialstruktur der Unternehmerschaft. Demographischer Aufbau, soziale Herkunft und Ausbildung der Unternehmer in NRW. Stuttgart, 1971, pp. 69–71.
45 From the family tree in Kelleter: Henckels, loc. cit.
46 More precisely "full marriages", those where the couples remain together until the end of the presumed fertility period of the wife (45 years of age). See A. von Nell: Die Entwicklung der generativen Strukturen bürgerlicher und bäuerlicher Familien von 1750 bis zur Gegenwart. Thesis, Bochum, 1973, p. 29.

course took very unequal parts in the definition of its aims. Generally the husband could rely on full support from his wife, he rarely encountered competition or criticism from her, for her position, self-awareness and satisfaction depended on family relationships to an even greater extent than his did. It would appear that during these decades women became more dependent and less influential the more the old links between the business and the family were broken. The housewife moved away from the world of business and work, without yet having full sovereignty in the house and the family.[47]

Second, the multiplicity of functions must be mentioned in order to explain what held these families together. It gave the family a central place in the thoughts and feelings of its members and supported a collective identity which went on from one generation to another. We have already considered many of these functions, the economic and educational particularly. There were many others. Religious observances were often largely in the family circle. Social life and games, music and other leisure pursuits were preferred at home. Family occasions such as marriages and christenings were great celebrations in the old middle and upper bourgeois families. On a wedding day the father might try his hand at writing a poem or the children would put on a play.[48] There were very few alternative means of entertainment – the father had access to some but generally these were much less highly developed than later and this lack of outside attractions strengthened the family.

There was also a shortage of alternatives in another respect. The belief must have gone very deep that in cases of individual misfortune or failure one could only expect help – to a better or worse degree – from the family. Only they would rescue a member from ultimate failure. In cases of bankruptcy and sickness, after accidents or the misfortunes of war the family came to the victim's aid as best they could.[49] Particularly during the first half of the nineteenth century there were hardly any other forms of protection or insurance, apart from the church and communal poor relief, and this must have seemed to most "respectable citizens" a nightmare and not a support.

---

47 For contrast see the extremely active, almost independent role played in the enterprise by the wife of Henckels in Solingen around 1815: Kelleter: Henckels, loc. cit., p. 129; the same applied to the wives of Hamburg merchants in the late 18th century: Schramm: Neun Generationen, p. 206; on the active roles played by the mother and grandmother of Alfred Krupp around 1800 see Berdrow: Familie Krupp, loc. cit., p. 247 f., 276. On the patriarchal role played by the father of the family in entrepreneurial households in the second third of the 19th century: Zunkel: Der rheinisch-westfälische Unternehmer, loc. cit., p. 73 f.; Köllmann: Barmen, loc. cit., p. 118; on the tradition of the patriarchal and autocratic head of the household: Möller: Kleinbürgerliche Familie, p. 10 ff. On the change in the role of women during the transition from the 18th to the 19th century see esp. K. Hausen: Die Polarisierung der "Geschlechtscharaktere" – eine Spiegelung der Dissoziation von Erwerbs- und Familienleben, in: W. Conze (ed.): Sozialgeschichte der Familie in der Neuzeit Europas. Stuttgart, 1976, pp. 367–93.
48 See the examples in Zunkel: Der rheinisch-westfälische Unternehmer, loc. cit., p. 71, 73; Berdrow: Familie Krupp, p. 284 (on the christening of Alfred Krupp in 1812); Schramm: Neun Generationen, p. 206 ff.
49 See G. Hahn: Untersuchungen über die Ursachen von Unternehmensmißerfolgen. Thesis, Cologne, 1956, p. 37 f.; Zunkel: Der rheinisch-westfälische Unternehmer, loc. cit., p. 73. On the objective limitations on the role of the family as support during the Napoleonic wars from 1806–15 see Schramm: Neun Generationen, p. 365. When Friedrich Krupp lost his house and his position in 1809 the young family moved into the mother's house, where other married brothers and sisters were living (Berdrow: Familie Krupp, p. 249). Paul Bredt moved back into his parents' house with his five children in 1879 when his wife died suddenly. See Bredt: Das Haus Bredt-Rübel, p. 85.

Since the reforms of the turn of the century guild and corporative institutions had been weakened and in some cases destroyed; new institutions of self-help were emerging only slowly; public insurance systems were not set up until the late nineteenth century and even then they did not include the bourgeoisie. One has to consider, however, whether during the first half of the century closely tied minorities, especially religious communities and sects did not develop a solidarity which functioned similarly to that of a family – perhaps even better – in providing a degree of protection and insurance, that they too formed social networks and helped to solve economic problems like those discussed above.[50]

Patriarchal authority and multi-functionality had strengthened and stabilised the middle class, farming and noble families for many generations. A third element now developed: it was in strong contrast to the two others and if not entirely new, did gain in importance with the increasing separation of the household and the enterprise and the still very limited liberation of family life which this brought. It was the romantic, idealised and emotional attitude which began to characterise the concept of the family, at first in the educated classes of the "Vormärz", then invading the entrepreneurs' households as well. The sources are scarce and seldom clear: how much is the expression of genuine love and affection in these families and how much is rhetoric, unthinking adoption of current modes of thought? What were the survival chances for delicate emotions in these multi-functional family groups, still with so many objective obligations and ties, in the early bourgeosie? There are a few instances to suggest that the chances were not lacking and that they were rather increasing than decreasing. Love and affection between affianced and then married couples, between parents and children, above all between brothers and sisters, formed ties which often bound members of a family more closely than the authority of the father or the force of contingency, but at the same time they brought greater individualisation and might stand in the way of the rationale or family sense which transcended the individual and his needs.[51]

For the families could only exercise the functions outlined above if their identity consisted of more than the sum of their individual members, if there was a family

---

50 For an example of one of the rare unmarried entrepreneurs: Gottfried Henckels, 1804–58, for whom obviously his relations with the Gichtelianer sect sufficed, fulfilling the role the family would otherwise have taken, even aiding the recruitment of senior staff (Kelleter: Henckels, pp. 138ff., 153). Werner E. Mosse assumes that there was less long-term cohesion in Jewish families, although there are spectacular cases of the contrary, than in comparable non-Jewish families. C. Wilson points out that the solidarity of non-conformist religious sects in England furthered economic growth. He goes on: "The Meeting House or Chapel extended the ties of the family, and you lent or borrowed within your known community with a confidence hardly yet to be extended beyond such limits." (The Entrepreneur in the Industrial Revolution in Britain, in: Explorations in Entrepreneurial History, Vol. 7, 1954/5, pp. 129, 45, here 131).

51 There are many instances from Hamburg in the later 18th and early 19th century in Schramm: Neun Generationen, e.g. pp. 202, 206ff., 381. On the relation between Werner Siemens and his fiancée and later wife Mathilde, daughter of a professor, in the 1850s see the correspondence between them in Heintzenberg: Aus einem reichen Leben, pp. 48–98, esp. pp. 50, 51, 52, 62, 63, 70, 72, 82f., 85, 87; on the close relation between Werner Siemens and his brothers and its importance for the business pp. 13, 14f., 19, 33, 64, 68, 320. Werner Siemens, the elder, had promised his mother shortly before her death to provide for his younger brothers and sisters, (pp. 60, 95). A similar promise was given by three brothers on the death-bed of their widowed mother in 1855: Schramm: Neun Generationen, p. 217. For the issues under discussion here the relations between brothers and sisters were more important than those between married couples.

sense which went beyond the happiness of individuals and was to a certain extent held to be superior to it. Only in this way could the family fulfil the legitimation function described above; only in this way did it serve as motive and reason for a decision not to consume but to accumulate. In fact we find the traces of such a supra-individual family sense in our sources. Werner Siemens, by then a successful entrepreneur, wrote in a private letter to his brother of an intention which he had had for a long time "to build up an enterprise which will last, which may perhaps one day under the leadership of our boys become an enterprise of world renown like that of the Rothschilds etc. and make our name known and respected in many lands!" and he concludes: "For this great plan the individual, if he regards the plan as good, should be prepared to make sacrifices".[52]

Particularly in the older, very self-confident commercial families, which have sometimes been compared with "dynasties", we might well find the beginnings of an emphatic, supra-individual family sense, transcending generations. And in fact they did plenty to encourage this. It is the fourth factor which favoured strong family cohesion. Again we can take the Siemens family, although they are rather an ideal and hardly representative example. When the firm of Siemens & Halske was founded in 1847 the family already had a "carefully and faithfully recorded family tree" going back through eight generations to the time of the Thirty Years' War. The record was first drawn up in 1829 and it was revised and supplemented several times in the following decades. The family had a coat-of-arms and a motto. After 1873 family reunions were held regularly, at least every five years; generally there were more than fifty and sometimes more than a hundred persons present. In the same year a family foundation was set up, its purpose "to give every member of the family of Siemens the possibility of proper education, both physical and intellectual".[53] Later family bulletins were issued (after 1905) and a family archive was set up in the old family home in Goslar (in 1931), where a Siemens library was also assembled with no lack of biographies of the more distinguished members.

Of course one cannot generalise from this. Nevertheless coats-of-arms and seals were frequent among the larger commercial bourgeois families. The older members of the wealthier Hamburg merchant families regularly had their portraits painted so as to leave a better record for posterity; later they were sometimes content with photographs. The family Bible was handed on from generation to generation and major events – births, marriages and deaths recorded in it with a respectful commentary for the benefit of future generations. The use of the same Christian names through many generations also symbolised and strengthened the family tradition, as did the early tendency to keep written records. Sometimes there were even rather legendary accounts of the family's origin.[54]

52 Werner to Carl Siemens 4.11.1863 in: C. Matschoss (ed.): Werner Siemens. Ein kurzgefaßtes Lebensbild nebst einer Auswahl seiner Briefe. Vol. 1, Berlin, 1916, p. 218; similarly on 25.12.1887, ibid., Vol. 2, p. 911, and to his son Wilhelm, his successor in the business, on 22.12.1883, in: Heintzenberg (ed.): Aus einem reichen Leben, loc. cit., p. 320.

53 See H. Siemens: Stammbaum der Familie Siemens. Munich, 1935, p. 26 (quotation), p. 18. Eligible acc. to §2 of the statutes were those persons numbered in the family tree and their legitimate offspring, but not adopted children.

54 See Schramm: Neun Generationen, loc. cit., p. 429 (portraits), 238 (the tradition of handing on names, which after the early 19th century gradually gave way to the desire for greater individual-

c) Where such a sense of family tradition and identity was at work, transcending individuals and generations and reminiscent of the behaviour patterns of the nobility, it certainly also furthered the cohesion of the immediate family circle, the single household, but at the same time pointed beyond it. Many of these families could only fulfil their economic functions because they were not totally absorbed in their own small household but found part of their identity in more distant kinship relations.[55] These were of course much looser than that of their immediate circle; they may have remained latent for years but could be actualised in case of need – within clearly recognisable limits – for the solution of problems. It was only in exceptional cases that the family in the wider sense, the kinship group or "clan", had a clear focal point and centre, and even so this could never develop the power and authority which the father exercised in the individual household. There were no clear external limits to these wider circles of relatives, indeed they changed according to the standpoint of the individual household concerned. That is also the reason why it is difficult to reconstruct them. Strong love and affection between their members were probably rather rare – with a few important exceptions such as closer relations which may have existed between brothers and sisters who had then founded their own families. What kept these "clans" together in such a way that they could function as described?

It is tempting to argue somewhat in a circle: the multiplicity of functions in view of the lack of feasible alternatives. How else could networks of familiarity have developed? How could the family help an individual in need if it was not itself part of a greater circle which offered protection and a distribution of risk? Also, there were few means of reducing unfamiliarity outside the direct circle in those times. Maintaining kinship ties would then seem to be a most natural strategy. Anyway, since the education process was so closely bound up with the family, since marriage partners were so consciously chosen, stressing the trend to social endogamy, kinship relations meant much more than they mean today: usually the same religion, similar values, a similar style of living and similar origins.

The tendency of families to cling together even in their outer circles was also strengthened by the tendency of the old entrepreneurial families to stay in one place. In the old industrial areas there was little geographical mobility among the entrepreneurs.[56] Relations living in the same place, if not in the same house, met frequently, even if this did not apply to all of them. "Many entrepreneurs' families had evolved a custom of meeting once a week. The Möllmanns' family day was Sunday, the Baums' Thursday. Friedrich von Eynern and his young wife Emilie Rittershaus had to devote virtually every other day, and very certainly every Sunday, to the family".[57] On journeys relations were visited, indeed these people travelled, as they said, "down the

isation); Moennich: Aufbruch ins Revier. loc. cit., p.61 (family legends). The family Bible with its entries was used as a source by Bredt: Haus Bredt-Rübel.

55 See R. Braun: Sozialer und kultureller Wandel in einem ländlichen Industriegebiet (Zürcher Oberland) unter Einwirkung des Maschinen- und Fabrikwesens im 19. u. 20. Jahrhundert. Erlennach/Zurich/Stuttgart, 1965, pp. 106f. This shows how small families which were differently structured and had particularist inclinations rather hindered the development of larger enterprises and groups of enterprises.

56 See e. g. Adelmann: Führungsschichten, p. 181.

57 Zunkel: Der rheinisch-westfälische Unternehmer, p. 73; Schramm, loc. cit., also mentions family days, p. 253.

cousins' road"[58] through Germany. For the rest many a household, many a sister, cousin or uncle may well have withdrawn from the net, refused closer contact and ignored the family bulletins. The system was flexible enough to go on functioning.

VII. Tensions

These particular qualities will show how the narrower and wider family circles of the commercial bourgeoisie could exercise the economic functions outlined above as frequently as they did. The families had maintained sufficient *traditional features* to be able to perform economic functions as the old "ganze Haus" with the enterprise and the family, servants and apprentices under one roof could do. Among these traditional features were: a large number of children, the patriarchal authority of the father and head of the household in the closer family circle, the tendency to inherit an occupation and enterprise and to social endogamy, the widespread network of kinship relations with which the smaller units were surrounded, the creation of a family identity which went beyond individuals and generations, and the importance of the multifunctionality of the family in view of the lack of alternative resources or institutions provided by the market or the state.

On the other hand these families constituted a *new element* in their environment. They were not supporting a craft shop as in the pre-industrial age or a farm which was largely selfsufficient, this was an industrial enterprise, functioning (or not functioning at all, as the case might be) according to capitalist laws, expanding, centralised. As middle class families they tended to be self-determinant, following their own rules and at some distance from the new economic rationale.

This basic tension caused repeated friction: either the needs of the enterprise infringed the principles and rules of the family, or the claims of family life threatened to disrupt the rationale of the economic sphere.

In the craft families in the eighteenth century a marriage for the son or daughter which was economically and socially "desirable" and as such planned and determined by the parents, may not have conflicted very much with the ideals and desires of the couple themselves.[59] The ideal of marriage as a self-determinant partnership only possible on a love basis, which became established mainly in the middle classes by the "Vormärz" at the latest was not in keeping with this type of "marriage of convenience". But was not the instrumentalised marriage of convenience an essential part of the family network we have just described and its economic and social functions? There can be no doubt that there were increasing conflicts between the "rational" marriage policy and the desire on the part of the young people for wedded bliss in the new style. No doubt there were marriages which were a sad contrast to what they claimed to be, full of inner conflict and compromise, tension and hypocrisy, a continuance of the old split between love and marriage which the younger generation was fighting against. What did this mean for the inner credibility of the family, which the

---

58 Berdrow: Familie Krupp, p. 258.
59 See Möller: Kleinbürgerliche Familie, p. 305 f.

popular encyclopedia of Brockhaus in 1834 described as "sacred" and was so frequently praised and celebrated as a private sphere free of conflict and instrumental-
isation?[60] Did the economic and social function it served not in turn affect the family
in such a way as to weaken its substance and hence erode the base on which it could
serve those functions? The sources are very discreet in their treatment of this inner
core of modern family life.

However, the marriage policy of the great entrepreneurial families was at least
slightly adjusted to the new ideas. We have already pointed out that although the
tendency to social endogamy did not decline there was a slackening of the tendency,
so frequent in the eighteenth century, consistently to form dynasties by frequent in-
ter-marriage between two or three families and of the tendency to marry into the same
industry or branch. The economic aspects of marriage would appear to have given
way more to the social functions, which suggests that the choice of marriage partner
was less frequently the result of a deliberate family strategy and more frequently the
result of existing social contacts, friendships and arrangements. Within these limits
the couples will have been able to choose freely, guided not first and foremost by the
business policy of their families' enterprises even if they did regard a "suitable" marriage as important, welcomed a dowry and generally regarded parental approval as
essential. Of course the marriage partner had to be suitable – not only socially and
economically but in religion as well, and this is in itself a restriction on purely economic considerations. However, it is hardly surprising in view of the great weight
placed on religion in everyday life and the attitude of the early entrepreneurs. We do
not often find an entrepreneur's son marrying hastily for love; the flower girl, the
hireling's daughter, the young girl in the factory would not have been considered. In
any case the son of an established merchant or entrepreneur did not marry in the first
full flush of passion. He generally married late, later than the sons of petty bourgeois
families or the educated classes and certainly later than the members of the lower
classes: at 33 on average between 1750 and 1849 according to A. von Nell's survey in
Lower Saxony. However, these young men generally married very much younger
girls, on average aged 22. The sons of the Bielefeld bourgeoisie in the nineteenth century also tended to wait until their thirtieth year before marrying a girl aged on average 22.[61] That was roughly the age in which according to another more comprehensive study entrepreneurs had finished their education and training at school, in apprenticeship and dependent employment and could for the first time take independent control of a business.[62] So the sons of the bourgeoisie concentrated on their business training for a relatively long time. They did not marry until they were economically and occupationally established.[63]

---

60 On these claims and this idealisation of the bourgeois family of the time: Schwab: Art "Familie",
    loc. cit., p. 291–97; Mitterauer/Sieder: Vom Patriarchat, p. 160.
61 Von Nell: Entwicklung loc. cit., p. 74, 75; for comparative figures see pp. 72, 107, 108. The Biele-
    feld data is from a random sample of 14 marriages from 1830 to 1910, by K. Ditt (Note 30).
62 See Stahl: Elitenkreislauf, loc. cit., p. 242. Heirs generally began to take over their father's business
    on average a year earlier (at 29).
63 With the effect of putting off his marriage from Werner Siemens in a letter of 13. 3. 1852, in: Heint-
    zenberg: (ed.): Aus einem reichen Leben, p. 60. Several authors have noted that the tendency of
    the bourgeoisie not to marry until a certain degree of commercial success had been achieved was
    apparent at the end of the 18th century as well. See Möller: Kleinbürgerliche Familie, loc. cit.,
    p. 171, esp. Note 6.

There still remained an element of calculation in the choice of a partner. No doubt there were marriages purely for money and cases where the father dictated the choice to his heir. And families will certainly have tried to prevent economically less desirable marriages and – as in one example – kept possible suitors away from the wealthy aunt or the niece who would inherit and who was thought to be not of the soundest of intellects but very anxious to marry, even going to the point of appointing a trustee.[64] Generally, however, marriage was not calculated like a business investment or transaction. The sources rather give the impression that the sons increasingly – though the daughters less so! – had room for independent initiative and made good use of it. However, they too kept within clearly defined limits, marrying only after careful consideration of all the aspects involved and in consultation with their parents or an uncle.[65] The reality was somewhere between a love match and a marriage of convenience and no doubt there were strong variations.

But the world of business penetrated the family sphere in other respects as well, causing changes, tension and "costs". The father influenced the sons' choice of occupation and often maintained his will over theirs.[66] The eldest son or at least one of the sons generally had to submit to the requirements of the family business[66a] and prepare himself systematically – like the crown prince – for his succession. This may well have been a heavy burden if it proved too great a strain or forced the young man contrary to his inclinations and ability. If there were several sons to a marriage this lessened the likelihood of conflict. The most suitable son could then be chosen.[67] These bourgeois families were certainly flexible enough to do that; unlike the nobility or the

---

64 See Zunkel: Der rheinisch-westfälische Unternehmer, loc. cit., p.73, esp. Note 46; see also Schramm: Neun Generationen, loc. cit., p.248 and on Charlotte Wilhelmine Honsberg in Wuppertal around 1800, "weak in the head but very anxious to marry" Bredt: Haus Bredt-Rübel, loc. cit., p.45f.

65 See examples ibid., pp.381f. (1813/14); Kelleter: Henckels loc. cit., p.154f. on the marriage of one of the heirs in 1840; Mönnich: Aufbruch, loc. cit., p.95; the letters from Werner Siemens to his fiancée, later wife (Note 51 above). One often has the impression that there were economically more rational alternatives for the entrepreneur in some cases. This also applies to Alfred Krupp's late marriage to Bertha Eichhoff, daughter of a public servant, and certainly to that of his son Friedrich Alfred to Margaretha von Ende in 1882 which the father had prevented for years (Berdrow: Familie Krupp, pp.316, 369f.).

66 See also H. Münch: Adolph von Hansemann. Munich, Berlin, 1932: Bredt: Haus Bredt-Rübel, p.73.

66a For an example see W. Kurschat: Das Haus Friedrich & Heinrich von der Leyen in Krefeld. Thesis, Bonn, 1933, p.32.

67 Werner Siemens seems to have taken it for granted that his eldest son Arnold, born in 1853, would take on the business. His second son, Wilhelm, born in 1855, was apparently first intended to go into parliament or act as the "scientific spirit of the business". The third, Carl Friedrich, was not born until 1872, in the father's second marriage and was too young to be considered for the succession, which was decided in the early 1880s. However, the eldest son proved little suited to the task. The succession then came to the second son, whose diary entries during his youth show considerable torments of self-doubt. Nevertheless, he went into the business in 1879 (without finishing his studies), where he took over various functions (with interruptions due to illness) and took over the direction of the firm in 1890. The founder, born in 1816, had therefore to carry on as head of the firm, which was growing rapidly and increasingly over-straining him, for a few years longer than he intended. See A. Roth: Wilhelm von Siemens. Berlin, Leipzig, 1922; and the diary of Wilhelm von Siemens in the Werner von Siemens Institut (Archiv) 4/Lf775. – For an example of a hard education as heir to a business which went ruthlessly over the boy's preferences, see that of Friedrich Krupp, son of Alfred Krupp: N. Mühlen: Die Krupps. Frankfurt, 1965, p.59f.

landowners they did not have fixed rules of inheritance and this made them economically very much more viable. A son-in-law or nephew could come into the business if there were no son or the sons were eminently unsuitable. Adoption as in Japan was apparently rare. But we do not know what conflict or heart-ache the question of the inheritance may have caused within the family.

Only closer analyses of the inheritance and dowry practice and of marriage policy altogether would show whether the choice of an heir who seemed most suitable to take over the business and the priority accorded to business interests and the general interests of the family in deciding the inheritance was purchased at the expense of other sons and daughters as can be shown, with the appropriate variations, in the case of noble families.[68] Certainly, handing on to the next generation proved a vulnerable point. Generally it would have been more in the interests of the business to maintain the accumulated capital (and not to distribute it), nor to set too many successors at its head, even if they were equally entitled to be there but to make the best qualified the head of the firm and the overall successor. But this often conflicted with the principles of justice and loyalty within the family. There is Berdrow's rather restrained account of the delay in handing over the steel works to Alfred Krupp in 1848, which must have put family feelings to a hard test and left at least one permanently damaged victim: brother Friedrich, out-bidden, who left Essen, virtually to go into banishment, becoming more and more of a strangeling, even if financially secure. There are other cases of dispute over the inheritance between the mother and children after the death of the father who had headed the business.[69] Generally an enterprise does appear to have been left to more than one person.[70]

The entrepreneurs of the Industrial Revolution, whether they founded their businesses or inherited them, would appear to have been familiar with the dilemma of having to choose between the interests of the firm and the loyalty or fairness to the closest members of their family. They resorted to various means to cope with this, sometimes handing the business on during their lifetime, reserving to themselves a regular income and a certain right of participation on matters of principle. Sometimes they founded or bought additional works in order to be able to leave one to each son,[71] though this was hardly possible in very capital-intensive industries. Sometimes they distributed shares to their children, imposing the condition that these could not be taken out of the business for some time, and not granting full codirection rights to prevent the number of managers growing to the detriment of efficiency, but leaving the direction of the enterprise to the person most suited. It is the beginning of a separation between shareholding and control in a family business. Some of the wills and contracts were very complicated.[72] But over the longer term it was not always possible

---

68 On the other hand it must be borne in mind that industrial enterprises and capital are on principle easier to divide than the land owned by the nobility and the rights this brings. See the excellent discussion of these problems by H. Reif, in: J. Kocka et al.: Familie und soziale Plazierung, Opladen 1980, p. 34–44. He also discusses the case of the nobility ibid., pp. 67–126, and in his book (see Note 2).

69 See W. Berdrow: Alfred Krupp, Vol. I, Berlin, 1927, pp. 221–7; on brother Friedrich ibid.: Familie Krupp loc. cit., p. 361 f. See also Note 78 below.

70 See the figures in Stahl: Elitenkreislauf, p. 284.

71 For instance in the Düren paper industry: Decker: Betriebliche Sozialordnung, p. 31, 104, 105 (esp. Note 43).

72 For examples see H. A. William: Carl Zeiss 1816–1888. Munich, 1967, p. 91–102; on obligations

to prevent heirs from claiming their full shares in the form of cash or too many or un-suitable heirs from demanding participation in the direction of the business.[73]

The only safe possibility was to change the firm into a joint stock company, a solu-tion which became increasingly popular even during the "Vormärz". The form cho-sen was that of an "Aktiengesellschaft" or "Kommanditgesellschaft auf Aktien"; in 1892, the legal form of the "Gesellschaft mit beschränkter Haftung" (GmbH) was created, providing a solution to the particulary needs of the family firm.[74] Even if the old family business often continued for a long time under the new guise, these changes did constitute an important step on the way to the gradual withdrawal of the business from the family context which was becoming increasingly necessary through the growing irreconcilability of family and business interests.

Testamentary or contractual arrangements regarding inheritance and succession or changes in legal form and the arrangements which frequently had to be made be-tween brothers and relations concerning capital participation and profit-sharing and business rights and obligations of various kinds meant that formalized contractual aspects penetrated deep into family relationships where they perhaps constituted a certain alien element. They changed one dimension of family life, institutionalising it and making it more "fixed" in order to meet the requirements of the business better.[75]

The conflict between the claims of the rapidly growing business and the family which was responsible for it could of course also negatively affect the course of busi-ness, hindering efficiency. If the owner of a factory had many sons and daughters and wanted to give them all fair shares the inheritance could prove a considerable burden on the enterprise,[76] with shares in the capital to be handed out or current earnings dis-tributed, unless it proved possible to establish a family or business interest which was accepted as superior to the claims of individual heirs or to find other ways of avoiding distribution.[77] For this reason crises over inheritance were frequent in family firms.[78] Such crises could also arise over the problem of selection of the management. The

---

laid on sons and grandsons see Kurschaft: Haus von der Leyen, loc. cit., p. 17 for the will made by Heinrich von der Leyen (Krefeld) in 1782.

73 See S. Haubold: Entwicklung und Organisation einer Chemnitzer Maschinenfabrik. Thesis. Bonn, 1939, pp. 32ff.; H. Rachel & P. Wallich: Berliner Großkaufleute und Kapitalisten. Vol. 2, Berlin, 1967, pp. 222, 223; Witt: Triebkräfte, p. 97.

74 See Herrmann: Entwicklungslinien loc. cit., p. 15, for an early example in 1834; see also Mönnich: Aufbruch loc. cit., p. 91 ff. on Hoesch 1871; Kelleter: Henckels, loc. cit., p. 181 on the change to a partnership limited by shares (1882); on the possibility of changing the legal form to that of a "GmbH" and Stumm's influence on the 1892 legislation: Hellwig: Unternehmer, loc. cit., p. 423 f.; on the frequency of the change even in the second generation Stahl: Elitekreislauf, loc. cit., p. 258.

75 For an example see the "Siemens'sche Vermögensgemeinschaft" of 1897 (or earlier) which col-lected the family capital, had statutes, and was administered by two employees. Clearly this was the only way to handle the family's claim to disposition and management, which was anchored in shareholdings, in view of the size of the enterprises, their spread and the capital involved. So a semi-public sphere developed between the level of the enterprise and the really private sphere of the individual members or branches of this huge family. See Kocka: Unternehmensverwaltung, loc. cit., p. 453.

76 I.e., if the enterprise was not sold to satisfy the claims of the heirs.

77 See A. Paulsen: Das 'Gesetz der dritten Generation'. Erhaltung und Untergang von Familienun-ternehmungen, in: Der praktische Betriebswirt. Jg. 21, 1941, pp. 271–280, here 278 f., and above.

78 From 1870 to 1879 in Henckels: Kelleter, loc. cit., p. 175 ff. After the death of the father there were law-suits over the inheritance. For a time the widow thought of selling to meet the various claims.

recruitment of the successor (or successors) in the direction of the business was primarily according to family criteria. But although an entrepreneur's son may have had all the advantages we described earlier in terms of up-bringing and experience this did not always guarantee that he would prove efficient at the job. If he were not, the business, which was still very dependent on the personality and ability of the head of the firm, could easily weaken or even disintegrate.[79] So dependence on the family could negatively affect the efficiency of a firm. Nor was it apparently always easy to prevent heirs who wished to do so from participating in the direction. On the other hand the factories of the Industrial Revolution could rarely be divided without seriously impairing business efficiency. This caused considerable coordination problems, as when seven members of the family wanted to take an active part in the direction of a small Düren textile firm, all claiming to represent the enterprise.[80]

The recruitment of members of the family to work below management level could also prove problematic. Of what use was the most loyal of men if his technical qualifications and general efficiency were not up to the job?[81] Moreover even in the early period it could happen that quiet, restrained growth was preferred for family considerations and many a chance to expand was not utilised because it would have made capital and staff from "outside" necessary, which might have jeopardised the family influence.[82]

VIII. Conclusion and Outlook

But these were exceptions. Generally we can say that in the first decades of industrialisation in Germany the family was one of those non- and pre-capitalist institutions which were a prerequisite, stimulus and vehicle of the process of capitalist industrialisation. It is hard to say how this process could have gone on without these families and their resources. Family structures and processes furthered capitalist industrialisation very much more than they hindered it. Family sense proved a strong motive to entrepreneurial behaviour. The desire to serve family interests, which were perceived as going beyond the individual and one generation, provided an ideological legitimation and in some cases motivation for growth-oriented entrepreneurial policy. The family helped to qualify the early entrepreneurs more than any other institution through "inheritance" of knowledge and skills and social benefits of many different kinds. The family made many a contribution to capital formation and its financial re-

---

79 In the 1880s at Siemens. See J. Kocka: Siemens und der aufhaltsame Aufstieg der AEG, in: Tradition, Jg. 17, 1972, pp. 125–42.
80 Leopold Schoeller & Söhne in 1862 in Düren. See Decker: Betriebliche Sozialordnung, loc. cit., p. 31.
81 Examples from Krupp and Siemens in Berdrow: Familie Krupp, p. 349 ff. Kocka: Unternehmensverwaltung, loc. cit., p. 352 ff.
82 See R. Braun: Sozialer und kultureller Wandel, p. 106 f.; H. J. Habakkuk: Industrial Organisation since the Industrial Revolution. Southampton, 1968, p. 12; D. S. Landes: The Structure of Enterprise in the Nineteenth Century, in: XIe Congrès International de Science Historique. Stockholm, 21.–28th August, 1960). Rapports V. Upsala, 1960, p. 115. See also the scepticism of the Stinnes brothers and sisters with regard to the joint stock company: they were only prepared to accept this in 1848 as an emergency and transitional arrangement until the family business could be re-established: Hermann: Entwicklungslinien, loc. cit., p. 14 f.

sources were of major importance. Family relations helped to solve early management problems; they served to provide information, to create trust, furthered cohesion and created a sense of class in the emergent bourgeoisie. They provided contacts which could be used for many purposes, created a sense of belonging together which helped entrepreneurial success. There were other functions which these families performed and which we have not been able to discuss here, for instance their role as models and ideology for industrial staff policy and administration; much has been written on this under the heading of "patriarchalism". Some of these functions were more dependent on the household family, some rather performed by the more distant circles of kinship relations.

We have put special emphasis on two of the prerequisites for this major positive contribution which family structures and resources made to the development of early industrial capitalism. Firstly the low state of development of viable alternatives: neither the market nor state institutions were developed enough in the first two thirds of the nineteenth century to be able to solve the central problems of early enterprises. Recourse to the family proved a viable and sometimes the only solution. Secondly the economic functions of the family can be explained through its structure and position in the strategically important sections of the commercial bourgeoisie. No doubt there were family structures which were less favourable to the process of capitalist industrialisation.[83] This article has made only a preliminary contribution to research on the – generally traditional – characteristics of entrepreneurs' families which enabled them to take on these economic functions. The entrepreneur's family has been described as a transitional phenomenon between the "ganze Haus", with the business and the family under one roof, and the middle class family of the modern type. This duality led to tension between some of its tasks and functions on the one hand and its claims and aims on the other, – tensions which were ultimately due to the principal structural difference between the family and the market as outlined at the beginning of this article.

We have discussed some aspects of the relation between the family and capitalism in the early phase of industrialisation. During the following decades[84] this relation changed; it became looser and its dis-functional elements became more pronounced. Roughly speaking we can identify three complex processes of change as responsible for this:

Firstly: on an advanced stage of development the industrial economy needed help from the family very much less than in its initial phases. Public institutions were increasingly taking over the function of educating and training the entrepreneur. The capital market was becoming developed; with the help of the banks and modern company law new non-family means of financing were being opened up. With more efficient methods of industrial management recourse to family relations was less and less needed. Cartels and groupings with a formalised, tendentially bureaucratic structure were making the family rather superfluous and hopelessly old-fashioned as a basis for the formation of concerns. The means of communication were being improved. The family and more distant relations remained important for the establishment of social cohesion in the group of leading entrepreneurs. But there were now

83 See Braun: Sozialer und kultureller Wandel, loc. cit., p. 106.
84 Exact dating is not possible of course here. But roughly the reference is to the last decades of the 19th century and the 20th.

other factors as well: common experience at university, in the student corporations, in spas; cross-membership of supervisory boards and the resultant network of relationships; the centralisation of administration in Berlin; joint work in associations. The changing capitalist industrial system created its own institutions and these ensured its maintenance and further development. To a certain extent what Max Weber said with regard to the religiously motivated spiritual ascetic also applied to the family: "The victorious capitalism . . . no longer needed this support once it had become established on a mechanical base."[85]

Secondly: if in later decades entrepreneurs held to family strategies for the solution of their problems, although more efficient alternatives were by then available, this often had a negative effect on their business, especially in the large enterprises, where the requirements were in any case rather dis-proportionate to the resources of the family. Most of the examples of the inhibiting effect of family ties come from the later period. It is only after the late nineteenth century and in big business especially that the limits of the family business and the dis-functional elements in the relation between the family and industry emerged clearly although, as we have seen, they were at least latent in the initial phase.

Finally the family itself changed in a way which made it less and less of a suitable vehicle for these economic functions. The average number of children dropped; the ability to take on the entrepreneurial role declined, particularly in the third generation,[86] partly as a result of economic success which opened up new worlds to the children. Internal processes of individualisation went on in the family. The transfer of functions to alternative structures outside the family and the loosening of family ties reinforced each other.

However, these are only tendential changes. At the end of the 1930's Otto Suhr reckoned that of about 4,200 firms in mechanical engineering 120 were more than hundred years old and nearly half of these were still in the hands of the founder family.[87] Even today there are still many successful family businesses. Especially small and medium-sized companies still very strongly depend on the family background. So even in the age of advanced manager capitalism family ties have not only had a negative effect, on the contrary.[88] As far as Schumpeter's grim prognosis that capitalism will dry out if there is no motivation left at all from the family sphere[89] is concerned, the last word has not yet been spoken.

---

85 Weber: Protestantische Ethik, loc. cit., p. 188.
86 Stahl's quantitative examination (Elitenkreislauf loc. cit., p. 255f.) of management through successive generations would appear to confirm this "law of the third generation", which certainly did not apply in the pre-industrial age: in or immediately after the third generation direction of the enterprise often passed out of the family's hands (esp. p. 264). Examples of the collapse of entrepreneurial families, which had been successful for generations or their retirement from business life around the middle of the 19th century can be found in Zunkel: Der rheinisch-westfälische Unternehmer, p. 112ff.; see also Kurschat: Hans von der Leyen, p. 90ff., 135f. Hypotheses in Paulsen: Das 'Gesetz der dritten Generation', esp. 274f. (the dangers of success) and p. 278f. (inheritance problems).
87 Familientradition im Maschinenbau. Untersuchungen über die Lebensdauer von Unternehmungen, in: Wirtschaftskurve. Jg. 1939, Heft 1, pp. 29–50, here pp. 32, 34.
88 Examples from the Wilh. Reich in Kocka: Entrepreneurs and Managers, loc. cit., p. 583f. H. Böhme, Emil Kirdorf: Überlegungen zu einer Unternehmerbiographie in: Tradition, Vol. 13, 1968, p. 294.
89 See Schumpeter: Kapitalismus, loc. cit., p. 258ff.

The Social Integration of Entrepreneurs in Westphalia 1860–1914

A Contribution to the Debate on the Position of Entrepreneurs in Society of Imperial Germany

Hansjoachim Henning

The extensive discussion on the role of the entrepreneur in the state and society during the second half of the nineteenth century[1] often makes us overlook that the entrepreneurs were not only a separate and distinct, economically determined interest group in society but that they were also bound to the other groups by personal ties. An examination of the direction, intensity and motivation of these ties and the extent to which they may have been influenced by economic and social factors will enable conclusions to be drawn about the entrepreneurs' image of themselves and their image as a group. These two aspects in turn give rise to the question of the social position of the entrepreneurs and its determinant features. The following article is an attempt to outline this.[2]

The sources available were in addition to the printed biographical data[3] the regis-

1 See for example Kaelble: Industrielle Interessenpolitik in der Wilhelminischen Gesellschaft. Der Centralverband Deutscher Industrieller 1895–1915, Berlin, 1967; ibid: Industrielle Interessenverbände vor 1914, in: W. Ruegg, O. Neuloh (ed.): Zur soziologischen Theorie und Analyse des 19. Jahrhunderts, Göttingen, 1971; H. Jaeger: Unternehmer in der deutschen Politik, Bonn, 1967; H.J. Varain: Interessenverbände in Deutschland, Cologne, 1973; S. Mielcke: Der Hansa-Bund, 1912–1914, Göttingen, 1976; P. Ullmann: Der Bund der Industriellen 1895–1914, Göttingen, 1976; H.J. Puhle: Parlament, Parteien und Interessenverbände 1890–1914, in: Michael Stürmer (ed.): Das kaiserliche Deutschland, Darmstadt (2nd ed.), 1976; J. Kocka: Unternehmer in der deutschen Industrialisierung, Göttingen, 1975.

2 These are the results of a preliminary and as yet incomplete examination of material which is being prepared on the social behaviour and social structures of the West German propertied class ("Besitzbürgertum"). On the educated classes ("Bildungsbürgertum") see H. Henning: Das westdeutsche Bürgertum in der Epoche der Hochindustrialisierung 1860–1914, Part I. Das Bildungsbürgertum, Wiesbaden, 1972. Studies undertaken so far in this field are very helpful but they are very superficial in regard to the questions raised here. Cf. Erich Dittrich: Zur sozialen Herkunft des sächsischen Unternehmertums. Neues Archiv für sächsische Geschichte 63 (1942); Kurt Weidenfeld: Die Herkunft der Unternehmer und Kapitalisten im Aufbau der kapitalistischen Zeit. Weltwirtschaftliches Archiv 72 (1954); Gerhard Adelmann: Führende Unternehmer im Rheinland und in Westfalen 1850–1914, Rhein. Vierteljahresblätter 35 (1971); Helmuth Croon: Die wirtschaftlichen Führungsschichten des Ruhrgebietes in der Zeit von 1890 bis 1933. Blätter für deutsche Landesgeschichte 108 (1972). Dittrich comes closest to indicating some of the basic trends in the recruitment of entrepreneurs, but he does not succeed in assessing them. Croon only touches on the problem, while Adelmann only examines the occupational origin, again without quantification. Friedrich Zunkel: Der rheinisch-westfälische Unternehmer 1834–1879, Cologne and Opladen, 1962, gives helpful information, although he aims to describe the type rather than the group behaviour. The study by P. H. Martes (see below) is also very informative.

3 Biographisches Jahrbuch und Deutscher Nekrolog. Ed. A. Bettelheim. Vols. 1–18, 1897–1917; Deutsches Geschlechterbuch. Genealogisches Handbuch bürgerlicher Familien. Neuer Reihe. Ed. Strutz u. Fr. Wilh. Euler. Glücksburg, 1975 ff.; Neue Deutsche Biographie. Ed. Historische Kommission bei der Bayerischen Akademie der Wissenschaften. Vol. I ff. Berlin, 1953 ff. Westfälische Lebensbilder. Ed. A. Börner et al. Vol. I ff. Münster 1930.

ter of births, marriages and deaths[4] and the records on rank and association business[5] in the state archives in Münster. With the exception of the information from the registry office all the data was treated as random samples. For the surveys in the registry offices the municipal and Land districts of Dortmund, Münster, Arnsberg, Coesfeld and Tecklenburg were chosen so as to enable a consideration of the influence of agrarian, pre-industrial and highly industrialised structures on social behaviour. The main source of information was marriage certificates, as these yielded data on the origin, marriage partners and – through the names of the witnesses – circle of friends of a group. This approach yields a very broad regional cross-section of trends in social behaviour even if there are divergent individual cases.[6]

The second half of the nineteenth century was a period in which the social structure was already determined by industrialisation and the resultant competitive society. But in the nobility, the military profession and the public service groups still existed with some of the criteria of a class society, so that status symbols could evolve from dual sources. In this study the question of group relations is to be handled by considering the personal and social ties of entrepreneurs with other social groups, taking as indicators of personal ties origin and marriage partners, and of social ties the circle of friends. This will enable conclusions to be drawn on the accepted status symbols.

However, difficulties arise in defining what the term "entrepreneur" covers. If the entrepreneur is defined as a person who acts independently and on his own initiative in taking decisions on the use of production factors and/or bears the risk of production and/or distribution, the field to be considered will be very wide. In terms of occupation it ranges from the independent tradesman to the major industrialist, including both the rentiers and the representatives of the senior managemant, as the rentier bears the risk while the director determines its nature.[7] Very certainly by reason of their function members of the senior management must be included, even if part of their remuneration made them dependent.[8] Where the basic position is on principle the same – "independence" (self-employment) as the nineteenth century understood this – it may be assumed that in such a large group different patterns of social behaviour will emerge and that these may be due both to the material position and to the weight of the resultant functions. Preliminary examinations have confirmed this in that the behaviour patterns of the "Kommerzienräte" (Commercial Councillors) clearly differ from those of other entrepreneurs, even before the title was acquired. As conditions were set for the acquisition of the title (after 1865 an independent fortune

4 Collection in the State Archives. Detmold.
5 State Archives, Münster, quoted as StAM: Oberpräsidium 1458–1490, 1514–1515, 3794–3797.
6 For more detail on the procedure see H. Henning: Bildungsbürgertum . . . loc. cit. p. 67 ff.
7 See Kurt Weidenfeld: Die Herkunft . . . loc. cit. p. 256.
8 The lack of stress on functional differences is to prevent the many persons who fulfilled several different functions or parts of functions from not being included per definitionem in the social field under review or from being too strongly aligned in patterns whose relevance for social behaviour still has to be examined. On functional differences between entrepreneurs, managers and capitalists see J. Kocka: loc. cit. p. 14f. Kocka, who follows the usual terminology, overlooks the importance of "independence" (self-employment) as a constituent feature of the bourgeoisie's self-awareness. The formal recognition of this by the state was the precondition which enabled members of the boards of joint stock companies to be elected to Chambers of Commerce after 1872. Cf. H. Henning: loc. cit. pp. 34 and 106 and Lutz Graf Schwerin von Krosigk: Die große Zeit des Feuers. Tübingen, 1958, Vol. II, p. 29.

of M 750,000 and after 1893 of M 1 million)[9] the entrepreneurs can be divided with the help of this fixed and yet variable threshold into two sub-groups with different patterns of social behaviour: the major entrepreneurs, which includes Commercial Councillors and those who would qualify for the title, and commercial entrepreneurs, which covers the rest, tradesmen, merchants and factory owners.

Of course the title "Commercial Councillor", which was generally acquired late – up to about 1890 by those appropriately qualified between the age of 55 and 60 and after 1890 at about 50[10] could not affect personal ties and only influenced social contact for part of the man's career. But as the conditions for its acquisition were either handed on or established in the early years of a major entrepreneur's activities they did determine his behaviour before an official norm could cramp his spontaneity and so the use of this criterion, which, in contrast, for example, to the tax class is recognisable in almost every source, would appear to be justified.

Moreover, defining the "major entrepreneur" by qualification for the title of Commercial Councillor does not involve a limitation to a particular period, as the requirements for the acquisition of the title changed in the course of time. We can use the title to characterise the major entrepreneurs both at the beginning and at the end of our period, although their financial position, like that of the factory owners generally, changed considerably with the rapid economic growth. Differentiating entrepreneurs according to the type of business they represented would not appear to be so appropriate[11] as no clearly definable criteria are available for this. Business performance and a strong financial position or creditworthiness may be necessary for the major entrepreneur and the factory owner, but performance is the only criterion applicable to the director of a company. Clearly considerable assignation problems arise.

In the period and region under review the group of major industrialists was very small. According to a list in the "Oberpräsidium" (the equivalent of the Lord Lieutenant's office) in Münster[12] only 27 Commercial Councillors, including all those who moved in or out of the district, lived in the province of Westphalia in 1885. Three of these were "Geheime Kommerzienräte" (Secret Councillors – a higher rank). The corresponding figures for 1900 were 51 and 5 and for 1910 81 and 11. It was possible to obtain data on integration behaviour for 106 members of this sub-group. The subgroup of factory owners and merchants is very much larger: estimates on the basis of the commercial census of 1907 put it at about 96,000.[13] 1200 documents relating to this group have so far been evaluated.

---

9 Cf. the Order by the Prussian Minister for Trade, Commerce and Public Works of October 8, 1890, only the contents of which are known. The general file StAM 190–1 (old register) has not been kept nor is it in the archive. Strangely enough the Order was not published in the circulars on general administration by the Ministry either, from which we may take it that the expectations and actions of prospective Commercial Councillors were not to be made too public. On the general aspect see the Order by the "Oberpräsident" (Lord Lieutenant) to the "Regierungspräsident" (Chief Executive) of Minden of February 25, 1895: the main requirement for the appointment as Commercial Councillor is in addition to considerations of the general public interest "considerable, secure capital assets, independent of the business concerned." StAM Oberpräsidium, 1514, Vol. II.

10 Cf. records StAM Oberpräsidium 1515, Vol. I.

11 Adelmann would appear to indicate this. loc. cit. p. 337.

12 Cf. records StAM Oberpräsidium 1515, Vol. I.

13 The census gives c. 152,000 self-employed without members of families helping in the business.

I. The Major Entrepreneurs

1. Origin

Table 1 shows that the major entrepreneurs in all sectors, who reached the peak of their influence between 1860 and 1889, were mainly recruited from among their own ranks. That applies particularly to the owner-entrepreneurs. In this sub-group as a whole they predominated over members of the higher management throughout the period under review in a relation of 3 : 2, while they were at an advantage of 3 : 1 in recruitments from their own ranks and the number of owner-entrepreneurs who moved into higher management is a small minority at ∼ 5%.

Reasons can be given for the predominance of the owner-entrepreneurs. As a whole these may explain the tendency of major entrepreneurs to rise from within the ranks but they do not account in every case for individual decisions.

During the period under review the joint stock company was the main form of enterprise in the basic materials industry but even here not every member of the senior management had such prospects that he could one day be recommended for the rank of Commercial Councillor. The rise of the directors to the ranks of major entrepreneurs was only just beginning.

But in Westphalia the initial phase of industrialisation and with it the time when the inventor entrepreneur could rise rapidly from other social groups was already

---

Of these c. 56,000 were independent craftsmen who do not count for our purposes. On the scope of the samples see Hans Kellerer: Statistik im modernen Wirtschafts- und Sozialleben. Hamburg, 1962, p. 124 ff.

Table 1. Major Entrepreneurs in Westphalia

Origin from	1860–64			1865–69			1870–74			1875–79			1880–84		
	S[1]	SM	M	S	SM	M	S	SM	M	S	SM	M	S	SM	M
Private enterprise	5		1	2		2	2		1	10	1	2	6		1
of which:															
Wholesale trade	1			2		1	2		1	2			1		
Heavy industry	4		1			1				2	1		2		1
Retail trade										2			3		
Commerce		1				2				4	1	1			
Crafts	1					1				1					
Indep. scholars		1				1				1					
Academic public. servants		2							1		1	1			1
Non-academic public servants									1					1	
Farmers										1	1				
Employees															
of which:															
commercial															
technical															
Workers															
Military															

[1] S = Owner-entrepreneurs, SM = Owner-entrepreneur moving to senior management, M = Senior management. *Sources:* Biographical hand-books, company "Festschriften"

over. It was no longer first and foremost technical knowledge and technical or craft skills which could make the owner of an enterprise into a major entrepreneur – what he needed now was capital to secure him the controlling influence in a company. Then he could use his commercial skill to expand it. The capital and the ability to use it were generally inherited, in other words they were largely the result of the work of the preceding generation. This constituted the objective prerequisites for the high percentage of recruitment from within the ranks of this sub-group.

But there were also subjective motives. The 1850s and 1860s were years of measured cyclical upswing only interrupted by brief if at times strong fluctuation. As the time offered favourable prospects of increasing the inheritance and carrying on the work of the older generation the elder sons tended to follow in their father's footsteps while the younger sons moved into the respected positions of academically educated public servants.[14] The inflow to the group of major entrepreneurs from the wholesale trade and non-commercial largescale production proved more steady and less cyclically dependent than that from heavy industry. This could suggest that in the industrial sector the view of an entrepreneurial position as extending through generations with a consequent longterm ability to take risks was only gradually emerging, a result both of the very high risks which entrepreneurs had had to take during the early years of industrialisation and the not as yet very high esteem in which entrepreneurs from the secondary sectors were held.[15]

The influence of the subjective assessment of the situation on recruitment can be seen from the reaction of the major entrepreneurs in the secondary sector to the world

---

14 Cf. Henning, loc. cit., p. 286 f.
15 Cf. Friedrich Zunkel: Beamtenschaft und Unternehmertum beim Aufbau der Ruhrindustrie 1849–1880. Tradition 9, 1964, pp. 263, 265.

1885–89			1860–89				1890–94			1895–99			1900–04			1905–09			1890–1909			
S	SM	M	S	SM	M	in %	S	SM	M	S	SM	M	S	SM	M	S	SM	M	S	SM	M	in %
2		3	27	1	12	71,4	6	2	6	3	1	7	3	1	3			8	12	4	24	80
1			9		1					1			2	1					2		1	
1		1	9		5		3			2		3	2	1				3	6	1	8	
			5				1					1							1		1	
		2	4	1	6	28,6	2	2	3		1	3	1		3			5	3	3	14	27,5
			1		1	3,6		1														2
			1		2	5,3					1			1						1		2
			1	1	5	12,5	1	1		2			1					1			3	8
			1		1	3,6	1														1	2
			1	1		3,6																

economic crisis of 1857/58 and the collapse of the "Gründerkrach". In each of the following five-year periods the trend to self-recruitment dropped markedly and at the same time the sons of major entrepreneurs tended to withdraw from the professions of independent scholarship.[16] Not only the younger sons but a growing number of elder sons went into the public service after an academic training.[17] The preference for a "safe" profession in view of the crisis was clear. But this did not last long. As soon as it became apparent that the risks were not as great as had at first been feared, and when the "Reich" administration changed in 1879 to a system of protective tariffs, thus opening up better prospects particularly for the basic materials industry, the trend to recruitment from within the ranks increased again.

In contrast to owners among the major entrepreneurs only just on one third of members of the senior management had come from their own sub-group, and within this share descendants of industrial entrepreneurial families were in a clear majority. This was the result of the growing preference in the secondary sector for the joint stock company, in which entrepreneurial families could acquire dominant shareholdings and interest. Often the change in the legal form of an enterprise virtually coincided with the change in the generation. Recruitment was continuous with no particular points of emphasis.

The second largest inflow at over a quarter was from the subgroup of factory owners and retail traders. They provided recruits to the groups of owner-entrepreneurs and senior management in a ratio of 3:2, so that the rise to the position of owner-entrepreneur predominated. This was particularly the case in times of cyclical upswing which furthered mobility in that they offered persons with small amounts of capital – half of these recruits came from the retail trade! – but considerable knowledge and ability opportunities for a fast expansion of their activities.

The smaller number who moved into senior management, on the other hand, tended to do so rather in times of slower economic growth. They were mainly men with only some private means but relatively great business experience and a background of commercial or technical and commercial training. It was not the size of their fortune but their ability which took them up the ladder. Their ability had been schooled – so to speak – on the lower rungs of entrepreneurial decision-making – they all came from manufacturing enterprises – and perhaps it was this experience of the capitalist outlook which gave rise to the dynamic that made them, in number at least, the equal of the inflow to the group of major entrepreneurs from within the ranks. No members of any other social group succeeded in this. Of course it must be remembered that these men rose at a favourable time. The move into a leading position came either in a period of re-expansion after a crisis, as was the case, for example, with L. Baare, Fr. Grillo and A. W. Kisker, or in a period of slower growth when the restructuring of the production apparatus was to release new impulses. That was the case with V. Brügemann, Fr. Springorum and R. Windmöller. At such times the influence of the banks was also greater, and it is possible that they were glad to see men in leading positions in the companies they were financing who came from outside the traditional circles of major entrepreneurs.[18] It was the social counterpart of the pres-

16 Henning, loc. cit., p. 507, Diagram 13.
17 Ibid., p. 504, Diagram 7.
18 Cf. for instance the attitude of the banks to L. Baare and Fr. Grillo. Lutz Graf Schwerin von Krosigk: Die große Zeit des Feuers. Vol. I. Tübingen, 1957, pp. 592 and 533.

sure to modernisation, concentration and the growing influence of the banks caused by the re-structuring process in industry.

Nevertheless it should be remembered that nearly three quarters of all major entrepreneurs between 1860 and 1889 came from their own group and the closely related circles of factory owners, merchants and so on. Any further inflows remained fringe phenomena. Only recruits from the ranks of academically trained public servants deserve mention, accounting for one eighth.

Most of these men became major entrepreneurs through moving into the senior management. That was due to the fact that the sons of public servants generally had no capital of their own and could only make a career through their own ability. Certainly the basic materials industry offered them favourable opportunities for that, the qualification as "Bergassessor" (senior mining official) was held in high esteem[19] and probably contributed in no small measure to making academic studies a firm component in the career pattern of the following generation. The other social groups of the self-employed and public servants contributed little to swell the ranks of the major entrepreneurs and no inflow at all came from other persons in paid employment.

Between 1890 and 1910 the trend in recruitment to the ranks of major entrepreneurs did not change but its intensity changed. Now only a good third came from within the ranks and within this third the inflow to owner-entrepreneurs slackened noticeably: it now held the balance with the inflow to the senior management. Above all the inflow to the owner-entrepreneurs from the tertiary sector dropped to just on a quarter of the frequency in the previous period, an example of social overlapping and the loss of social positions for a traditional group of entrepreneurs through the changes in company structures. Recruitment of owner-entrepreneurs from heavy industry also slackened but remained at about two thirds of the former frequency. This was probably due to the same causes as affected the inflow from the tertiary sector; however, new developments in the chemical and electrical engineering industries for instance still offered possibilities for economic independence on the scale of large enterprises as well.

Recruitment to the senior management from the sub-group of major entrepreneurs grew as compared with the preceding – and longer – period. There were two reasons for this. Firstly members of owner-entrepreneur families adjusted to the new situation brought about by the changes in company structures and – like Delius, Hoesch, Meininghaus or Mummenhoff, for example – took posts in the senior management, helped by their generally not inconsiderable capital holdings. So the concentration process did not, as has occasionally been argued,[20] bring increasing entrepreneurial resignation, entrepreneurial activity simply appeared in a different form. Secondly the now established management itself began to develop dynasties, as can be seen from the examples of Dresler, Baare, Brügemann, Springorum or Fleitmann. If this was possible in enterprises where what mattered was the majority holding the capital inherited from the father's generation must have played an important part. Among this guarantor of economic independence men who rose up the ladder assimilated the behaviour patterns of their former target group. By handing managerial

19　Cf. Walter Serlo: Die preußischen Bergassessoren. Essen (5th ed.), 1938.
20　Cf. for example Gerhard Adelmann: Führender Unternehmer in Rheinland und Westfalen, 1850–1914. Rhein. Vjbll. 35, 1971, p. 338.

positions on like a family fortune they were treating the claims of other shareholders like their own property and exercising a power which went beyond that of traditional class élites insofar as they were not, like these, acting on the basis of particular, generally known and accepted legal norms. This is one of the signs of élite formation in the sub-group of major entrepreneurs which marked them off from the top layer of the wealthy bourgeoisie.[21]

In the second part of our period, however, the inflow from within the ranks was no longer the main trend in recruitment to the group of major entrepreneurs; the inflow from the subgroup of factory owners, merchants and so on had gained a clear lead with the inflow from the production sector in a big majority. This was certainly the result of social betterment. A move to the position of owner-entrepreneur or that of senior manager was generally the result of the expansion of an enterprise in the favourable economic climate with its steady growth trend. But that was only the case for one third of the inflow. The majority of the others went into senior management, not on the basis of their capital holdings but through practical and theoretical knowledge and ability, with an increasing share of academic qualifications.

This would appear to confirm that the typical way of climbing in the competitive society of the bourgeoisie was, as in the educated classes, through performance[22] and not the privilege of wealth. But it is striking that recruitment outside the sub-group was almost exclusively from the status-related subgroup of entrepreneurs of small and medium-sized means. Relations with all other social groups had slackened further in comparison with the preceding period and that also applied to the group in which performance was a status symbol: the academically trained public servants. Their share of recruitment to the ranks of the major entrepreneurs, which had degenerated to a fringe phenomenon, suggests that performance was not in fact sufficient for entry here. On the contrary, the importance of the inflow from the ranks of small and medium-sized entrepreneurs and the almost total lack of any inflow from any related non-status group shows that economic independence, which was itself a status symbol, and the experience of business decisionmaking which it entailed, helped men to rise to senior managerial positions. So the major entrepreneurs attracted a recruitment potential from which they could expect a high readiness to assimilation.

Of course the process was not guided or steered – that would hardly have been possible. It was more likely a combination of the desire of men on the way up to move into new fields of activity, as these were opened up through the re-structuring of company forms, and the tendency of shareholders to choose persons of similar status, even if they came from a different group or field of activity, to enlarge their own élite circle. Insofar the major entrepreneurs developed a behaviour pattern similar to that of the Prussian nobility who preferred to supplement their ranks with newly ennobled senior public servants and members of the military profession.[23] In each case the

---

21 On the terminology see Wolfgang Zapf: Wandlungen der deutschen Elite. Munich, 1965, p. 35 f.; Wilhelm Stahl: Der Elitekreislauf in der Unternehmerschaft. Frankfurt, Zurich, 1973, p. 12 ff.

22 Cf. Henning, loc. cit., pp. 288 and 484.

23 Cf. Nikolaus von Preradowich: Die Führungsschichten in Österreich und Preussen (1804–1918). Wiesbaden, 1955, p. 162. The further remarks which are based on this observation on the effects on the bourgeoisie as a whole are largely doubted. Cf. e. g. on the educated classes Henning, loc. cit., p. 489.

development began at a time when there were more influential positions to be filled than men to fill them; for the nobility this situation arose with the expansion of the army, and for the major entrepreneurs with the increase in the number of senior management positions as the number of joint stock companies rose. Choosing the man for the job, i. e. a man from the top of the most closely related status group, was always a means of securing influence. Optimal recruitment was all the more important to the major entrepreneurs as after 1876 associations began to be formed in which the size of membership brought a certain weight and strengthened the local or regional influence of the entrepreneurs.

The increasing integration of Westphalian major entrepreneurs with the core group of the propertied class in addition to recruitment from within their own ranks, which is observable in both the periods under review, cannot, in view of the great distance maintained to other groups in society, be interpreted as social mobility; it was mobility within the group, the characteristic way for an élite to supplement its numbers when its aim is to preserve its functions.[24]

---

24 A comparison with research up to now is difficult as these writers either do not consider the entrepreneurs at all as a social group or take them globally. To name those who take the first approach – and this is not to diminish the wide recognition which the many individual achievements have earned – Adelmann, loc. cit., Helmuth Croon: Die wirtschaftlichen Führungsschichten des Ruhrgebietes in der Zeit von 1890–1933. Blätter f. dt. Landesgeschichte 108 (1972) and ibid. in: Herbert Helbig (ed.): Führungskräfte der Wirtschaft im 19. Jahrhundert (1790–1914). Part II. Limburg, 1977; Konrad Fuchs: Wirtschaftliche Führungskräfte in Schlesien. Zs. f. Ostforschung 21 (1972) and the otherwise very valuable study by Friedrich Zunkel: Der rheinisch-westfälische Unternehmer 1834–1879, Cologne and Opladen, 1962. The second approach is chosen by Wolfgang Huschke: Forschungen über die Herkunft der thüringischen Unternehmerschicht des 19. Jahrhunderts (= 2nd supplement to the periodical "Tradition"), Baden-Baden, 1962; Erich Dittrich: Zur sozialen Herkunft des sächsischen Unternehmertums, N. A. f. sächs. Geschichte 63, 1942, and Wilhelm Stahl, loc. cit. The three authors recognise a high inflow from the crafts to the groups of entrepreneurs and they conclude from this that the entrepreneurs were highly mobile. See e. g. Stahl, loc. cit., p. 107. Admittedly Stahl may be very restricted by his material which was limited to the selection criteria of the Neue Deutsche Biographie. However, Hartmut Kaeble, who uses the same material and therefore must be subject to the same limits (Sozialer Aufstieg in Deutschland 1850–1914, in: Konrad Jarausch (ed.): Quantifizierung in der Geschichtswissenschaft. Düsseldorf, 1976, p. 286) comes to the conclusion, although he uses the concept "entrepreneur" without differentiation, that the main recruitment tendencies were "self-recruitment and supplementation from the ranks of the commercial middle classes. In its most general form this observation corresponds with the regional results in this study. "Restaurateurs and above all the craftsmen", in Kaelble's view, play virtually no part in the inflow to the ranks of the major entrepreneurs, and this refutes the thesis that the industrial sector was a "launching pad" (W. Köllmann: Der Prozess der Verstädterung in Deutschland in der Hochindustrialisierungsperiode, in: R. Braun et al.: Gesellschaft in der industriellen Revolution. Cologne, 1973, p. 251 ff.) for this sub-group; Kaelble would also like to see this modified (loc. cit., p. 296). A comparison with Kocka, loc. cit., p. 37 ff., is not necessary as his periods have only vague limits and he does not reflect the latest state of research in every regard. Otherwise he would presumably have noticed that during the second half of the nineteenth century the self-awareness of the educated classes continues to dominate and remarked upon its affinity with the entrepreneurs – using the term in the widest sense (Henning, loc. cit., pp. 286 and 291 f.), for the upper ranks of the public service were increasingly recruited from the entrepreneurs – not vice versa – who copied the career patterns of the public service. Hence – consciously or unconsciously – they took the principle of performance as a suitable, democratic means of selection in the industrialisation process as well. It was with this concept that the enlightened bourgeoisie had largely broken the privileges of the nobility at the beginning of the nineteenth century. Kocka cites the "national overtones" of the "progress

II. Marriage

The data on the marriage ties of the major entrepreneurs is very much sparser than that on their origin. As might be expected with the predominantly genealogical interest occasionally the names of wives are mentioned in the sources but not the occupation of the father-in-law. So far it has only proved possible to obtain definite information on the marriages of Westphalian major entrepreneurs in 46 cases, but even with these extreme caution must be exercised in deriving behavioural patterns.

Table 2 shows that the Westphalian major entrepreneurs during both phases of the period under review married into their own subgroup in by far the greater majori-

---

rhetoric" (cf. pp. 39 and 40) in vain! As the barrier to mobility between the educated classes and the entrepreneurs was already being broken down particularly in the highly industrialised areas before the beginning of the national over-estimation of industrial interests, the national element did not give rise to any affinity between the two groups. Toni Pierenkemper, Die westfälischen Schwerindustriellen 1852–1913, Göttingen 1979, p. 43 ff. comes to a similar conclusion. Yet, when interpreting his figures, he neglects the perceptible differentiation of the social throng and speaks of a "recruitment mainly from the same social strata." For Pierenkemper this is representative of the German society (p. 169). Even though he rightly stresses the most important trend, he completely undervalues the perceptible throng from ranks with the same status, but with a lower economic position or from other classes. Most of all he distorts the mobility of other middle class groups within the period under review, which was not determined by self-restrictment. Of the regional studies Paul Hermann Martes: Zum Sozialprofil der Oberschicht im Ruhrgebiet, dargestellt an den Dortmunder Kommerzienräten, Beiträge zur Geschichte Dortmunds und der Grafschaft Mark 67 (1971), p. 167 ff., esp. pp. 195 f. and 200 ff. comes to roughly the same conclusion as this study. However, it still needs to be shown that Martes decided not to weight his material and preferred the genealogical survey.

Table 2. Marriage

Marriage into:	1860–64				1865–69				1870–74				1875–79				1880–84			
	S¹		M		S		M		S		M		S		M		S		M	
	S	M	S	M	S	M	S	M	S	M	S	M	S	M	S	M	S	M	S	M
Private enterprise	2	3			2	1							1	4			1	2		
of which:																				
Wholesale trades		1			1															
Heavy industry	2	2			1	1							1	4			1	2		
Retail trade etc.																				
Commerce											1		1							
Crafts																				
Indep. scholars														1						
Academic public servants											1									
Non-academic public servants																				
Farmers														1	1					
Employees																				
of which:																				
commercial																				
technical																				
Workers																				
Military											1									

¹ S = Owner-entrepreneurs, SM = Owner-entrepreneurs moving into senior management, M = Senior management. *Sources:* Biographical hand-books, company "Festschriften"

ty of cases. Up to the mid-1870s there were still some signs of a limited mobility but this then disappeared except for a few fringe cases. Where there was mobility it was into the farming community and here – as the survey showed – the group of major landowners. But a survey of marriage certificates will not reveal whether these major landowners were not in fact former entrepreneurs, so that here too there may have been – hidden – ties to the same sub-group. But contacts which might have been expected from the recruitment pattern, i.e. marriage into the circles of academically trained public servants, had by then shrunk to insignificance. The distance to the other bourgeois groups in society was considerable. Like recruitment the marriage ties of major entrepreneurs with their own sub-group show some differentiation which suggests that marriage was not only a question of personal inclination but also a matter for social and economic considerations. Owner-entrepreneurs, for example, preferred to marry into each others' families, often preferring the same industry[25] and as far as possible comparable wealth. It was a way of eliminating competition or at least weakening it. In extreme cases we even find children of major shareholders of the same enterprise marrying.[26] It is also clear that members of the senior management tried if possible to marry into owner-entrepreneurs' families, although towards the end of the second phase marriages with families in the same position increased.

25 On the integration within industry shown in Table 2 see e. g. the relations of the Berger-Harkort, Bröckelmann, Delius-Tiemann, Kisker and Klein (Siegen) families. For approaches on the comparable trend among members of the senior management see W. Serlo: Westdeutsche Berg- und Hüttenleute. Essen, 1938, pp. 69 and 240.

26 Cf. e. g. the relations between the Delius, Tiemann and Kisker families in the area covered by the Bielefelder Webereien AG. Gustav Engel: Gedanken zur Hundertjahrfeier der Bielefelder Webereien AG. Bielefeld, 1965.

1885–89				1860–89					1890–94				1895–99				1900–04				1905–09				1890–1909				
S		M		S		M			S		M		S		M		S		M		S		M		S		M		
S	M	S	M	S	M	S	M	in%	S	M	S	M	S	M	S	M	S	M	S	M	S	M	S	M	S	M	in%
1		1		9		6	3	72	1		1		1		2				2		4		3		2		7	5	66,6
					2																2	1			2	1			
1		1		9		4	3		1		1		1		2		2		2		2		2		2		5	4	19.05
				1				8							1						1				1		2		
				1				4					1												1				4.76
				1				4																	1				4.76
				1	1			8											1								1		4.77
				1				4																					

Particularly members of the senior management loosened their ties to their own origin groups outside the group of major entrepreneurs when marrying. This suggests that the members of senior managements when marrying into old families in their industry were seeking not only the economic advantages of the dowry but above all the social consolidation of their positions. For the older generations this clearly included not only wealth – these men had that or had secure prospects of it – but even more prospects of economic independence over several generations, which became a status symbol. This trend hardly changed up to the First World War. That members of the senior management increasingly tended to marry into families of the same rank suggests that the efforts of the preceding generation had up-graded the social position of these social newcomers, who began to follow the traditional marriage patterns of their target group as they had the recruitment patterns. But the trend to direct links with the target group still predominated. If nevertheless the inclination to marry into their own ranks tended to fall slightly this is not so much a sign of social mobility as the opening was only to the next most closely related status sub-group and excluded all the others. One motive for this, in addition to the affinity between the two sub-groups noted in the question of origin may be suspected in the importance of the milieu of origin. This came to acquire greater social importance particularly in the border area between the two sub-groups as the economic position of the commercial entrepreneurs improved with the improvement in the general economic climate. A further reason for the weakening of the trend may be that the process of qualification tended to last longer for men who had to climb the ladder as academic studies grew in importance. Many had chosen their marriage partner before entering their social target group although the behaviour pattern still tended to be followed.

So the marriage patterns of Westphalian major entrepreneurs show a desire for considerable social exclusivity both in relation to other social groups and in trends within the subgroup, and newcomers tended to adjust to this. The mobility barrier was outstanding entrepreneurial achievement; the status symbol economic independence preserved through generations with means well secured. The pressure on men who climbed to adjust points to the existence and cultivation of a class consciousness resulting from the status symbol. It set standards for marriage for which a comparison with the behaviour of traditional class élites is very appropriate: in marriage a man was expected to maintain his social standing, pay due regard to the advantages of property and so preserve his status symbol. To what extent this behaviour was the result of a general group consensus can be seen from the social sanctions which were imposed on those who did not conform.[27]

So in both origin and marriage we see that in the major entrepreneurs of Westphalia in the second half of the nineteenth century the region had acquired a new social élite. During the process of industrialisation a sub-group of the entrepreneurs had taken on a status and functions which marked them off from their former social milieu, that of the wealthy bourgeoisie. They were able to limit their recruitment to one status-related sub-group of the bourgeoisie and erect a high barrier to mobility. Their functions gave them a sense of power and this together with the social distance

---

27 A Commercial Councillor who in advanced years married a sales girl very much younger than himself was socially ostracised. StAM Oberpräsidium 1514 Vol. III.

they had created gave them a sense of class.[28] This in turn formed and determined a pattern of behaviour which was directed to the preservation of functions. In this the major entrepreneurs showed a quality which in its sense of superiority and power was hardly less than that of other class élites. So in their personal behaviour and the mentality this reflected the major entrepreneurs came close to other class élites although no actual integration was apparent.

However, one important difference must be emphasised. The other class élites saw their power as resulting from their rights but they believed that this was integrated into a general whole and should be exercised for the benefit of that whole. However much the concept and the means may be open to interpretation the nobility followed the crown for this reason and the public servants saw their duty to governors and the governed in the same light. Whether the same could be said of the major entrepreneurs could well form the subject of a more detailed examination. But the fact can hardly be ignored that however wide the range of activities of the major entrepreneurs was, satisfying their own interests took up a large part of it.[29]

III. Social Contacts

As in the case of marriage ties, only a general tendency can be ascertained for the social relations of the major entrepreneurs, as the state records on associations only contain lists of names in exceptional cases.[30] However, we can recognise three categories of social relations, in which the measure of publicity of the contact is a not inconsiderable indicator.

If social contact was very largely of a private nature for the major entrepreneurs, it was also very largely limited to their own equals. Competition in business did not necessarily prevent personal friendship or at least friendly relations. On the contrary, we can see that business matters formed part of private contact. Meetings in centrally situated elegant hotels were by no means a rarity, with both private and business relations playing a part. Often enough the business discussions took up the lion's share of the time but they never excluded the personal contact altogether.[31]

One interesting fact emerged from the examinations: what was said on these occasions reached the ears of the Chief Executive with remarkable speed and was communicated directly to the King.[32] There are, however – understandably – no signs that this form of private social contact ever went beyond the group itself.

---

28 See Zapf, loc. cit. p. 41.
29 See the qualification report by the Chief Executive in Minden (Qualifikationsbericht des Regierungspräsidenten), 6. 9. 1900: ". . . public opinion would find it incomprehensible if a man whose only achievement is to earn a lot of money and spend only the barest essential were to be given the very highest mark of honour (i. e. awarded the title of Commercial Councillor)." StAM Oberpräsidium 1514, Vol. II.
30 Records StAM Oberpräsidium 3794 and 3795.
31 Cf. for example the administration („Zeitungsberichte") report by the Chief Excutive in Arnsberg of 14. 4. 1905. StAM Oberpräsidium 1407-reports 1905.
32 See Fn.[31].

This was the case at official events, celebrations of business, personal or family occasions. The heads of the local and state authorities and officers stationed in the locality were invited to company jubilees, family festivities and honorary dinners.[33] However, their presence was more of a decorative element than indicative of real personal contact.

The older generation of major entrepreneurs appear to have sought social contact in circles outside their own group, in clubs, societies for the patronage of musems etc., selected shooting parties and so on,[34] where they met university-trained public servants, independent scholars and other entrepreneurs. Membership of these circles brought not only social contact, which was important for the maintenance of the proper local position, it also served business interests, for the entrepreneurs met the groups from whom the civic councillors and local election committees serving the parties of the establishment came. This form of social contact often resulted in the major entrepreneur taking on the role of local patron.[35]

The younger generation[36] appear to have sought to represent their interests – here in the widest sense of the word – in person above local although not on parliamentary level.[37] They had their departmental directors, for example, elected as civic councillors, which was easily possible through the threeclass election system.[38] This took them rather out of local events and it was not without effect on their standing in other social groups. Generally they retained nominal membership of the clubs and associations which their fathers had joined and they did not cease to act as patrons. But their involvement was less personal and this had the appropriate effect.

It was only in interest groups, self-administrative organs and nationalist propaganda activities that the contact of major entrepreneurs went beyond their own subgroup and status-related groups. Here again, however, it was filtered as they took over leading functions in these associations, so that their rights and activities again created a distance between them and the ordinary members.[39] Often they were regarded as representing the employers generally although they had little contact with the majority of them.

In the propaganda associations the major entrepreneurs again took on the role of patron or functionary, with the same social result. The importance attached to their

---

33 Records StAM Oberpräsidium 1406, 1407, 350, Vol. X, 351, Vol. X, 352, Vol. X (Zeitungsberichte des Regierungspräsidenten).

34 Cf. Helmuth Croon: Die wirtschaftlichen Führungsschichten, loc. cit., p. 155.

35 Records StAM Oberpräsidium 3688 and 3795. For details see the qualification report on Fr. Grillo by the Chief Executive in Arnsberg of 13. 9. 1882, for Fr. Vohwinkel of 21. 6. 1889 and for Ed. Kleine of 11. 6. 1907. StAM Oberpräsidium 1514, Vol. I and II.

36 On the change in generation see Croon: Führungsschichten, loc. cit. p. 145.

37 After about 1910 mention of posts on civic councils becomes less frequent in qualification reports by the chief executives, while activities in interest associations, chambers of commerce and in the provincial parliament are more frequent. Records StAM Oberpräsidium 1515.

38 See Croon: Führungsschichten. loc. cit., p. 154. On the problem as a whole ibid.: Die gesellschaftlichen Auswirkungen des Gemeindewahlrechtes in den Gemeinden und Kreisen des Rheinlandes und Westfalens im 19. Jh. Research report for the Land of North-Rhine Westphalia, No. 564, 1960.

39 This is very apparent in the Deutscher Flottenverein and the veteran associations. Records StAM Oberpräsidium 3797: Of 87 persons proposed by the Chief Executive for the province committee of the Flottenverein 24 (27.6%) were major entrepreneurs. For the veteran associations see H. Henning: Kriegervereine in den preussischen Westprovinzen. Rhein. Vjbll. 32 (1968), p. 471.

participation can be seen from one little event. When after many efforts a provincial branch of the "Deutscher Flottenverein" was finally to be established in Westphalia as well in 1899 the "Oberpräsident" (roughly the equivalent of the Lord Lieutenant) ordered a special compartment to be attached to a train to take 40 major entrepreneurs who had been personally invited from Münster to Dortmund, while the other guests – about 250 altogether – had to make their own way to Dortmund.[40] The social distance, which was respected by the other social groups, as well,[41] could hardly have been better illustrated.

Altogether, therefore, the social behaviour of the major entrepreneurs confirms the picture which has already emerged from their personal ties. In Westphalia they were an élite and their social exclusivity, although it was softened somewhat by the degree of publicity attached to their social contact, was never given up.

Despite this élitist attitude and a social order which was still arranged on the class system the Westphalian major entrepreneurs showed little inclination to enter the nobility. Only three of the 106 who have been identified made an application for entitlement – strangely enough during the second phase of our period – and none of the three came from heavy industry.[42] That the applications were not successful, despite the great wealth of the applicants and efforts to enter into ties with landowners among the nobility through the marriage of their daughters, may be illuminating for the criteria which the Prussian nobility observed over the enlargement of its ranks but it does not tell us much about the efforts of major entrepreneurs to rise. On the contrary, the minute percentage of applications shows – in contrast to a widely held view which is derived from different periods[43] – that as a part of the "bourgeoisie" as a whole the major entrepreneurs were not interested in attempting to enter the nobility. That is particularly striking in a province such as Westphalia, which had a high degree of industrialisation to provide a source of new wealth, major landowners as a source of old wealth and, having belonged to the Prussian crown for a relatively long period, might have been thought to offer the appropriate climate and incentives. But here of all places the ties between feudalism and capitalism were extremely weak! There can be no doubt that the major entrepreneurs, a power élite created through the process of industrialisation, adopted a behaviour pattern which was very similar to that of the nobility but they were not interested in personal or social integration. The

---

40 Invitation from the Oberpräsident of March 15, 1899. StAM Oberpräsidium 3797.
41 See also the clear distinction in social level in the composition of the Board of Management and the general membership of the Westdeutscher Verein für Kolonisation und Export. Figures on this but not a full interpretation in Klaus J. Bade: Friedrich Fabri und der Imperialismus in der Bismarckzeit. Freiburg, 1975, p. 140 f.
42 Among 15 recorded applications from members of the bourgeoisie, including requests for restitution of a former title. Records StAM Oberpräsidium 1473 Vols. I–III. Pierenkemper (p. 73) mentions the same number of knightings, amounting to 1.2% of his range of investigation. Yet, on page 39 he speaks of "common knightings" among the big entrepreneurs without analysing the contradiction between the accepted position and his own findings. Has a stereotype to be kept up at any price?
43 See e. g. Zapf, loc. cit., p. 41 and the literature quoted. Examples taken from east of the Elbe are generalised and taken to represent the Reich as a whole. Families who "continued to rise over several generations" are related to the Kaiserreich, which had hardly experienced two generations. Although sociological methods should be precise a few names are taken as illustrating a dominant trend.

apparent contradiction can only be explained by the fact that the major entrepreneurs were a sub-group of the bourgeoisie, which in the nineteenth century was rising at the expense of the nobility on the strength of the area in which it could operate freely, the business world. These people may have believed that they could only make themselves felt and maintain their position if they adopted the same forms of behaviour as the existing power élite but they were anxious to stress their social independence. This may be a sign of the largely unreflecting opposition to the nobility which was a dominant feature of the bourgeoisie in the nineteenth century and had even found its way into light literature around the middle of the century.[44] Further examinations would be needed to show whether these observations do not in fact indicate a greater preponderance of that bourgeois attitude in the Germany of the nineteenth century, the general lack of which has been postulated,[45] forming the basis for the thesis of the existence of a feudal-capitalist upper class.

II. The Commercial Entrepreneurs

1. Origin

On the question of recruitment to the group of merchants and factory owners, who are here, for want of a better term, grouped under the name of commercial entrepreneurs, Fig. 1 shows a generally much greater social mobility than was apparent among major entrepreneurs. There are three main trends:

1. Nearly 50% of commercial entrepreneurs came from among their own ranks.
2. Roughly 25% came from the independent crafts.
3. About 15% came from the non-academic public service.[46]

During the period under review the dominant trend in selfrecruitment remained the same, although it fluctuated considerably at times, while the second and third trends declined slightly. No sharp break is discernible, only in the social fringe areas is a more lively inflow observable after 1880/85 from the economically independent groups.

The high share of self-recruitment was mainly determined by the material prospects which opened up for those who pursued their occupations with energy and insight. This can be seen very clearly from a comparison with the cyclical curve. The first clear decline in self-recruitment came after 1870, at the time of the "Gründerkrach" and at the beginning of a long period of slow economic growth, when prospects for entrepreneurs were generally regarded as deteriorating. It was only after the first "slack years" were over that self-recruitment accelerated again, to show an-

---

44 Cf. Karlheinz Wallraf: Die "bürgerliche Gesellschaft" im Spiegel deutscher Familienzeitschriften. Thesis, Cologne, 1939, pp. 14 and 22.

45 See e. g. G. A. Ritter and J. Kocka: Deutsche Sozialgeschichte, Dokumente und Skizzen. Vol. II 1870–1914. Munich, 1974, p. 68 f.

46 In interpreting Diagram 1 it must be borne in mind that the survey was taken from the marriage register and so reflects social status at the time of marriage. The time when the occupation was chosen is more indicative of the motives in recruitment. Hence the interpretation is based on this moment, i. e. about 10 years before the mark on the diagram.

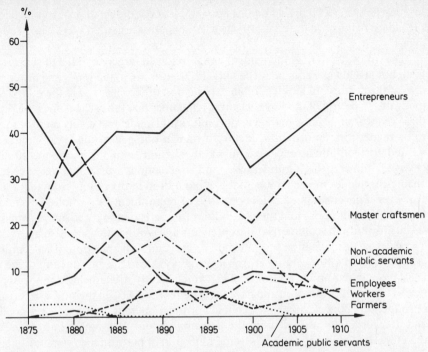

Fig. 1. Origin of Commercial Entrepreneurs in the Province of Westphalia. *Sources:* Register of births, marriages and deaths in STA Detmold; biographical hand-books; company "Festschriften"

other sharp drop towards the end of the 1880s. During this period industrial unrest broke out on a larger scale for the first time, in some cases involving conflict with workers who were unofficially organised. At the same time the new state social insurance appeared as a negative influence on company profits and was regarded as a risk for the employers as its effect could not be controlled. At the beginning of the great upswing after the second third of the 1890s self-recruitment rose again clearly and this time without a renewed drop. The parallelism between the development of self-recruitment and the cyclical curve is very apparent and it shows that at times when business was going well the elder sons were generally very willing to follow in their fathers' footsteps and take on the risks of the life of a commercial entrepreneur, carrying on their fathers' heritage by maintaining their economic independence. Economic independence was a status symbol for the bourgeoisie in the nineteenth century and it clearly exercised sufficient attraction to prevent the elder sons of entrepreneurs from taking refuge in the security of public service even in times of economic downswing if they possibly could. It was mainly the younger sons who did this.[47] The elder preferred to take a position on the commercial or technical staff of an enterprise.[48] This could be regarded as a transition phase, which made the lack of econom-

47 See H. Henning: Bildungsbürgertum . . . loc. cit., p. 286. The sons of commercial entrepreneurs were the second strongest source of recruitment to the academically trained public service up to 1890 and up to 1914 the strongest.
48 According to surveys taken from the same registers as those used for the commercial entrepreneurs recruitment to the ranks of commercial and technical employees from the commercial en-

ic independence bearable. The work was similar and it did not block the way back to
the father's status. On the contrary, the wider experience gained was often an advantage.

The inflow from the independent crafts followed largely parallel to self-recruitment but at a lower frequency. The only differences are in the 1860s and around the
turn of the century. In looking for an explanation of the clear rise in the inflow from
the crafts at the end of the 1860s we must remember that the cyclical upswing during
these years brought good market opportunities and made it relatively easy for a move
to be made from craftsman to factory owner in one generation. Less capital was
needed for equipment and investment. It was not until the economic situation
changed following the "Gründerkrise" and larger amounts of capital were needed to
enable companies to keep going that we find a drop in the inflow from this source.
However it never dropped below one fifth of recruitment as a whole. This is clear
proof of the will to rise and the possibilities for craftsmen to do so and it shows the
social affinity of the commercial entrepreneurs as a group to this status-related group.
The marked disinclination of craftsmen to move into the position of entrepreneur
around the turn of the century is probably mainly due to the introduction of the new
legislation on self-administration in 1897 which greatly strengthened the social position of the master craftsmen and gave them better prospects in their own sphere. The
introduction of the electric motor enabled production in the crafts to be rationalised
and it accordingly profited from the economic boom. We may deduce from this,
therefore, that material prospects as the reflection of performance were the decisive
factor in recruitment from the crafts as well.

The inflow from the ranks of the non-academic public service, on the other hand,
did not as a whole follow the cyclical development. Until the mid-1880s it moved
rather anti-cyclically and can probably be regarded more as the result of a re-orienta-
tion in the possible education pattern of the sons of public servants. The increasing
industrialisation and the wider range of technical training available made it seem appropriate for these young men to choose to train, if they had the inclination, through
general schooling and – for example – an institute of higher technical education,
which was shorter and less expensive than a university education and will have been
more in keeping with the rather straitened circumstances in which the family always
had to live.[49] This clearly began to appear to a growing number of the non-academic
public servants, who were very status-conscious, as a suitable path for their sons to
take, even if it did not, as the father's profession did, reward individual achievement
with a system of entitlements.[50] But the opportunities which this route offered for individual performance were regarded certainly not as a loss, rather as a gain in social
status. This suggests that even in sections of the educated classes material possession
resulting from individual achievement was coming to be regarded as a status symbol
equal to education and hence an element in social success. That the entrepreneurs
had always esteemed the social status of the public servants can be seen from the very

trepreneurs was 35.9% in 1985, rising to 50.4% in 1900, thus compensating for the decline in recruitment to the commercial entrepreneurs from their own ranks.

49 See H. Henning: Bildungsbürgertum ... loc. cit., p. 154 ff.

50 The inflow of sons of non-academic public servants to the ranks of the technical employees,
which shows a marked rise after the mid-1880s, indicates the same. Recruitment was 15.4% in
1884 but 23.6% in 1890. STA Detmold, register of births, marriages and deaths.

considerable and steady inflow from their ranks to these professions.[51] So these movements from one group to another were not without their social aspects and depending on the extent to which the individual could rise, they led to an increasing integration between the educated classes and the propertied classes, largely in the petty bourgeoisie but among the upper bouregoisie as well, a sign of considerable social mobility within the class as a whole.

However, there were limits to this internal mobility: the contribution which the academically educated groups made to swell the ranks of commercial entrepreneurs in Westphalia can hardly be regarded as a fringe phenomenon. But as a considerable number of commercial entrepreneurs moved into this group,[52] mobility between the propertied and the educated classes was more one-sided in the upper than in the lower ranks and the integration correspondingly less close. The effects of a class consciousness based on rights and educational privileges were still plain. The commercial entrepreneurs, on the other hand, who were the core group of the propertied classes, proved much more adaptable in their attitude to non-bourgeois groups. The inflow from the ranks of workers and employees was several times higher than that from the academically educated upper bourgeoisie. So social barriers did not prevent a person rising from the non-bourgeois groups into this class.

We can say therefore that a general tendency is observable in the recruitment patterns of the entrepreneurs: the main ties were with the economically independent groups but an inflow was possible from other groups as well. These people did not apparently have a very marked sense of class, personal achievement and the material possessions which it brought were enough. This raised the status of those who came from the petty bourgeoisie and increased the degree of integration between the bourgeois groups. Apart from this the inflow was not determined largely by social aspects but by economic prospects. The principle of performance furthered the material attitude.

2. Marriage

As can be seen from Fig. 2 the marriage ties of commercial entrepreneurs show a similar distribution to that of their origin. A division according to frequency will show three main trends; there is also broad social distribution in the fringe areas of the group.

The dominant trend was marriage into the same group. This was not subject to any real fluctuations nor are any differences recognisable between the generations. The trend as it emerges here gives the impression of a firm tradition. A slight decline during and after the "Gründerkrise" is quickly made good as the economic climate improves again.

Since this line does not fluctuate in comparison with the cyclical trend we can take it that the desire to marry into their own group was as strong a motive for the commercial entrepreneurs as material prospects. It secured status for the members of the second generation and brought the social consolidation of his economic position for the

---

51 See H. Henning: Bildungsbürgertum ... loc. cit., p. 141 and p. 501.
52 Loc. cit. p. 287 and p. 429.

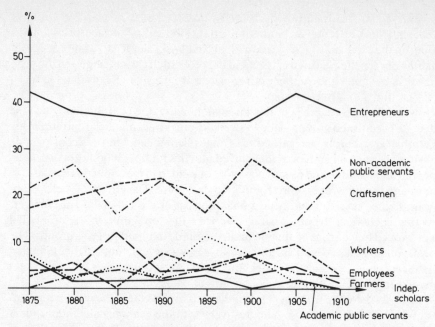

Fig. 2. Marriage of Commercial Entrepreneurs in Westphalia. *Sources:* Register of births, marriages and deaths, STA Detmold ; biographical hand-books ; company "Festschriften"

newcomer. It is a social aspect, but although it may have determined behaviour patterns in marriage, it did not have a socially exclusive effect.

In the second and third strongest trends in marriage patterns we can recognise a difference between the generations. The older generation of commercial entrepreneurs shows as second most frequent choice marriage into the group of master-craftsmen, with the trend declining slightly. In addition to the fact that the entrepreneurs were here marrying into a group with the same status symbol and – as the frequency of these marriages shows – did not regard the difference which did exist as a social disqualification, there were two further motives. The first was of a material nature. The craftsmen may not have had great fortunes but they had secure assets and means. The dowry they could give will have been very welcome particularly in times of slow economic growth, during the 1880s, for example. It will have been a support especially for those entrepreneurs who, like all the retail trade, hotel-keepers or small dealers in agricultural products, depended on short-term consumption where growth was slow in this period.[53]

The second motive was social but it proceeded from the craftsmen themselves: the sense of tradition, indeed we can even speak of a sense of class, in the crafts. The sons of craftsmen married into their father's group, even if economically they had outgrown it. Nevertheless, this motive was rather weaker than the material considerations: individual samples show that roughly a quarter of the commercial entrepre-

---

53 See W. G. Hoffmann: Das Wachstum der deutschen Wirtschaft seit der Mitte des 19. Jahrhunderts. Berlin, et al. 1965, p. 700.

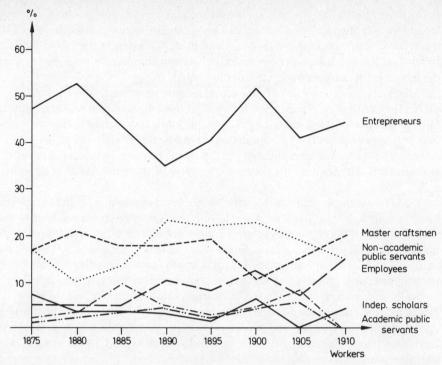

Fig. 3. Social Contact of Entrepreneurs in Westphalia. *Sources:* Register of births, marriages and deaths, STA Detmold; biographical hand-books; company "Festschriften"

neurs who married into the crafts were themselves the sons of craftsmen. The others were climbers, that is they came from the non-academic public service or they were the sons of experienced entrepreneurs themselves. So the crafts exercised a kind of directive function for the accumulation process at the core of the propertied class.

The third most frequent choice of marriage partner in the older generation of commercial entrepreneurs was in the group of non-academic public servants.

Here there were no economic considerations and the motive was purely social. With a marriage into these circles an entrepreneur could raise his position in society by acquiring "better class relations". The hotel-keeper or factory owner, who became the son-in-law of a district secretary or tax collector, saw his own achievement crowned and consolidated by the link with an "old class" which had a firm social position and the aura of proximity to the King. That the desire for social consolidation obviously played such a large part shows that at least some of the entrepreneurs were still not really sure of their social standing and this was certainly one of the results of the hierarchical structure of the state.

The younger generation of commercial entrepreneurs were at first less interested in marrying into the crafts. It was only as the economic climate began to improve again that these ties become more frequent. So we see that this trend moves conversely to recruitment which suggests material motivation: the craftsmen were now earning well and could offer a handsome dowry. There is a further factor which points to the strength of the material motivation for these marriage ties: before the cyclical upswing it was largely the sons of craftsmen in the younger generation who married the daughters of craftsmen, proof of the traditional loyalty to the old milieu. After 1895 this type of marriage almost disappears and it plays no part in the generally rising trend. Taken as a whole, however, marriage between commercial entrepreneurs and the daughters of craftsmen still stays in third place.

Marriages into the circles of non-academic public servants moved into second place. This trend moved parallel to the cyclical upswing and as it was generally acknowledged that nothing was to be got from the public servants the dominant motive here will have been social. This applied to the younger generation as well as to their fathers. The desire for consolidation of the social position obviously grew all the stronger the better secured the economic position of the commercial entrepreneur was.

Beside these three main trends a wide fringe area is apparent with great social mobility in marriage patterns. Marriage into different status groups considerably widened the ranks of the commercial entrepreneurs, another sign that as a group they did not have an exclusive sense of class. But here too we find a delimitation. It is the same as in origin: separation from the academic groups. Again the initiative probably came from the academic groups as we see that the converse move was gladly accepted.[54]

So the commercial entrepreneurs also largely tended to marry into their own circles or into the group with the same status symbol, that of the crafts. Again marriage mainly strengthened ties among the petty bourgeoisie, while the lack of mutual contact between the propertied and the educated classes prevented similar integration in the upper ranks. Once again the commercial entrepreneurs proved to be the core of the propertied class and marriage into their circles was regarded by the petty bourgeoisie as a social achievement. In addition to considerable material expectations on the part of individual entrepreneurs, which were feasible on marriage into a similar status group, we can recognise the desire for a social documentation of the economic position which had been achieved. The broad fringe area shows how willing the commercial entrepreneurs were to open their ranks to non-bourgeois entrants.

3. Social Contacts

The entrepreneurs' social contacts show a similar picture[55] to that of their marriage ties, with three main trends and a broad social spectrum in the fringe area. This is hardly surprising, since it was from the social contact that the marriage ties largely resulted.

Most frequent was social contact within the group. The tendency to this was very much stronger than in recruitment or even marriage. That may be due to the fact that the individual generally has a wider circle of acquaintances than relations and that he seeks acquaintances and forms friendships with people who are similar to himself.

The second most frequent group of social contacts was with the master craftsmen. However, ties with this group weakened after 1890 and even more so after the turn of the century, being replaced by friendship and contact with the non-academic public servants, who had formerly occupied only third place. The noticeable social distance

---

54 See H. Henning; Bildungsbürgertum . . . loc. cit., p. 291.
55 See Fig. 3.

from the crafts and the growing affinity with the public servants suggests that the younger generation of entrepreneurs placed greater value on the social position of those with whom they maintained contact than their fathers did. They wanted social recognition or social consolidation from their contacts and friendships; these motives are particularly clear among the younger generation because the economic position of the non-academic public servants fell far behind that of the entrepreneurs when the economic upswing started. That entrepreneurs increasingly sought contact with this group shows that the material considerations were being supplemented by a socially oriented component. The public servants were "an old class" and in this way they became integrated into the bourgeois competitive society.

The entrepreneurs met the public servants in the various associations which they joined, in male choirs,[56] shooting clubs,[57] veteran organisations[58] and so on. As long as the social contact remained within bourgeois groups the degree of its publicity brought no gradation in intensity. However, publicity did affect the social behaviour of entrepreneurs towards nonbourgeois groups. They did not lose their readiness to integrate with alien status groups but it was less marked in social contact than in their personal ties.

This type of social contact was largely limited to employees and the "better" workers in the pre-industrial spheres, that is, those who were integrated into the bourgeoisie. The industrial workers were pushed into a vacuum and formed associations of their own.[59]

So the entrepreneurs largely sought personal contact within their own ranks and with status-related groups. After about 1890 they increasingly used this to document their social position. In this they did not on principle abandon their readiness to social integration but it was reduced and limited largely to those non-bourgeois groups who could most easily conform to the bourgeois status symbols.

III. Conclusion

During the whole period which we have examined here the major entrepreneurs appear as a sharply separated social group, offering only very limited possibilities for persons from the most closely related status group, the commercial entrepreneurs, to

---

56 See for example the social composition of the "Lyra" Warendorf, "Liedertafel" Soest, "Münsterische Liedertafel", "Einigkeit" Bochum or the Male Voice Choir in Siegen. Records StAM Oberpräsidium 3794 and 3795.

57 Records StAM Regierung Münster Vol. 1151.

58 See H. Henning: Kriegervereine . . . loc. cit., p. 467f.

59 See for example the report by the Chief Executive in Arnsberg to the "Oberpräsident" of December 3, 1897. According to this members of the male voice choir "Sängerbund" Hoerde included "traders, medium craftsmen, petty officials and better-class factory workers." StAM Oberpräsidium 3794. On April 27, 1904 the "Landrat" in Bochum reported to the Chief Executive in Arnsberg that a large number of railway officials had left the Langendreer veterans' association when the number of workers rose. "In view of the social conditions I regard it as urgently necessary to keep the old members of the guard, most of whom come from better families, in the association." StAM Regierung Arnsberg 1 Pa No. 17.

rise. After 1870 social mobility, which had at first been recognisable as a fringe phe-
nomonen, virtually ceased to exist. What remained was a behaviour pattern which re-
sembled that of the nobility in a hierarchical society, but which presupposed wealth
as an inherited and personal attribute. The degree of wealth was a determinant for
membership of the group as it brought with it the corresponding capacity for decision-making. A further criterion was the importance attached to decision-making
functions outside the sphere of the enterprise and which also depended on the degree
of wealth. This brought both the pressure and the inclination to the – discreet – exercise of power. These were the common characteristics of a group which had developed into a new élite with an appropriate sense of class. The major entrepreneurs had
moved so far away from their own social origin that we can only speak in very restricted terms of integration with the bourgeoisie, although the nomenclature remained
bourgeois. However, the bourgeois constituent values of the will to perform and the
resultant social mobility and the privileges which derived from the concretisation of
individual achievement remained the legitimation of the will to command and
awareness of power which characterised this new élite.

So the major entrepreneurs were consistent in their lack of interest in mixing with
the old upper classes and as they themselves did not have historic rights to legitimise
their new position they were not or only very hesitantly accepted by the crown and the
nobility as a new leading power. Ultimately, therefore, they took up a socially exclusive position between the different social groups.

The entrepreneurs formed the core of the propertied class, integrating with status-
related groups and so displaying the tendency of this class to cling together. The common interest was the accumulation of material possession, which also explains the affinity of the different groups. But if the desire for material possession was largely
economic it was not conceived in the sense of re-distribution and hence of a class position; the individuality of the desire and the imponderabilities which material possession brought, for instance in social standing, were among the determinant features
of this class. This also explains the desire of the commercial entrepreneurs to consoli-
date their social position. That was the main motive for their marriage with members
of the non-academic public service class, as they were not as yet accepted by the academic public servants. Contact was only possible with these circles if it proceeded
from the public servants themselves. As a group, therefore, the commercial entrepreneurs were socially mobile; the main focus was on bourgeois groups but they permitted recruitment from non-bourgeois groups if those who rose were prepared to take
on the characteristics of the bourgeois society.

The World Economy in the 20th Century – Continuity and Change

Wolfram Fischer

When the Board of the German Historians' Association asked me to give the concluding lecture on the world economy in the twentieth century at its congress I had to find a way of making at least a few conclusive and well-founded remarks on this vast subject within the space of one hour.

There were three possibilities that I considered: it would have been appropriate to talk about "Hamburg and the World Economy in the Twentieth Century". That would have limited the range and given the subject a particular perspective. I rejected this because it seemed to me too narrow an approach and because I did not feel that I had enough specialised knowledge on Hamburg to be sure of getting my local colour right. The second possibility which I considered was to discuss the relationship between the economy and politics in the twentieth century in a global context. That would have been most in keeping with the tradition of the study of German history. I rejected this as well because I was afraid that I would become too much embroiled in the polemical discussion of current theories on imperialism or dependency without being able to give adequate reasons for my views. I therefore decided in favour of the third alternative, which is to concentrate on the phenomenon of the world economy itself, take its structure and changes as the subject of examination and include political decisions only as one group of several determinant factors.

But what is the "world economy"? "The term is used rather carelessly and generally equated with international trade relations", said A. Predöhl in his introduction to the problems of the world economy.[1] This is not correct, he argues, since a large part of trade takes place within the hage national territories of the USA and the Soviet Union. But the foreign trade of individual nations, which appears in the statistics as international trade, will be larger the more national frontiers there are. Predöhl concludes from this: "By the world economy we should therefore understand those relations between the individual economies of the world, independent of national frontiers, which make these individual economies dependent on each other for their essential needs."[2] This definition seems to me simple and clear, and despite possible difficulties in interpreting what "essential needs" may be in any one case I should like to adopt it with one variant. Mutual dependence, according to this definition, is the decisive criterion but there is another, the globality of relations, and Predöhl does not devote enough attention to this. It is for both these reasons that the Soviet Union, the People's Republic of China and the whole of the Eastern Bloc have so far remained

---

1 Andreas Predöhl: Das Ende der Weltwirtschaftskrise. Eine Einführung in die Probleme der Weltwirtschaft. Reinbek b. Hamburg, 1962, p. 10.
2 Predöhl, p. 11.

on the fringe of the world economy while small states such as Hongkong, Singapore, Switzerland and even Taiwan and South Korea are important centres.

However, in this article I am not going to concentrate on individual states but firstly on large regions which can be defined by their state of economic development and their geographical position, and then on sectors of the world economy as a whole, that is, agriculture, industry and services. I shall be using terms which have been evolved for purposes of economic analysis, such as "terms of trade", the price relations between various groups of goods, or economic units such as the gross national product and the national income, as well as statistical instruments used to measure economic movements, such as the trend, long fluctuations or the growth rate; I shall only marginally touch on economic policy institutions and organs such as the world monetary system.

In the first section of the article I shall discuss the main structural features of the world economy before the First World War, during the inter-war years and after the Second World War. In the second I shall deal with growth trends and fluctuations in growth. The third section will deal with the position of the developing countries in the world economy, while in the last section I shall make a few remarks on the conclusions which may be drawn from these facts and applied to the study of history and practical economic policy.

I. The Structure of the World Economy in the Twentieth Century

By the end of the nineteenth century the world economy had taken on a very characteristic structure. There was a clear geographical centre in North-West and Central Europe, with subsidiary cores on the outer fringes of Europe, a second core which was in a process of rapid development in North America and a fringe core just developing in East Asia and Oceania. The rest can easily be categorised as the periphery. Among the most salient features of this world economy were that trade relations within the core and between the core and the subsidiary core areas were very much more intensive than relations between the cores and the periphery; above all, they were very much more intensive than relations within the periphery, which covered the major part of the world's surface and accounted for about two thirds of the world's population, which was estimated at 1.6 billion in 1900.

That has not greatly changed today. Especially trade relations between what we now call developing countries have remained through all the ups and downs of cyclical movement, through world wars and political upheavals minimal in comparison with trade between the highly developed industrial regions. Certainly we must make allowance for the built-in "bias" in favour of Europe, with its many national frontiers, in considering any statistics on world trade, but even so the result is clear: in the twentieth as in earlier centuries the European countries largely traded with each other; in second place came North America, Oceania and Japan, followed by the rest of Asia and Latin America in a very low third place, while lowest of all is the volume of trade with Africa, which was almost entirely under colonial domination. In 1913 Europe accounted for just under two thirds of world foreign trade, and more than three quarters of this was within Europe and the European settlement areas in North America and Oceania. In 1971 55.3% of world exports were in trade between nations which the United Nations Organisation calls "developed market economies"; if Eastern Europe is included, the figure, despite the low volume of trade between the first and second worlds, is still just under two thirds – as it was before the First World War. Only 3.7% of world exports were among the under-developed market economies themselves. In the period between the wars (1928) the core and its subsidiary areas actually accounted for more than three quarters of world trade.[3]

Thus, Europe and the areas of European settlement overseas formed the real network of world trade, and the other regions participated in specific categories, which may have been of great importance to them but which compared with the whole were only marginal.

If we now turn to the explanation for the predominance of the Western industrialised countries (and Japan) in world trade we will need to take a look at the composition in terms of groups of goods. We shall follow international practice here in distinguishing between primary and secondary goods and among primary goods in making a further distinction between foodstuffs and raw materials, and within industrial products between consumer and investment goods. It is striking first of all that before the First World War and between the wars the share of the two main groups shows an astonishing degree of constancy. Measured in current prices, the percentage of primary goods fluctuated from 1876 to 1937 only between 61.3% and 64.3%. It was only after the Second World War that this dropped to 33.2% (1970).[4] So the post-war period brought a considerable shift in favour of industrial products. We shall come back to this.

However, a considerable change had already taken place earlier, and this becomes plain if we study the sub-groups of these aggregates. In primary goods the share of foodstuffs and agricultural raw materials had already dropped before the First World War, while that of minerals had risen. In industrial goods there was a fall in the share of consumer goods and that of investment goods – machines, chemical and electrical products – rose.[5] This trend intensified in the period between the wars.

In the period after the Second World War this structural change took on dramatic proportions, and machines, vehicles and chemical products are now the most important goods being traded internationally.

It is tempting to explain the constant predominance of the industrial countries and the growth in the share of industrial products in world trade with the terms of trade, i.e. the relation of export to import prices for a country, a group of countries or a product or group of products. But a closer examination of the changes in the terms of trade between the main groups of goods and then between regions will show that these are by no means straightforward; there are long fluctuations, first favouring primary goods, then industrial products, while the different composition of exports which individual countries offered on the world market permitted great differences

3 P. Lamartine Yates: Forty Years of Foreign Trade. A Statistical Handbook with Special Reference to Primary Products and Underdeveloped Countries. London, 1959, p. 32f.; A. G. Kenwood and A. L. Lougheed: The Growth of the International Economy, 1820–1960. An Introductory Text. London, 1971, p. 224; United Nations Statistical Yearbook, 1975, p. 438.

4 Yates: p. 37, Table 9. Kenwood and Lougheed: p. 287, Table 23; United Nations Statistical Yearbook, 1976, p. 55.

5 Kenwood and Lougheed: p. 102f.

in the terms of trade within the industrialised and the non-industrialised world. There is no clear trend which might be seen to operate as a kind of law. The producers of raw materials and foodstuffs are not condemned to receive fewer and fewer industrial products for their goods, nor does it follow from the rise in the world population and the growth in demand in the industrial countries with their growing wealth that raw materials and foodstuffs are becoming so scarce that their prices are going to shoot up relative to those of industrial products. Fluctuations in both directions, the regularity or irregularity of which needs to be examined in each case, characterise the picture over the last hundred years and at least at times the fall in transport prices has enabled both sides to gain in world trade.[6]

Before discussing these fluctuations in more detail we must complete our picture of the structure of the world economy by taking a brief look at world production as well as world trade. Here too we are primarily concerned with cross-section analyses to show the structure at specific points in time. Again we choose for these the period immediately before the First World War, the years of stability between the wars and the years just before the oil crisis. We shall limit ourselves to a few points.

It is well known that as a result of the industrialisation of the core region world industrial production was already very unevenly distributed before the First World War. The USA was already in the lead after the 1880s, followed second by Great Britain and after 1906/10 by Germany. In 1913 the regions of the industrial cores and their subsidiary areas accounted for 87% of world industrial production. Among the territories now known as developing countries India was in the lead, if only because of her size. However, she only accounted for 1.1%, leaving barely 12% to be shared between the rest of the world.[7]

In the years between the wars the relations shifted further in favour of the United States and some of the new industrial countries, while the shares of Germany, Britain, France and the USSR dropped. Taken together, however, the same core countries still produced around 85% of the world's industrial goods.[8]

The old industrialised countries (together with Japan and the Soviet Union) remained predominant after the end of the Second World War as well. Immediately after the war (1947) the USA and Canada together were in fact producing about half of the world's industrial goods and North-West Europe only 20% but again taken together the market economy countries and Eastern Europe still accounted for 82%. Among the developing countries India was again in the lead with 0.9%, closely followed by Argentina.[9] As Western Europe recovered, the share of the industrial na-

6 Kenwood and Lougheed, p. 171; League of Nations: Industrialisation and Foreign Trade. Geneva, 1945. And: United Nations: Relative Prices of Exports and Imports of Under-developed Countries. New York, 1949; William Arthur Lewis: Economic Survey 1919–1939. London, 1949; Charles Kindleberger: The Terms of Trade. A European Case Study. Boston and New York, 1956. For a critical summary see Paul Bairoch: The Economic Development of the Third World since 1900. London, 1975.

7 League of Nations: Industrialisation and Foreign Trade, p. 12 ff.; Derek H. Aldcroft: Die Zwanziger Jahre. Von Versailles zur Wall Street 1919–1929 (Geschichte der Weltwirtschaft im 20. Jahrhundert. ed. Wolfram Fischer, Vol. 3), Munich, 1978, p. 337, Table 15.

8 Ibid. As neither Switzerland nor Holland nor Norway nor Spain and Portugal are included in these statistics on the core, the share is actually higher.

9 Wladimir S. Woytinsky and Emma S. Woytinsky: World Population and Production. New York, 1953, p. 1005.

tions appears to have climbed again, reaching over 85% by the beginning of the 1970s.[10]

In the distribution of raw materials production, considerable changes took place in individual goods, but these are only dramatic in the case of mineral fuels. In 1913 oil played a minor role. The main source of energy was coal and 87% of this was mined in Europe and the United States and exported, especially from Great Britain, all over the world. In the years between the wars oil began to grow in importance. Oil production continued to grow through all the crises and wars but until the beginning of the 1950s it was one industrial country, the United States of America, which dominated the world market as supplier. The rise of the Near East from a share of 9% in 1948 to 38% of world production in 1974 is the most striking phenomenon. During the same period the share of North America dropped from 60% to 20% and it is now roughly the same as that of the Soviet Union. In natural gas the North American share is still at 53%. But there are still major industrial raw materials which are produced largely in the industrialised countries, and the high growth rates are in the big, relatively young industrial countries such as Australia, Canada, the USSR and in the future probably China as well.

Only tin is still the domaine of four developing countries, Malaysia, Bolivia, Thailand and Indonesia. The dependence of the industrial countries on developing countries, which in 1913 was only the case for rubber and tin, has certainly increased, but it is very unevenly distributed. Even in oil the OPEC countries do not have a monopoly; they simply head price developments as any strong cartel would. There has only been a very slight shift in the world economy as a whole in favour of the raw materials countries.[11]

We know less on the distribution of world agricultural production. In 1953 the Woytinskys, two of the great authorities on world statistics, commented: "Precise evaluation of world agricultural output is next to impossible".[12] For the years 1934/38 they give an estimate by the International Institute of Agriculture in Rome, according to which Europe (but not including the Soviet Union), North America and Oceania, in other words the market economy countries without Japan, together accounted for 48% while all the territories largely settled by Europeans accounted for around two thirds.[13] This share is likely to have grown rather than diminished by the early 1970s.[14]

To complete our picture of the structure of the world economy we need to take a look at the tertiary sector and try to estimate the share which the different regions

10 As far as I know the UNO publications do not give direct figures on the distribution of industrial production. However, it can be deduced from the indices for the individual groups of countries that a) the growth in industrial production was highest in the European Eastern block countries, b) it was somewhat higher in Western Europe than in North America and Oceania and c) the market economy developing countries had only marginally higher growth (from a very much smaller base) than the market economy highly industrialised countries. The overall weight of the industrialised countries in the East and in the West must therefore have increased.
11 United Nations: Statistical Yearbook, 1962, p. 143 ff.; 1963, p. 312 ff.; 1975, p. 48 ff. and 186 ff.
12 Woytinsky and Woytinsky: p. 455.
13 ibid., p. 321 and 457.
14 This follows from the production indices of the United Nations for the same reasons as given in Note 10. (Rom) However, in the growth of agricultural production the European Eastern block only takes a middle place.

have in services. Here we encounter greater obstacles than in the case of physical production or the value of production, which we have used as a yardstick so far. For services fulfil quite a different function in underdeveloped countries from that in industrialised countries, where the relative growth in services is regarded as a sign of economic progress. As the input of capital into production (and communication) grows,
the productivity of labour grows with it and resources, especially labour, are freed for
the services sector. So the higher the degree of industrialisation and the higher the
productivity of labour, the stronger, generally, are services in an economy. As occupations in services bring on the average a higher income than jobs in the production
sphere, a growing share of services occupations generally also means a growing national income. But in many developing countries the size of the services sector is
largely the expression of lack of employment. Persons who are unemployed or un-
der-employed, who cannot make enough to live on in agriculture and have no industrial jobs offer services. In developing countries the size of the services sector is often
a sign of hypertrophy. Since 1900 the growth of the services sector in developing
countries has been roughly three times that of the share of employees in industry. But
one cannot conclude from this that these countries have made a leap forward in modernisation due to the import of higher technology. That may be the case in one or two
instances, but generally the high share of the services sector together with a dominant
proportion engaged in agriculture means that the country is industrially backward.

As services, like all the productive activities, are included in the national accounts, we will perhaps be able to form the clearest impression of the predominance
of the industrialised countries if we take as yardstick the distribution of world income. Admittedly the inaccuracies in the figures, particularly for data which goes
back before the 1930s, are enormous; nevertheless I should like to consider the results
of estimates by the Dutch economist L.J. Zimmermann, who has attempted to show
world income and regional income for the period from 1860 to 1960.[15] According to
this, slightly less than two thirds of world income was distributed among the industrialised countries (not including Eastern Europe) both in the pre-war period and in the
inter-war years, although their share of world population was only 21.5% in 1913 and
22% in 1929. In 1975 as well, according to the latest statistics from the United Nations,
the market economy industrialised countries account for almost two thirds (65.7%) of
the world's gross product, although their share of population has dropped back to
one fifth. The Socialist countries in Eastern Europe which have a population share of
9.1% account for 15.5% of the world's gross product. This leaves barely 19% for the
70% of the world's population which lives outside the industrial core areas of the
world economy.

To summarise the results of this first section we can say that the structure of the
world economy, if this is seen as the distribution of production, trade and income in
the various regions of the world, has shown a constant dominance of the areas settled
by Europeans on both sides of the Atlantic with fringe cores in Oceania since the later
nineteenth century. Only Japan has succeeded in joining the circle of nations which
shape the world economy, the Soviet Union, on the other hand, only in terms of pro-

15 L.J. Zimmermann: The Distribution of World Income 1860–1960. In: Egbert de Vries (ed.): Es-
    says on Unbalanced Growth. A Century of Disparity and Convergence. 'S-Gravenhage. 1962,
    p.37 and 52ff.

duction and hence income but not of integration of trade and investment. There have been shifts in emphasis within the core – until into the first decade after the war mainly in favour of North America and to the disadvantantage of Central and Western Europe – but what looked like a dramatic shift from the point of view of Britain or Germany, especially in the 1920s and 1930s, was relatively insignificant in a world-wide perspective.

This constant dominance of one group of economies is related to a structural shift, which appears to operate almost with the force of a law, within the highly developed industrial economies in favour of a more and more capital-intensive (and energy-intensive) production structure in industry and agriculture and communications and hence to a growing labour productivity and higher incomes for production factors. This development may have brought an intensification of the division of labour within the world economy, but this has been mainly within the dominant block of the developed market economies, and it has not brought a general increase in the dependency of this block on food and raw materials from the rest of the world. There has only been a clear increase in dependence for certain products, most important oil, and this can be compensated by the industrial nations through higher exports to these regions.

So even after de-colonisation the Third World has not succeeded in forming one or more regions of weight in the world economy or intensifying trade among own nations, which are still oriented to the dominant regions in the world economy and much more dependent on these than they are on the Third World.

II. Trends and Cycles in the World Economy

For more than 100 years economists have been trying to get a better grasp of the movements of economies over time and provide better explanations of the dynamics of modern economy. They have evolved various terms and methods for this, the most important of which for our purposes are the calculations of trends and cycles. That there should be regularities or rules in the ups and downs of observable and measurable changes in economic activity is one of the basic convictions of economists, but historians are traditionally rather sceptical about this. The historian would like to know what really happened, down to every detail. Economists search for laws which may explain the movements, even if they are now a little more cautious about estimating regularities. In the 1860s Juglar "discovered" the economic cycle, which generally lasts between 7 and 11 years. Later Kitchin established shorter fluctuations of about 40 months, the Russian economist Kondratiev found long fluctuations in the price level of between 50 and 60 years each and finally Kuznet established the investment cycle of altogether between 20 and 25 years. In all these calculations certain factors have to be disregarded so that the regularity of the fluctuation becomes more apparent: the long-term development, the trend, has to be ignored. Conversely the short-term cyclical or irregular fluctuations have to be eliminated when calculating the trend. It was the long-term trend which was of greater concern in the immediate post-war years than the short-term fluctuations. Since Keynes, many of those involved in the formulation of economic policy had come to believe that it was possible first to reduce and then to eliminate the fluctuations altogether by appropriate counter-steering. With the stronger interruptions to growth which set in after the late 1960s research on the cycle came back into its own and new empirical analyses of the economic development, such as Sir Arthur Lewis's "Growth and Fluctuations 1870–1913" (London, 1978) are an attempt to use both analytical tools at once.

Most of this research expressly or tacitly assumes that in the nineteenth century, especially during the final decades before the First World War, there was something like "normal" economic development. This was either covered over, sidetracked or interrupted altogether by the world wars and the problems of the inter-war years, and many believe that it reappeared after the Second World War or that a new "normality" established itself. Knut Borchardt discussed these question in relation to Germany at the last Historians' Congress in Mannheim, and he outlined the assumptions and consequences of the different perspectives for the interpretation of German history in the twentieth century.[16] The same can be done for the world economy in the twentieth century, for the inter-war years seemed to many countries to bring a reversal of past experience, a break in the trend. Great Britain especially seemed to be threatened with a stagnation which was often thought to be a reflection of the fact that this was a "mature" industrial economy with an old technology and structure which were obviously no longer capable of renovation and rejuvenation. But South-East Asia as well, although by no means a "mature" economy, did not really find its way back to the old growth path of before the war in the inter-war years.[17] It is interesting that estimates of the development in national incomes have shown that in other parts of the world as well the interwar years brought a break in growth.[18] One economist has actually calculated for Australia a real decline in per capita production between 1913 and 1929.[19] Even in the USA there was a slow-down in the growth of income. Only Japan, Latin America and China had, according to these calculations, higher growth rates in 1929 than in the period before the First World War, but in Latin America this was compensated by the rapid increase in population. For the world as a

16 Knut Borchardt: Trend, Zyklus, Struktureinbrüche, Zufälle: Was bestimmt die deutsche Wirtschaftsgeschichte des 20. Jahrhunderts? in: Vierteljahrsschrift für Sozial- und Wirtschaftsgeschichte 64 (1977), p. 145–178. Cf. also Dietmar Petzina: Krisen gestern und heute – die Rezession von 1974/75 und die Erfahrungen der Weltwirtschaftskrise (Vortragsreihe der Gesellschaft für Westfälische Wirtschaftsgeschichte H. 21), Dortmund, 1977.
17 For Europe altogether: Ingvar Svennilsson: Growth and Stagnation in the European Economy. Geneva, 1954. There is a great deal of literature on Great Britain, from which I have selected only one which has solid empirical proof: Derek H. Aldcroft: The Inter-War Economy: Britain 1919–1939. London, 1970. Aldcroft discusses this question in a broader context in Vol. 7 of the world economic history of the twentieth century quoted in Note 7. On S. E. Europe see esp. p. 134ff. Vol. 6 of the Handbuch der Europäischen Sozial- und Wirtschaftsgeschichte (Stuttgart Klett-Cotta as from 1979) will discuss this in detail. The chapters on S. E. Europe are by Berend and Ranki (Budapest).
18 Simon Kuznets: Modern Economic Growth: Rate, Structure and Spread. New Haven and London, 1966; ibid: Economic Growth of Nations. Total Output and Production and Production Structure. Cambridge, Mass., 1971.
19 N. G. Butlin: Australian Domestic Product: Investment and Foreign Borrowing, 1861–1939. Cambridge, 1962, esp. pp. 7 and 33; C. Foster (ed.): Australian Economic Development in the Twentieth Century. London, 1970, esp. Chaps. 2, 5 and 6; Aldcroft: Die Zwanziger Jahre, p. 326ff.

whole a decline in the average growth rate from 2.2% to 1.7% has been calculated, per capita from 1.5% to 1.0%, in other words a drop of a full third.[20]

This slow-down in growth, it should be noted, took place before the catastrophic effects of the world economic crisis took hold, thus bringing a real and in some cases very abrupt decline in national incomes. Although many at the time believed that the crisis followed a period of great upswing, the "Golden Twenties", other researchers soon began to ask whether the whole period between the wars was not in fact one of stagnation and interruptions to growth and the collapse after 1929 only the dramatic peak of what was in fact a long-term structural crisis. But however one looks at it, the preparations for war, the war itself and the period immediately following brought an upswing which neither A. Hansen in 1938 nor Schumpeter in 1939 had believed possible. It was stimulated first by the rearmament of Germany and Japan and after the 1940s by the enormous increase in production in the USA, which spread to the rest of the world after the war was over.[21]

Everywhere growth rates during the first twenty years after the Second World War reached proportions which were not only far above those of the inter-war years but those of the prewar period as well. While long-term overall economic growth in the leading countries had been around 2% before the First World War, now long-term average growth rates of 4 to 5% were being registered and Japan actually touched just on 10%.[22] Per capita for the Western industrialised countries this was an even greater rise over the pre-war period, since despite the various "baby booms" the rise in population was lower.[23] It is only in the last decade that growth rates have dropped again to a level which largely corresponds to that of the era before the First World War.

It therefore seems appropriate to postulate that the reconstruction period is over, that we have returned to the "normality" of the nineteenth century and in future can expect growth rates of 2 or at most 3%. According to this interpretation the long-term economic development can best be shown in the form of a linear trend, with the two inter-war decades bringing a deviation downwards and the two post-war decades a deviation upwards. As we do not know what is going to happen in future this view can neither be verified nor disproved. Those who accept it, however, will find themselves with a difficulty in interpretation. Why did the world economy react to the two world wars, which brought similar disruptions to "normality" by re-directing production factors, shifting trade flows and so on, in such different ways – to the first with a 20 to 25-year depression, and to the second with a similar period of prosperity? One possible explanation could be found in the work of Kondratiev and Schumpeter. Accord-

20 Aldcroft: Die Zwanziger Jahre. Von Versailles zur Wall Street, 1919–1929, p. 327, Table 11.
21 The importance of the war economy for the upswing in the USA and elsewhere has been convincingly shown: Alan S. Milward: Der Zweite Weltkrieg. Krieg, Wirtschaft und Gesellschaft 1939–1945. (Geschichte der Weltwirtschaft im 20. Jahrhundert, Vol. 5), Munich, 1977, esp. Chap. 3.
22 United Nations: Statistical Yearbook, 1969, p. 550 ff.; 1972, p. 613 ff.; 1975, p. 684 ff. See also Kenwood and Lougheed, p. 290 ff.; Angus Maddison: Economic Growth in the West. London, 1964, p. 29; ibid.: Die neuen Großmächte. Der wirtschaftliche Aufschwung Japans und der Sowjetunion. Bergisch-Gladbach, 1969, p. 93.
23 According to Lewis this was 1.2% on a yearly average for the industrial core countries (USA, Great Britain, Germany, France) in 1880–1910 and 1.15% in 1957–69 (W. A. Lewis: Growth and Fluctuations 1870–1913, p. 136). In Europe it had been below 1% since 1950 (United Nations, Statistical Yearbook, 1969, p. XXVII, 1976, p. 8.

ing to Kondratiev the long upswing phase which began in 1896/1900 should have been followed by a downswing in the twenties and this should also have lasted about 25 years, giving way to a new upswing phase towards the end of the 1940s. This should have lasted until the end of the 1960s or the early 1970s. The slow-down in growth since the last third of the 1960s in some of the industrialised countries was therefore to be expected.[24] Are we in fact in a new Kondratiev downswing?

If we are to answer this question we must first clarify the causes of these long fluctuations. Schumpeter saw them as waves of innovation followed by a slackening of innovative impetus. In his view the first Kondratiev upswing, from 1787 to 1842, was the phase of the Industrial Revolution, the second, from 1843 to 1897, the iron and steel phase, and especially the railway age. The third, after the turn of the century, which was later held to have been interrupted by the First World War, could be described as the age of electricity and chemicals. Then the upswing since the 1940s could be regarded as the (rather late?) impact of vehicle and air traffic, perhaps also as the age of computers and atomic power.

However, it is always difficult to prove such explanations empirically, for the obvious technical innovations of an age do not really have such a broad effect during that age that they could be described as the decisive motors of overall economic progress. The phase of the Industrial Revolution was still very largely agricultural. The iron, steel and railway phase is easiest to prove. But around the turn of the century electricity and chemicals were playing a smaller role in the world economy than agriculture, transport, the textile industry and mechanical engineering. Vehicle and air traffic come rather in a Kondratiev downswing. Atomic power and computers can be shown to be technical novelties at the end of the 1940s and in the early 1950s but it is only in the early phase that they can also be shown to be innovations in the sense that they further technical progress. During the post-war years it was mechanical engineering and chemicals, both of which emerged in the nineteenth century as industrial sectors, which dominated the spread of industrialisation, the modernisation of agriculture and the rise in productivity in both spheres.

It is even more difficult to produce empirical evidence of and reasons for the slackening of innovative impetus in the interwar years and during the last decade.[25] Motor transport and air traffic could – from the technological standpoint – have acted as innovative forces in the period between the wars – as they certainly did in the USA in the 1920s – if there had been sufficient purchasing power to stimulate demand, and the computer began its progress on a broad front at a time in which we may well be in one of Kondratiev's downswing phases.

In my view, therefore, the possibility of the effect of long waves which are due to the impetus of technical progress cannot be ruled out, but it cannot be exactly or adequately proven either.

---

24 The slow-down in growth rates predicted by the model, however, is only apparent in some countries, e.g. The Federal Republic of Germany and Sweden. In the case of the USA and Canada or Belgium for instance, it cannot be established. See U.N.: Statistical Yearbook, 1976, p.676ff.
25 Gerhard Mensch and Reinhard Schnopp: Stalemate in Technology, 1925–1935. Internationales Institut für Management und Verwaltung, discussion papers 1977. Wissenschaftszentrum Berlin, is an interesting attempt to do this. See also Gerhard Mensch: Das Technologische Patt. Frankfurt, 1975.

The historian is more likely to prefer a different explanation of the contrasting effects of the two worlds wars on the world economy. He will look for this in political and economic policy decisions. If one takes this path one will indeed find a large number of arguments which taken together will give a coherent explanation. I shall content myself with a few indications:

After the First World War it did not prove possible to build up a world monetary system which worked. The question of political debts was not solved in time and so the European economies remained with a heavy burden. The USA did not react adequately either politically or economically to the leading role which it had acquired. Instead of enforcing a solution to the question of political debts, opening their country to the exports of other nations and so helping the stagnating European economies to find their way back to the growth path of the pre-war years and create better export markets for the under-developed countries, the Americans retired to their own vast and almost self-sufficient domestic market. They did not make their currency a world currency nor their Federal Reserve system a world bank, lender of last resort, which would have helped to overcome the liquidity problems the rest of the world was struggling with. Great Britain concentrated too strongly on restoring the old parity to the dollar and gold and so imposed upon itself and the Commonwealth countries a devastating deflationary policy. Germany remained caught up in the trauma of the lost war and let the reparations become an internal bone of contention instead of courageously tackling the problem or coming to terms with it. The Eastern and South-Eastern European countries let the breaking up of the old empires affect their economies and so lost considerable chances of growth. France held to her antiquated agrarian structure and used the international position she had regained since 1926 not to cooperate but largely to thwart Anglo-American attempts to reach a common world monetary policy. And finally, every government proved inadequate to combat the world economic crisis because, instead of cooperating with each other, they pursued a "beggar-thy-neighbour" policy, took refuge in national rescue operations and hence did even more damage internationally.

In contrast, even before the end of the Second World War the USA had decisively grasped her leading role, created a new world monetary system, laid the basis for an at least partial liberalisation of world trade, and helped first Europe and then a number of other parts of the world with considerable public and private credit. The West Europeans took up the American initiative, and created in the European Community a greater market and a new dynamic centre of world trade to match the USA. Japan did not wallow in resentment but played an active part in the new and liberal world trade movement, creating for herself a primary position in it and in many instances forcing other nations to stand up to intense international competition. All the market economy countries pursued an active domestic economic policy designed to achieve and maintain full employment. This may have created some balance of payments and monetary problems, but it did secure growth.

All that is true. Nevertheless, again the effects of such a bundle of decisions on the world economy cannot be measured exactly. Of course it can be proved that, for example, trade among the countries of the European Community increased more strongly than world trade generally. But that need not necessarily be the result of the customs union or the common agricultural policy, it could be due to geographical proximity and comparable growth in all the partners. After all, as we have seen, even before the First World War the European countries largely traded with each other. And Switzerland and Austria, neither of whom are members of the EEC, have fully participated in the general growth and the increasing integration of the European economies.

So there is no clear proof that political decisions on major issues during the post-war years have been responsible for the difference in the general trend as compared with the inter-war years, any more than it can be proved beyond a shadow of a doubt that it was the effects of innovations or the lack of such innovations which caused the differences in the world economic situation. It is more probable that the two interacted and supplemented each other. So it is possible that the two world wars and their consequences did not so much deflect or interrupt the Kondratiev cycles as strengthen them.

But there is something to suggest that mistakes in economic policy decisions after the First World War and better decisions after the Second did role a major role. It is the differences in the development of international trade and national production in the pre-, inter- and post-war periods. Before the First World War world trade grew faster than world production, but not quite as fast as industrial production alone.[26] The liberal economists of the pre-war period saw in this something like a basic law of the world economy. Alfred Marshall, for instance, argued that the causes of economic progress must be sought in international trade.[27]

In the inter-war years on the other hand, world trade grew more slowly than world production, especially production of industrial goods, indeed it even grew more slowly than population. Many economists concluded from this that technical progress, industrialisation, growing real incomes and other factors necessarily led to a relative reduction in the international exchange of goods, since the spread of industrialisation reduced comparative cost advantages, created a general ability to produce industrial goods and hence reduced the need for imports. Finally it was argued that the geographical expansion of the world economy would come to a natural end as soon as practically all the regions were integrated into it.[28] The post-war period has shown that this "diminishing trade hypothesis" is certainly not a law, it is not even a long-term rule, for since the Second World War trade has again been growing much more strongly than production.[29] World trade has again become a motor of the world economy, an even stronger motor than it was before the First World War.

That of course has strengthened the conviction of those who see in a liberal world economy the optimal model for the welfare of nations. It is an important argument for the further liberalisation of world trade or against the imposition of new restrictions on imports. The fact that it is mainly the highly developed industrial nations which profited from this strong expansion of world trade, that trade between them expanded faster than trade between the industrialised countries and the less devel-

---

26 According to Kenwood and Lougheed, p. 86, the average annual growth rate in production was 2.1% between 1870 and 1914, while that of world trade was 3.4%. According to Yates, p. 31, the index of world exports in 1911/13 was 139 and for industrial production 378 (Base year 1876/80).

27 Alfred Marshall: Principles of Economics, 8th edition, reprint London 1959, p. 255.

28 The major advocate of this theory was the American Alvin Hansen. It is opposed i.a. by F. Hilgerdt in the "Summary of Findings" in his pioneering study for the League of Nations: Industrialization and Foreign Trade, pp. 116–120, but this did not appear until 1945.

29 Kenwood and Lougheed, p. 285.

oped nations has caused many of those involved in economic policy in the Third World at least to question the liberal principles of present world economic policy in the market economy industrialised countries and to demand a re-organisation which would institutionally favour the raw materials and food producing countries, for example by creating cartels for raw materials or minimum prices or guarantee a transfer of resources, e.g. through more untied development aid. Radical critics are actually asking for "de-coupling" from the world economy.[30]

Their argument is roughly this: international trade only furthers the development of those countries which are producing essential goods for the markets of the industrialised countries and which have the opportunity to make a profit on exports and thus form capital with which to develop their own resources and further their own process of industrialisation and the modernisation of their agriculture. It does not help those one-product countries which can only offer bananas, tea or coffee to the rich countries, or whose raw materials have been exploited by such countries without creating employment and hence income to any noticeable extent in the country itself. In these societies at best a "dual economy" can develop with an export-oriented modern sector which has little relation to the rest of the traditional economy.[31]

In fact there are a number of developing countries in which the growth of the export sector is hardly likely to result in a stimulus to general economic growth, as about 5 to 7% of workers are employed in enclaves producing goods, 90% of which are exported, while the other 93 to 95% of the workers are producing goods of which only 1% is exported. If these are sectors in which all or nearly all the technology has to be imported from the developed countries, as in mining or oil extraction, the income effect on the developing country is indeed minimal. In 1960, for example, only 0.6% of the work force of the developing countries were employed in minig, but this sector accounted for 40% of these countries' exports. The most extreme example is oil, which at that time accounted for one third of the exports of developing countries but provided work for only 0.02% of the people.[32] However, the oil states have either been able to nationalise the oil wells or force the oil companies to pay higher levies and now through the cartel they exercise they have created such fantastic profit margins for themselves that the resultant income has catapulted at least the sparsely populated among them, such as Kuwait, Saudi Arabia and the Sheikdoms on the Persian Gulf into the ranks of the countries with the highest per capita income in the world.[33]

In the third section of this article I shall be asking whether this is likely to prove a model for the solution of the problems of the developing countries, that is for two thirds of the world's population, and so we must take a closer look at the economic structure of these countries.

---

30 Detlef Lorenz: Weltwirtschaft zwischen Arbeitsteilung und Abkoppelung, in: Konjunkturpolitik. Zeitschrift für angewandte Konjunkturforschung 23 (1977), pp. 196–215. This also gives further relevant titles.
31 The basic formulation of this theory is in Râul Prebish: The Economic Development of Latin America and its Principal Problems. New York, 1950.
32 Paul Bairoch: The Economic Development of the Third World since 1900. London, 1975, p. 108.
33 In 1974 Kuwait had a national per capita income of 11,063 US dollars, Switzerland 6,790, Sweden 6,153, the USA 5,923, Canada 5,840 and the Federal Republic of Germany 5,480 (United Nations Statistical Yearbook, 1976, p. 689–691).

III. The Developing Countries in the World Economy

One could draw up a long list of the disadvantages from which the developing countries suffered in the world economy of the nineteenth and twentieth centuries; it would show a growing discrepancy between them and the industrialised states. Paul Bairoch has estimated that per capita income in these countries was about one sixth that of the industrialised countries in 1900 but only one thirteenth in 1970. One must add, however, that over the same period real per capita production by the developing countries almost doubled while in the industrial countries it quadrupled.[34] Of the well-known saying that the rich only get richer while the poor get poorer, only the first part apparently applies; the second only applies to the relation between them. One must also add that calculations of this kind do not show the differences between regions. Per capita income in Latin America, for example, was more than twice as high as that in Asia even in 1900; by 1970 it was 3.3 times as high. The differences between the developing countries have always been much greater than those between the industrialised countries. They have grown greater over the last century – and not simply since the oil cartel came into operation. If one leaves these differences out of account one can say that the developing countries will need about a hundred years at the growth rates they have shown in the two decades from 1950 to 1970 before they can reach the per capita income of the market economy industrialised countries.

Opinions may differ as to whether that is a long time or a short one. For those involved in the formulation of economic policy it is a long time, probably far too long. For the economic historian, on the other hand, it is short. After all, the British needed 200 years to move from the start of the Industrial Revolution to their present state of development; the Americans and the Germans at least 150, for the European countries only progressed half as fast in the nineteenth century as the developing countries after the Second World War. Even the Japanese needed a full century and they the best in the class.

Of course there are always a number of unknowns in such calculations. One of them is population growth. A change in the growth in population in the Third World of only 0.1% per year in either direction would cause a considerable change in the situation, for with the present population of 3 billion in the Third World and a growth rate of 2.1% per year, as has been the case in Asia over the last decade, the difference over 100 years would be $+2.465$ billion or -2.238 billion.[35] In the first case, therefore, per capita income would be considerably lower and in the second considerably higher. We know from German experience how quickly a growth in population can change to a decline, although this of course cannot simply be applied to the developing countries. As the birth-rate here has been so much higher than in Europe over the last few decades the share of young people in the population is so high that even if the birth-rate were now to fall dramatically the rise in population would still continue for at least one generation, as the children from the high birth-rate years of the post-war period reach child-bearing age. It is not until the second and third generation, when

---

34 Bairoch, loc. cit., p. 192.
35 Calculated from the Statistisches Jahrbuch 1978 for the Federal Republic of Germany (international surveys), p. 610–612 (population in 1977) and United Nations, Statistical Yearbook, 1976 (growth rates 1965–1975).

the effects of the Sundt Law, which shows how rises and falls in the population are transmitted through generations,[36] begin to ebb, that any real absolute changes in the growth in population in the Third World can be expected.

Movements in population, and especially the birth-rate, are one of the main differences between the industrialised countries and the Third World. The population of Europe did not grow either in the nineteenth or in the twentieth century with the speed with which the overseas population has risen, because in Europe the birth-rate started to drop almost as soon as the mortality rate dropped. In many African countries, on the other hand the birth-rate is still at more than $40^0/_{00}$, and in Niger, Mali, Malawi, Togo and Zambia it was over $50^0/_{00}$ on the average for the years 1970–1975. In some Latin American and Asian states it is nearly $50^0/_{00}$. Some of these are among the poorest countries in the world, Bangladesh and Afghanistan, for instance, but they also include oil-rich Saudi Arabia.[37] The growth in population and the density of population are for a considerable part of the developing world, especially South and East Asia, decisive factors in the persistence of poverty. The effect is particularly drastic in connection with the other main factor, the climate or the availability of natural resources. It is no coincidence that most of the developing countries and nearly all the 40 poorest nations of the world are in the tropics, while the two Latin American countries which already had the highest per capita incomes in 1900, Argentina and Chile, are in temperate zones. The relatively better development prospects for China in comparison, say with India are partly due to differences in climate. Drought and floods, tropical diseases and hunger have wrought havoc in the tropical regions over and over again for thousands of years. Under the influence of the West many of the tropical diseases have been eliminated or greatly reduced but this has only intensified the problem of overpopulation. From a moral point of view, it ist cruelly paradoxical that the most humane aspect of Western influence on the non-Western world, namely the improvement in medical care and supplies, has at the same time done most to perpetuate the economic problems of these countries. The more people survive the greater is the pressure on the means of subsistence of these regions. No "imperialist exploitation" of raw materials, no re-direction of trade or production through the need to adjust to the requirements of dominant industrial countries, no investment decisions by multinational enterprises has had such a far-reaching effect on the developing countries and their economies.

The effects of better medical care and hygiene will be further strengthened as soon as hunger, which is still a constant threat to 500 million people in the world and constitutes the second major cause of mortality, is overcome. In Europe in the pre- and early industrial age the improvement of the quality and supply of food was the strongest motor to population growth. The same is apparent in the developing countries today. In regions which are no longer threatened by periodic famine or endemic under-nourishment for instance most parts of Latin America, the average life expectancy is already over 60. In Asia only the most highly developed areas have reached this level. If the densely populated areas such as India and Bangladesh, where life expectancy is still at 36 (Bangladesh) and 41 (India) reach the European standard of liv-

---

36 A. E. Wrigley: Bevölkerungsstruktur im Wandel. Methoden und Ergebnisse der Demographie. Munich, 1968, p. 71.
37 United Nations, Statistical Yearbook, 1976, p. 79 ff.

ing, the pressure of population will grow even further. For the same reason a considerable growth in population must be expected in Black Africa, where in some countries, for example Gabon and Chad, life expectancy for men is still under 30.[38] For a large number of African states the population is expected to double over the 1975 figure by the year 2000.

Here we see the vicious circle of development policy in the densely populated, poorest regions of the world. Overpopulation, i. e. a population which is too dense in relation to utilisable agricultural land, and too low in agricultural productivity, are the main causes of poverty. But if agricultural productivity increases and with it food supplies, the population increases and the fruits of the improvement are soon consumed. Whereas in Europe, America and Oceania agricultural technology and chemistry have suspended the old law of diminishing returns on land and the productivity of agriculture has increased in the developed countries roughly fivefold since the beginning of this century, the law still applies in Asia, where in some regions agricultural productivity has actually deteriorated since the beginning of the century and in others it has increased only slightly, because more and more marginal land has to be taken into cultivation.

In the industrialised countries the number of male workers employed in agriculture has been reduced by half since the turn of the century, indeed in some cases by two thirds, as a growing number have found better-paid work in industry and the services sector. In the developing countries, on the other hand, the number of male workers employed in agriculture has doubled. The continuous inflow of labour into a sector which is in any case suffering from over-employment prevents a rise in the productivity of labour. Today in Asian and African agriculture, this is only about two thirds of what European agriculture had achieved by the threshold of the Industrial Revolution. This comparision will perhaps show more clearly than any other how far apart the industrialised countries and the developing countries are, not only today but even in comparison with what Europe had achieved 100, even 200 years ago, and what an immense amout of effort will be required to reach the goal of material welfare for the people of Asia and Africa which matches that of Europe today or even in 1900.[39]

Will industrialisation solve the problem? Much has been said on the success and failures of what has been attempted so far. Here, too, there are greater differences between the regions of the Third World than between the industrialised states. Argentina, Chile, Taiwan and Korea are not so far behind the industrialised countries as Afghanistan or the Philippines. But again we come up against a vicious circle. Apart from smaller countries, it can generally be said that industrialisation becomes easier if there is powerful demand at home for industrial goods. This was achieved in Europe largely through increasing the productivity of agriculture; this preceded the Industrial Revolution and ran parallel to it. On the other hand a lasting increase in productivity is hardly conceivable in these countries if industry and the services sector

---

38 United Nations, Statistical Yearbook, 1976, p. 79–82. Nigeria is the most densely populated country in Africa and babies born there in the first half of the 1970s had a life expectancy of 37 years. In comparison, in Europe the life expectancy for men was at the same time over 65 in every country except Albania, for women, again with the exception of Albania, over 70. In the Scandinavian countries, for example, it was 77.
39 Bairoch, loc. cit., p. 33, Table 9 and p. 42.

cannot absorb a considerable part of the agricultural population. If we follow Bairoch, the percentage of the population in the developing countries which is not engaged in agriculture should increase by at least 8% a year for at least a decade if the number employed in agriculture is at least to remain stable.[40] If it is gradually to decrease, the rise should be about 10%. That has never happened anywhere yet in the history of industrialisation. In the 12 years of explosive growth from 1953 to 1965 the number of non-agricultural workers grew in Japan at yearly rates of 3.8% and in the Soviet Union 3.5%.[41] These were probably the highest growth rates ever achieved in industrialised countries with a still powerful agricultural sector over a period of rather more than one decade. Individual developing countries may of course reach this for a time or even surpass it. The growth in the numbers employed in industry in Syria, Thailand and South Korea between 1965 and 1975, for example, indicates similar growth rates for the entire non-agricultural sector.[42] But it is hardly conceivable that all the under-developed regions could achieve such growth rates at the same time and, what would be necessary if the desired effect is to be attained, actually surpass it by a considerable amount.

So industrialisation alone will not solve the problem, certainly not in one or two decades. Nor will the services sector be able to develop such absorptive capacity, apart from a few exceptions, especially since, as we have seen, it is in any case tending to hypertrophy in under-developed countries. At least a very considerable part of the problem will have to be solved within the agricultural sector itself.

In almost all developing countries there are enclaves in agriculture which, like mining and oil production, are producing mainly for the world market. Some of these are extremely productive. At the beginning of the 1950s foodstuffs accounted for roughly one third of the exports from developing countries. In 1970, despite the rapid increase in the share of oil and minerals, they accounted for almost one quarter. This share is distributed among a wide range of products, none of which accounts for more than 5% of the exports from the Third World.[43] What is their influence on the productivity of tropical agriculture and the incomes of the developing countries? In comparison with mining production, the employment effect is generally higher, i.e. these exports create more incomes that remain in the country. The long fluctuations in the world economy have caused considerable fluctuations in the income which could be obtained for agricultural exports but the volume has grown virtually independent of the price.

The tropical countries fully participated with their agricultural exports in the last long upswing of the years before the First World War. According to W.A. Lewis, during the entire 40-year period before the war their growth rate was 3.1% a year, a high growth rate for such a long sustained period and certainly higher than the growth rate of the social product of the European countries in the same period. Then, however, a comparably long period of decline set in, which reached its lowest point, despite the improvement in the terms of trade, during the Second World War. After 1955 the growth rate did leap to 3.8% for one decade, thus exceeding the pre-war figure, but as

---

40 Bairoch, loc. cit., p. 39.
41 Calculated from Angus Maddison: Die neuen Großmächte. Der wirtschaftliche Aufstieg Japans und der Sowjetunion., p. 96, Table 14.
42 United Nations, Statistical Yearbook, 1976, p. 209–216.
43 Bairoch, loc. cit., p. 99, Table 31.

the terms of trade continued to deteriorate, it remained below the overall economic growth rates of the industrialised countries.[44]

So the key to economic success lies in subsistence agriculture. Rice is as the main foodstuff of Asia and most of the poor countries of the world a good indicator of the chances of improving the general standard of living. World production of rice grew from the beginning of the 1960s to the mid-1970s by 37.6% at a fairly constant rate. The main rice cultivators also succeeded in slightly improving the fertility of their land. But this still leaves the developing countries far behind the productivity figures in the rice-producing industrial countries. In Japan, for example, land productivity for rice was three and a half times as high in 1974 and in Australia it was 3.75 times higher than in India and six times higher than in Syria. For grain, which is gaining in importance as a foodstuff in Asia, too, the position is a little better. India, for example, succeeded between 1961 and 1972 in more than doubling production. The difference in yield per hectare to the most efficient West European countries, Holland and Sweden, is still great but many of the developing countries, above all Mexico and Egypt, can thanks to what is known as the "green revolution" show a yield per hectare which is much higher than that of the USA and Canada. Even India's yields are no longer so very far behind those of other big regions in the world.[45]

So is there a "Bias for Hope", as Albert O. Hirschman entitled a series of studies published in 1971 on the development in Latin America? Are the developing countries on the "Journey to Progress", to quote the title of another of his works on Latin America, or has Rául Prebisch's grim prophesy of 1950 come true, and can the situation only deteriorate for the developing countries as demand for their products grows more slowly, technical progress works to their disadvantage and their inadequately organised workers cannot fight for improvements? For Latin America with its reserves of land and mineral resources, its growing purchasing power – despite the still very high growth rate in population – has the economic prerequisites for steady progress. Here it is rather social and political problems which are causing the still very uneven distribution of income, wealth and power, but not natural conditions or international power relations that are blocking the way to a better life for millions of people. For the densely populated areas in South and South-East Asia and Black Africa it cannot be said with certainty that great strides will be made which could lead to self-sustained growth, but one cannot say that this is entirely impossible either. But the battle against hunger in these regions is not yet over and it cannot be won simply by changing one or two social or political conditions, because the causes lie much deeper. (Not in production conditions alone but in the productive forces, as Marx would say.) At best it will be decades before the population has a standard of living which corresponds to what Europe enjoyed in 1900.[46] I regard it as questionable whether de-coupling from the world economy would help these regions, as many critics of the liberal world economic order maintain,[47] for very few of these states have an ade-

---

44 W. Arthur Lewis: Growth and Fluctuations 1870–1913. London, 1978, p. 226 f.

45 Statistisches Jahrbuch, Federal Republic of Germany, 1976, p. 626 f.

46 The most comprehensive survey on Asian problems is still that in Gunnar Myrdal: Asian Drama. An Inquiry into the Poverty of Nations. 2 vols., New York, 1968, although the data is naturally now old.

47 In Germany i.a. Dieter Senghaas: Weltwirtschaftsordnung und Entwicklungspolitik. Plädoyer für Dissoziation. Frankfurt/M., 1977. More differentiated is e.g. Mahbub Ul Haq: The Poverty Curtain. Choices for the Third World. New York, 1976.

quate development potential in the form of material and human resources which might enable them to move out of poverty more quickly alone than with the help of capital and know-how from the industrialised states. If China, a non-tropical country with huge and as yet only partly exploited natural resources, has decided to take the path of closer integration into the world economy, this should surely apply even more to countries such as India, Bangladesh, Indonesia and Black Africa.

IV. Conclusion

And so we come to our final section. For reasons of space I have not been able to go into a number of questions which are of course of considerable importance for our subject. I have hardly touched on the questions of capital accumulation, investment ratios, international credit relations or development aid and I have only very briefly mentioned the world monetary system. Indeed I have left out the monetary sector as a whole. This is not a reflection of a decision on my part in favour of one of the sides in the eternal controversy between economists over whether the monetary or the "real" factors are the decisive influence in economic development or in initiating and overcoming growth fluctuations. Whatever the significance of the "money veil" may be it affects the level of production and trade and so it has at least been considered indirectly. At the beginning I explained that I would also largely have to leave out the role of state policy. But it is reflected in "real" results, and it seemed more important to me to present those. The same applies to the anthropological and sociological aspects of a consideration of economic structures and events. They are as interesting as they are relevant, but they are most useful when comparing different cultures and traditions, which I was not mainly concerned with here. What I was trying to show was first and foremost general economic conditions and events, long-term trends and medium-term fluctuations in the world economy. They also represent basic factors underlying of political history in the twentieth century.

What is the significance of emphasis on the elementary economic conditions for an interpretation of the history of the twentieth century and hence for the study of history today? In my view it helps to see both the political history and the economic and social history of individual countries and regions in a global perspective, throws a clearer light on the conditions and problems which political action faces and into which the social and economic developments in the individual countries are a part. You will have noticed that I have not mentioned national political figures at all and multinational companies only very briefly. That is not to suggest that they have no influence on the development of the world economy. But they all have to act under existing conditions, which can only be changed to a limited extent by energetic acts. They have all come up against the limits of what is economically feasible. Nor have I discussed interest groups, although many political historians regard them as major factors in modern history. Again their effect will become much clearer if it is seen against the background of basic general economic conditions, especially if one bears in mind what social transformations economic trends and changes can give rise to.

This again is something I have only been able to mention briefly, for instance in discussing the changes in the employment structure in the various regions of the world.

It seems to me both important and at the same time problematic that this approach means that the historian has to make use of analytical concepts and instruments which do not come from the academic discipline of history but from economics – if one were to change the perspective slighely they could come from sociology or anthropology. Without the use of these instruments, which have been evolved by generations of economists in systematic work on the "nature" of economic relations and behaviour, on economic equilibriums and regular and irregular movements, plausible statements would not be possible at all. That they do not always provide a theoretical explanation which is entirely free of contradictions does not diminish their value. As Maier-Leibnitz pointed out yesterday[48] major progress in physics only became possible when scientists stopped searching for complete theories. He rightly pointed out that social scientists make a big mistake if they insist that meaningful empirical work is only possible on the basis of complete theories. For progress in science we do not need formulae of global relevance, but we do need to pose precise questions which can be empirically tested.

But empirical testing of new questions would not be possible without recourse to the work of the innumerable statisticians who have developed the methods for collecting and analysing mass data and those who gather them in the statistical offices of the individual nations and the United Nations, who arrange them in systematic order and prepare them for publication. They created many of the sources I have used here. It must be remembered that this type of source already possesses a considerable degree of abstraction. Statistics are the formalised results of the actions of billions of people in billions of working days; they are based on a systematic survey and examinations of very different aspects of the daily lives of all the people on earth. They are not concrete realities like a person or a group of people. But they do express elementary factors concerning ordinary people, in their work, in their leisure and consumption. Statistics are difficult to handle and they hardly have the glamour of more vivid documents such as letters, autobiographies or even records. But they show what people live on in the literal sense of the word. For the historian there are certainly more rewarding tasks than sifting through them and interpeting them. But not to do this would really mean taking away the material basis of history. Marx quite rightly perceived this. But he was neither the first nor the only one to see that, nor can we conclude that the whole course of history can be directly or even indirectly reduced to this. So it was not a particular theory of history which caused me to choose this perspective but recognition of the value of this approach in a certain context and of the need for a presentation of the basic economic structures and developments in the twentieth century.

But there is a pragmatic component beside the scientific one in this approach. I am convinced that it enables us to draw lessons from history. Military history has always been studied with a view to improving later tactics by better understanding of the reasons for successes and failures. Economic history, and social or political histo-

---

48 This refers to the lecture given by the president of the Deutsche Forschungsgemeinschaft, H. Maier-Leibnitz, at the Historians' Congress, on the subject: Einflüsse der Naturwissenschaft im 18. und 19.Jahrhundert.

ry, can be pursued with the same aim in mind. The long and medium-term analysis of world economic structures and developments has shown how difficult it is to change basic conditions, and conversely what structural changes are "built into" the modern economy and will be quasi-automatic, which are possible or even necessary if the material prosperity of mankind is to be improved. The analysis has, in my view, told us something about the prospects for economic policy which is designed to serve this purpose.

Whether this aim is the right one to pursue is part of that sphere of values which I have not discussed. Certainly there may be higher goals for mankind than the improvement of material living conditions. But as long as two thirds of the world's population are on the verge of starvation the improvement of their standard of living is certainly not an unworthy aim. It may well be one of the most urgent tasks we are faced with.

Zeitschrift für Unternehmensgeschichte – Beihefte

Herausgegeben von Wilhelm Treue und Hans Pohl
im Auftrag der Gesellschaft für Unternehmensgeschichte e. V.

10. WILHELM TREUE
Dreimal 50 Jahre Gothaer Lebensversicherung
Ein Bericht über die letzten 50 Jahre – 1927–1977
1977. VI, 63 S., 4 Taf., kt. DM 16,–   ISBN 3-515-02667-3

11. HANS POHL/WILHELM TREUE
Die Konzentration in der deutschen Wirtschaft seit dem 19. Jahrhundert
Referate und Diskussionsbeiträge der 2. öffentlichen Vortragsveranstaltung der Gesellschaft für Unternehmensgeschichte e. V. am 28. Juni 1977 in Köln. Mit Beiträgen von Hermann J. Abs u.a.
1978. VIII, 88 S., kt. DM 12,80   ISBN 3-515-02734-3

12. HANS POHL, Hrsg.
Betriebliche Sozialpolitik deutscher Unternehmen seit dem 19. Jahrhundert
Referate und Diskussionsbeiträge des wissenschaftlichen Symposiums der Gesellschaft für Unternehmensgeschichte e. V. am 25. November 1977 in Hamburg
1978. VIII, 99 S., kt. DM 19,–   ISBN 3-515-02853-6

13. GÜNTHER SCHULZ
Die Arbeiter und Angestellten bei Felten & Guilleaume
Sozialgeschichtliche Untersuchung eines Kölner Industrieunternehmens im 19. und beginnenden 20. Jahrhundert
1979. XII, 409 S. m. 3 Abb., 22 Graphiken u. 56 Tab., kt. DM 76,–   ISBN 3-515-02885-4

14. HANS POHL/WILHELM TREUE
Stiftung und Unternehmung
Erfahrungen und Zukunftsperspektiven. Referate und Diskussionsbeiträge der 3. öffentlichen Vortragsveranstaltung der Gesellschaft für Unternehmensgeschichte e. V. am 31. Mai 1978 in Frankfurt a. Main
1979. VIII, 62 S., kt. DM 16,–   ISBN 3-515-03116-2

15. HANS POHL, Hrsg.
Berufliche Aus- und Weiterbildung in der deutschen Wirtschaft seit dem 19. Jahrhundert
Referate und Diskussionsbeiträge des 2. Wissenschaftlichen Symposiums der Gesellschaft für Unternehmensgeschichte e. V. am 7. Dezember 1978 in Sindelfingen
1979. X, 119 S., kt. DM 26,–   ISBN 3-515-03136-7

16. HANS POHL, Hrsg.
Entwicklung des Arbeitskampfrechts in Deutschland und in den westlichen Nachbarstaaten
Referate und Diskussionsbeiträge des 4. Wissenschaftlichen Symposiums der Gesellschaft für Unternehmensgeschichte e. V. am 7. Dezember 1979 in Hannover
1980. VIII, 82 S., kt. DM 17,–   ISBN 3-515-03380-7

17. REINHARDT HANF
Im Spannungsfeld zwischen Technik und Markt
Zielkonflikt bei der Daimler-Motoren-Gesellschaft (DMG) im ersten Dezennium ihres Bestehens
1980. X, 63 S. m. 18 Abb., kt. DM 17,40   ISBN 3-515-03385-8

18. HANS POHL/RALPH SCHAUMANN/FRAUKE SCHÖNERT-RÖHLK
Die chemische Industrie in den Rheinlanden während der industriellen Revolution
I: Die Farbenindustrie
1981. Ca. 230 S. m. 3 Abb., 1 Faltkte., kt. ca. DM 32,–   ISBN 3-515-03449-8

FRANZ   STEINER   VERLAG   GMBH · WIESBADEN

F. Lütge

Deutsche Sozial- und Wirtschaftsgeschichte

Ein Überblick

Reprint der 3. Auflage 1966.
Nachdruck. 1979. XVIII, 644 Seiten
ISBN 3-540-09444-X

Inhaltsübersicht: Germanentum, Antike, Christentum. Die soziale und wirtschaftliche Kultur der Frühzeit. – Die Neuformung der sozialen und wirtschaftlichen Kultur in der Karolingerzeit. Die Geburt des Abendlandes. – Die Entfaltung der sozialen und wirtschaftlichen Kultur bis in die Mitte des 14. Jahrhunderts. – Der Strukturwandel der sozialen und wirtschaftlichen Kultur im 14.–15. Jahrhundert und die Fortentwicklung bis zum Dreißigjährigen Kriege. – Das Zeitalter des Merkantilismus (Kameralismus). Die soziale und wirtschaftliche Entwicklung bis zum Siege des Liberalismus. – Die sozialen und wirtschaftlichen Verhältnisse im Zeitalter der entfalteten Volks- und Weltwirtschaft (19. und 20. Jahrhundert). – Ausklang. – Literaturverzeichnis. – Personen- und Sachverzeichnis.

Aus den Besprechungen:

„Lütges **Deutsche Sozial- und Wirtschaftsgeschichte** ist in anderthalb Jahrzehnten seit dem Erscheinen der Erstausgabe zum fachhistorischen Standardwerk geworden, eine stets bewährte Quelle umfassender und gründlicher Belehrung und eine zuverlässige und ertragreiche Arbeitshilfe im Hochschulunterricht. Die… dritte, wesentlich vermehrte und verbesserte Auflage geht, inhaltlich genau besehen, über ihren Titel hinaus, denn dieser „Überblick" – wie der Autor allzu bescheiden sagt – erschließt nicht nur die sozialwirtschaftliche Entwicklung des deutschen Sprach- und Kulturgebiets, sondern umspannt in allen sachlich entscheidenden Partien die Grundlagen und Wandlungen abendländischer Wirtschaftsordnung und -gesinnung und darüber hinaus deren vielfältiges Beziehungsgeflecht zu außereuropäischen Gesellschafts- und Staatsverbänden…"

Allgemeines Statistisches Archiv

Springer-Verlag
Berlin
Heidelberg
New York

W. Glastetter

Die wirtschaftliche Entwicklung der Bundesrepublik Deutschland im Zeitraum 1950 bis 1975

Befunde und Aspekte

1977. 90 Schaubilder, 133 Tabellen. VII, 261 Seiten
(Heidelberger Taschenbücher, Band 185)
ISBN 3-540-08075-9

Diese Arbeit zeichnet die wirtschaftliche
Entwicklung der Bundesrepublik Deutschland im
Zeitraum 1950 bis 1975 nach und weist auf wichtige
Tendenzen und Strukturwandlungen hin. Dabei wird
weder ausschließlich ein modell-theoretisches noch
ein deskriptiv-historisches Anliegen verfolgt; der
Zielinhalt bewegt sich vielmehr zwischen diesen
beiden Polen. Die Untersuchung stützt sich
ausschließlich auf empirische Daten, wie sie sich in
der Volkswirtschaftlichen Gesamtrechnung, der
Außenhandels-und der Zahlungsbilanzstatistik
niederschlagen. Die wirtschaftliche Entwicklung wird
unter verschiedenen Gesichtspunkten – Entstehung,
Verwendung, Verteilung, Finanzierung des
Bruttosozialprodukts, ergänzt durch die außenwirt-
schaftliche Verflechtung – dargestellt, und es werden
Verbindungen zwischen diesen Perspektiven aufge-
zeigt. Insofern stellt die Arbeit eine wichtige Ergän-
zung sowohl der theoretischen wie auch der poli-
tischen Diskussion dar. Sie eignet sich besonders
auch für wirtschaftstheoretische und -politische Lehr-
veranstaltungen, um die abstrakt-theoretischen
Begriffe und Darstellungen durch konkrete Informa-
tionen und praktische Anwendungsfälle zu illu-
strieren und zu untermauern.

Springer-Verlag
Berlin
Heidelberg
New York